What is Meaning?

Fundamentals of Linguistics

Each book in the Fundamentals of Linguistics series is a concise and critical introduction to the major issues in a subfield of linguistics, including morphology, semantics, and syntax. The books presuppose little knowledge of linguistics, are authored by well-known scholars, and are useful for beginning students, specialists in other subfields of linguistics, and interested non-linguists.

What is Morphology?
Mark Aronoff and Kirsten Fudeman

What is Meaning? Fundamentals of Formal Semantics
Paul H. Portner

What is Meaning?

Fundamentals of
Formal Semantics

Paul H. Portner

Blackwell
Publishing

BLACKWELL PUBLISHING
350 Main Street, Malden, MA 02148-5020, USA
9600 Garsington Road, Oxford OX4 2DQ, UK
550 Swanston Street, Carlton, Victoria 3053, Australia

First published 2005 by Blackwell Publishing Ltd

7   2009

Library of Congress Cataloging-in-Publication Data

Portner, Paul.
    What is meaning? : fundamentals of formal semantics / Paul H. Portner.
        p. cm. – (Fundamentals of linguistics)
    Includes bibliographical references and index.
    ISBN: 978-1-4051-0917-8 (hbk. : alk. paper) – ISBN: 978-1-4051-0918-5
(pbk.: alk. paper)
        1. Semantics.   2. Semantics (Philosophy)   I. Title.   II. Series.

P325.P635 2005
401'.43–dc22

                                                                    2004015923

A catalogue record for this title is available from the British Library.

Set in 10/12$^{1}/_{2}$pt Palatino
by Graphicraft Limited, Hong Kong
Printed and bound in Singapore
by C.O.S. Printers Pte Ltd

The publisher's policy is to use permanent paper from mills that operate a
sustainable forestry policy, and which has been manufactured from pulp
processed using acid-free and elementary chlorine-free practices. Furthermore,
the publisher ensures that the text paper and cover board used have met
acceptable environmental accreditation standards.

For further information on
Blackwell Publishing, visit our website:
www.blackwellpublishing.com

This book is dedicated to Sylvia. Together we've managed so much more than a book on semantics over the past few years.

Contents

Acknowledgments

There are a number of people I'd like to thank for their support as I've worked on this book. My students in introductory semantics classes over years have dealt with me as I've refined my way of presenting formal semantics, and have given feedback on previous versions of this material. My teachers at Princeton and the University of Massachusetts have helped me see more clearly what's of fundamental importance in semantics, and in particular I would mention Emmon Bach for writing his *Informal Lectures on Formal Semantics*, which showed me how much a book of this kind can be helpful to students of semantics. My colleagues at Georgetown, especially Raffaella Zanuttini and Elena Herburger, and the teaching assistants in my semantics courses have contributed a great deal to my teaching and scholarly life. My contacts at Blackwell, Tami Kaplan and Sarah Coleman, have pushed the project forward with me, reviewers, and their company in an efficient yet constantly pleasant way. Finally, my family has always believed in me, and this has given me the confidence to try this project; their help and that of Sylvia's family with our son Noah has given me the time to finish it.

This book offers one perspective on the subject matter of semantics, and of course I alone am responsible for errors and biases.

Paul Portner
Georgetown University, Washington, DC

1 The Fundamental Question

Semantics is the study of meaning. Those who make this field the center of their academic lives need to enjoy being seen as unimportant, because many people they meet during daily life believe that the study of meaning cannot be a serious, much less a scientific, pursuit. For the general public, an issue is "just semantics" if it has to do with mere matters of form, and accusing someone of focusing on semantics is a way of saying they want to avoid the heart of the matter. An interest in semantics sounds like a deep concern for details of etiquette: perhaps useful in certain contexts, like the diplomatic party or ivory tower, but something which tough-minded realists will brush right aside.

The reputation of semantics within its broader field of linguistics is the opposite of this popular one in many ways. Semanticists tend to use a lot of tools drawn from logic and even mathematics as they go about their jobs as university professors (and almost all of them are university professors; the rest mostly work for computer companies). Because of this, they tend to write down their ideas using all sorts of funny symbols (such as λ, $\exists$, and $\forall$). We call this approach to language *formal*, meaning that it is couched in these logical/mathematical languages. The formalism of semantics makes the field virtually impossible for the uninitiated to understand. It also makes it very difficult for those who don't have a native talent for abstraction and logic to become initiated. In other words, semantics is thought to be really technical and hard. (You can imagine what this means for the image of semanticists.)

Though semantics as practiced by the specialist is formal and abstract, at least it is this way for a reason: Formalization allows the construction of very precise theories, and precise theories are better because they don't allow the theorists to fudge the data quite so easily as less precise theories do. Semanticists have to be especially cautious in this respect, I believe, because discussion of meaning can very quickly turn into pointless contests between vague but strongly held opinions – exactly the sort of situation which the popular view of "it's just semantics" rightly mocks.

Let me give an example: suppose we wish to understand the difference in meaning between a simple past tense sentence like (1) and a present perfect sentence like (2):

(1)   Mary received the most votes in the election.

(2)   Mary has received the most votes in the election.

After thinking about the two examples for a while, an intuition about the difference may emerge. One common intuition is that (1) simply reports a past event, while (2) reports both a past event and a current result of that event, such as that Mary will be the next president. Armed with this intuition, one can then start looking at other present perfect sentences, and the idea that they report the present results of past events may seem better and better (*Shelby has finished his dinner* – so he's no longer hungry, *I haven't slept for days* – so I'm very tired, . . .). Then suppose we encounter the conversation in (3):

(3)   Speaker A: Will Mary be able to finish Dos Passos' *USA* trilogy by
        the next book club meeting? It's so long!
        Speaker B: Well, she has read *Remembrance of Things Past*, and it's
        even longer.

There is a current fact which speaker B is pointing out: that Mary might indeed finish the *USA* trilogy. Our intuition seems to be confirmed. However, we think about it some more, and there's a problem. The fact that Mary might finish the book isn't really a result of her reading *Remembrance of Things Past*. The fact that she read *Remembrance of Things Past* is merely evidence for what she might be able to read in the future. Is there something else which speaker B's sentence is trying to report, some other situation which really is a result of her reading *Remembrance of Things Past*? One suggestion: the result is that she has read a really long book before. But notice that this alleged result is itself reported with a present perfect sentence (*She has read a really long book before*), suggesting that our explanation is getting circular, and in any case this "result" is rather ephemeral. Any other possibilities? There are plenty of concrete results of her reading *Remembrance of Things Past*: she has confidence in her ability to read long books; she knows who Albertine is; and infinitely more.

But this raises another problem: How does speaker A know which of these speaker B has in mind? This debate isn't going to get anywhere unless somebody provides a precise explanation of what they mean by the term "result." A formal theory of events and results and time might well be of help here.

Returning to the main thread of discussion, formal theories have some other advantages as well. They are good for implementation in computational settings and for exploring the relations between semantics and the other sub-disciplines of linguistics which have a formal flavor, like syntax, as well the interdisciplinary field known as cognitive science, in particular computer science, psychology, philosophy, and neuroscience. While indirect, these are also good reasons to study semantics in a formal way.

Nevertheless, even if you grant that abstraction and formalism are excellent things for those working at the frontiers of research, you may still want to think about the nature of meaning from a scientific perspective while not taking on the task of learning a lot of formal logic. The goal of this book is to help you do that. It is also designed for those of you who may be undertaking to learn the technical side of semantics, and feel you need a bit more guidance as to what those formulas are really all about.

In order to study meaning, we have to begin with some basic understanding of what sort of thing a meaning is. Trying to answer the question, "What is a meaning?" in its most general sense is a scary task mostly undertaken by philosophers! But we need to begin this book with at least a few basic considerations.

1.1   What is a Meaning?

In ordinary life, we sometimes find ourselves talking about the meanings of words and sentences. For example, I am at home reading, but find myself confused. I don't know what something means. If I ask my wife the meaning of a word, she will give me an answer:

"What does 'kakapo' mean?"
"It's a kind of parrot."

Or,

"What does this character mean?" → 狗
"It means 'dog'."

When I ask what a word means, I typically get more words – perhaps in the language I used in my question, perhaps in another, but nonetheless more words. Can meanings be words? The answer is obviously "no," if we want to approach meaning as scientists. Because, supposing that the meaning of "kakapo" is "a kind of parrot," what about the meanings of "kind" and "parrot"? More words. Eventually identifying the meaning of a piece of language with more language is bound to become circular, as a word is defined in terms of some of the very words which it helps define.

> Pick a simple word and look up its definition in the dictionary. Then look up the crucial words in that definition, and so forth. Do the definitions become circular?

A more sophisticated view similar to this one is known as *meaning holism*. Most famously supported by the philosopher Quine,[1] the theory of holism claims that the meaning of a word or phrase or sentence depends on its relationships with other words, phrases, and sentences. For example, it might be argued that part of what makes up the meaning of *tall* is that it's opposed to the meaning of *short* (something that seems quite plausible). More precisely, holist theories tend to be *functional* in the sense that it is some aspect of the use of a piece of language which makes for its meaning, so we should really say that part of the meaning of *tall* is that if you call something *tall*, you should not at the same time call it *short*, and if you call something *tall* you should be willing to also call it *not short*. The big issue for holism is to find a way to say which of the relations among words, phrases, and sentences are important to semantics. Radical holism takes the position that there is no line to draw between connections of this plausible sort (*tall* with *short*) and all of the connections among words, phrases, and sentences (*tall* with *I like beans and so I plan to make red bean soup for dessert*). In that case, the semantic system of a language will be a complex, interconnected network, and all meaning will be relative to the whole system. It's difficult to see how meaning can be studied in a scientific way from this perspective. (I should say that it's hard to assess whether holism is in general incompatible with scientific linguistic semantics because over the years a wide variety of theories have been labeled as "holistic."[2])

Linguists who study meaning don't believe that the study of meaning should be unscientific. They feel this way in the first instance (I believe) not because they are better philosophers than Quine and his followers, but because their experience with language shows them that the way languages express thought is not as arbitrary as the holist's way of looking at matters would lead you to expect. Instead, they find overwhelming evidence for deep and consistent patterns in how languages express meaning, patterns which are in need of scientific explanation. We'll see some of these patterns in the chapters to come. Thus, though the initial intuition that we started with, that the meanings of words involve their relations with other words, is probably correct in some sense, it does not by itself provide a basis for the scientific study of linguistic meaning. Therefore it has not been incorporated much into the thinking of formal semanticists. It is more relevant to the practice of the field of semiotics, the study of symbolic systems generally (including language to the extent that it has something in common with such things as the "meaning" of foods and clothes).

If meanings aren't words, our next guess might be that meanings are something in the mind: concepts, thoughts, or ideas. When you understand the meaning of the word *dog*, your mind (and brain) change in certain ways. At some point you form a concept of dogs (let's indicate the concept with capital letters: DOG). Then, you associate this concept with the English word *dog*, and from then on you have an ability to use the word *dog* whenever the concept DOG is active in your thoughts. From here it's a short step to saying that DOG is the meaning of *dog*. This theory would explain the patterns in how languages express meaning in terms of the nature of concepts, and perhaps ultimately in terms of the way the brain is structured. Let's call this perspective the idea theory of meaning.[3]

One obvious challenge for the idea theory is to come up with a sound psychological theory of what concepts and ideas are. This psychological theory needs to provide a concept or idea for every meaningful piece of language. Thus, there will need to be ideas and concepts associated with each of the following (at least in any situation in which they are meaningful):

Dogs and cats
The picture of my wife
Three
Whatever
The president lives in Washington, DC.
Had been sleeping
Why
Who said that we had to be at the airport so early?
-*ed* (the past tense marker)

The idea theory needs to say what idea is associated with *whatever*, *why*, or *three*, and this doesn't seem as easy a project as explaining what idea is associated with *dog*. At least, the idea theory provides no quick and easy path to a complete theory of meaning. But even if it's not going to be easy, the idea theory may work. Certainly, something is going on in our minds when we use words and phrases, so in some sense there are ideas associated with all meaningful language. Don't we just have to discover what they are (hire more psychologists!) and use them to explain meaning?

The question which the scientist of meanings needs to ask is not simply whether our concepts and ideas play a role in how we use language in a meaningful way – of course they do. The real issue is whether those concepts and ideas have the right properties to explain everything we need to explain about meaning. In other words, we can consider what we know about meaning already, and then check out whether the idea theory is consistent with that knowledge. Well, what do we know about meaning? Here are some basic points:

i   Sometimes pieces of language have the same meaning – they are SYNONYMOUS.

Dog
Canis familiaris

Mary kissed John.
John was kissed by Mary.

ii   Sometimes pieces of language conflict with each other in terms of their meanings – they are CONTRADICTORY.
The pig is on top of the turtle.
The turtle is on top of the pig.

iii   Sometimes the fact that one piece of language is an accurate description of a thing or state of affairs automatically guarantees that another is an accurate description of it too – the first ENTAILS the second.
Robin
Bird

The circle is inside the square.
The circle is smaller than the square.

The idea theory can say a bit about what it is for *Mary kissed John* and *John was kissed by Mary* to be synonymous. Suppose that in my mind I have ideas, or concepts, of Mary, of John, of kissing, and of "pastness." These ideas are combined into some kind of aggregate idea, the one associated with the sentence *Mary kissed John*. The idea theory would then want to say that *John was kissed by Mary* is associated with same aggregate idea, and this is why the two sentences are synonymous. The second sentence has all the same pieces as the first, put together in a different order, plus an additional one, the passive voice (the fact that the sentence takes the form . . . *was kissed by* . . . instead of . . . *kissed* . . .). In some way, the idea associated with the passive voice exactly undoes the effect of putting *Mary* as the subject of the sentence in one case, and *John* as the subject of the sentence in the other. In other words, the sentence without passive voice, *John kissed Mary*, is not synonymous with *Mary kissed John* – clearly – and it's the passive voice which gets into the aggregate meaning of *John was kissed by Mary* and sets things right.

I think it's clear that the meaning associated with the passive voice will not be the kind of thing that we typically call an "idea." This meaning has a grammatical nature, having to do with the order in which John and Mary are mentioned in these sentences. This suggests that, if the idea theory is to work at all, ideas will have to have a language-like nature. That is to say, because the meanings of certain pieces of language are deeply tied into the grammar of that language, ideas themselves will need a grammar. If our ideas have a grammar, they are a language, and we are thinking of them as a *language of thought*.[4]

An important objection to the idea theory arises from the famous "Twin Earth thought experiments."[5] The basic idea of the Twin Earth thought experiments is that we can learn a lot about the nature of the mind and language by imaging a world which is exactly like our earth except for some specific differences, and then examining whether those differences seem relevant to how our minds or language work. The following kind of Twin Earth thought experiment is relevant to whether we should accept or reject the idea theory of meaning. One thing we're absolutely sure about is that when we use a common term like *water*, we are referring to a very definite kind of thing in the natural world. In fact, when we use *water*, we're referring to H_2O. Now, imagine some people inhabiting a planet very much like ours. This planet is, in fact, so very much like ours that if you went there, you couldn't tell you weren't on earth. Everything on Twin Earth is just like on earth. There's even a copy of you there (and while you're visiting Twin Earth, he or she is visiting our earth). This Twin Earth only differs from earth in one way, and that is that everywhere we expect to find water there, we find another substance, XYZ, which looks, feels, and acts just like water, but which is actually not water. So, obviously, when the Twin Earth people who speak a language very similar to English say *water*, they are referring to XYZ, and not H_2O. This implies that Twin Earth English and our earth English are not quite the same language. The word *water* differs in meaning between them.

Since Twin Earth is just like earth, each person on earth has a twin there. And this twin is exactly like the true earthling in every respect (except that instead of H_2O, there is XYZ in his or her body). Importantly, the mental life of the earthlings and their twins on Twin Earth are identical. Despite the fact that their mental lives are identical, they don't mean the same thing by the word *water*. This implies that the meaning of *water* is not determined solely by the what goes on inside the head of people who use the language, and this is just to say that meanings are not ideas. Rather, what a word refers to is partially dependent on the environment in which people who use a language live. Given that you live surrounded by H_2O, *water* will refer to water and not XYZ. (If you want to make Twin Earth a bit more consistent, you can say that people who know a lot about chemistry there know that XYZ is common there, but H_2O is not, and conversely on real earth. All that matters for the thought experiment is that some people – not knowing much about chemistry – have no clue about what XYZ or H_2O are. These people and their twins will have the same internal mental concepts associated with the word *water*, but will mean different things by it.)

Another important conclusion about the idea theory can be drawn by considering the meanings of individual words like *dog*. I have formed a concept of dogs through my experience with them. In particular, when I think of dogs I often think of the fluffy gray-and-white, mid-sized ones called Keeshonds, because this is what my dog Shelby is. For me, DOG has many components drawn from Shelby's appearance and behavior. Most people, though, have never heard of or seen a Keeshond, as I can attest from Shelby's celebrity whenever we go for a walk through town. Let us call these people "the unfortunate ones." The concept of DOG held by the unfortunate ones lacks many of the most prominent features of my concept DOG. Since we have different concepts of dogs, and according to the idea theory the concept equals the meaning, this would seem to imply that the word *dog* means something different for me and for the unfortunate ones. So, when they ask me "What kind of dog is that?" their question actually doesn't mean the same thing for me and for them. This conclusion seems somewhat implausible, for even if two people with different experiences with dogs ask that question, they are nevertheless probably looking for the same kind of answer from me.

You might say that my concept of DOG and the unfortunates' concept are similar enough to count as the same because of the fact that they are concepts of the same things out there in the world, namely the members of the species *Canis familiaris*. In other words, all the unfortunates and I aim to use our concept of DOG to classify and think about the members of that species, and on this ground our concepts are different versions of the same thing. But this concession weakens the idea theory tremendously. It turns the idea theory into a side-trip on the road of understanding meaning. As illustrated in diagram 1, if we're going to explain the meaning of *dog* in terms of the concept DOG, and the concept in terms of the animals which it describes, we might as well explain the meaning directly in terms of the things, avoiding the detour through ideas. This is the view which is adopted within the theory of meaning presented in this book.

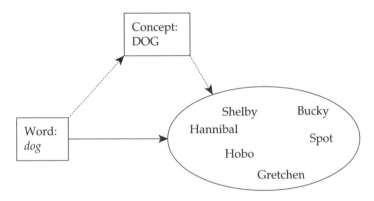

Diagram 1

The reason that the word *dog* means the same thing for you and for me is not that we have the same mental constructs relating to the word. Rather, it's because of our intention to apply the word *dog* to the same things out there in our environment, namely the dogs. (Of course we may not agree about precisely which things these are. You may honestly think that Shelby is a kind of small bear, and refuse to call him a dog. But still our intentions are the same: to call everything by the word *dog* which really is a dog. It's just that you are failing to do so, due to ignorance.)

Notice, by the way, that none of this implies that we don't have concepts of dogs and other things – of course we do! – or that these concepts aren't crucial in how we use meaningful language in the correct way. It doesn't imply that we lack a language of thought (or that we have one). It doesn't mean that semanticists can't contribute to studying the psychology of language. In fact, I am convinced that semantics has an important part to play in the study of cognition. It simply says that meanings aren't ideas. Whatever the relation between meanings and ideas may turn out to be, they aren't the same thing.[6]

If meanings are not in the relations among pieces of language, and are not ideas, what else could they be? Another type of answer which is influential within philosophy says that they are social practices.[7] The idea is that when somebody says something, it should be thought of as a kind of move in a giant language game which we all play. This game has rules, and these rules imply things like "If somebody makes the move of saying 'What time is it?' to you, an appropriate move for you to make is to say 'It's 6 o'clock' (if it is 6 o'clock)." Of course this is, in fact, an appropriate response, so any type of semanticist is going to want an understanding of meaning which explains why it is appropriate. But an advocate of the social practice theory of meaning goes beyond this to argue that this is all there is to meaning. So an important task is to explain precisely how each meaningful piece of language comes to have the roles in the language game which it has. Take for example the response "It is 6 o'clock." It is an appropriate response only if you think it is in fact 6 o'clock, and this is somehow based on the fact that it is comprised of the pieces *it*, *be*, present tense, *6* and *o'clock* put together in a particular way. (If these same pieces were put together as "Is it 6 o'clock?" it would not be an appropriate response.) Perhaps we can say that there is a social practice (a rule of the language game) which says something like this:

If the previous move was an utterance of "What time is it",
  then an utterance of the form "It is X o'clock" is a candidate appropriate move, and
  if the clocks in the neighborhood look roughly like this: ①,
    then it is an appropriate move to make the utterance with X filled in as "6."

This social practice theory has not had much impact on linguistically oriented semanticists for three reasons. First, there seems to be a fundamental conflict with one of the basic insights of modern linguistics (not just semantics) that our languages are not arbitrary social conventions, but rather reveal deeper universal patterns which spring from the way our minds are built. These patterns call out for scientific explanation, and it seems hard to explain them on the basis of the notion of game-like social practices. In this way this perspective on meaning suffers from the same problem as the first approach we looked at, the one which said that the meaning of an expression comes from its relations with other expressions of language. However, it is not clear to me that there is a fundamental conflict here. It could be that a follower of the social practice theory could say that language is a very special kind of social practice which is instinctual and which has rules that are to a large extent determined by a part of our brains which is responsible for making us follow them.

The second reason that the social practice theory has not been seen as relevant to linguistic semantics is that it does not seem to provide an important role to the intuition that "It is 6 o'clock" is an appropriate response because it *is* 6 o'clock and you want me to believe this. It is this aspect of language which seems to distinguish it from true games. In baseball, a player will try to catch the ball before it hits the ground because this will help achieve the goal of winning, and that's it. But you answer my question not just because the rules of the language game tell you that you have to (or else you "lose"), but because you recognize that I want to know a certain piece of information, which I can get if you say "It's 6 o'clock." Any other way of giving the same information, or other relevant information, would also be an appropriate move (think about *It's dinnertime* and *I don't know*). Gathering these moves together under a collection of rules which tell you what you can do in response to my making the move of saying "What time is it?" would just miss the reason why they are appropriate. So advocates of the social practice theory must provide a notion of "the information provided by a sentence" which is compatible with the fundamental idea that language is a social practice. This is a difficult task, and there is controversy about whether they can succeed. If they can, then it is possible that the social practice theory is compatible with the ideas about meaning presented in this book.[8]

The third reason that linguistically oriented semanticists tend not to pursue the social practice theory is that they feel that we already understand a great deal about how meaning works in language. The main point of this book is to introduce you to the most important of these insights. But these insights have not been achieved in terms of the social practice theory, or the other theories discussed above for that matter. Rather they have been achieved in terms of some ideas about meaning which I'm about to get around to introducing. Until some other way of thinking about meaning shows that it helps us understand something about how language works that we didn't understand before, semanticists – like other scientists – will see little reason to change.

1.2   Meanings are Out in the World

This discussion so far points to the conclusion that meanings are not internal to language, are not in the mind, and are not merely social practices. Rather, they are based in language- and mind-external reality. The meaning of the word *dog* implies that it describes all of those things that actually are dogs, regardless of our ability to define it with words or to formulate an appropriate mental concept.[9] The point is even simpler to see in the case of names. The name *Confucius* refers to the ancient Chinese philosopher, and this is the basis of its meaning (indeed this may be all there is to its meaning). The fact that people may have very different ideas about Confucius, including some very vague ones like "he's just some ancient Chinese philosopher" which would not distinguish him from lots of other individuals, doesn't prevent them from all meaning the same person when they say "Confucius."[10] Of course many names can be used to refer to more than one person. But in a given situation, a speaker intends to refer to just one of them, and if everything goes well, she will. The ability to do this does not depend on the speaker and hearer sharing some idea about the person which would serve to pick him or her out of a lineup. For example, someone could ask "Who was Alexander?" and refer to the ancient general, not any other Alexander, even though that person didn't know any more about him than that he's some long-dead guy.

1.3   We Should Think of the Meaning of Sentences in Terms of Truth-Conditions

So far we've thought in a bit of detail about the meanings of some nouns like *dog* and *Confucius*. What about other types of language? The traditional next move in building up a comprehensive semantic theory is to think about the meaning of complete sentences. Following this tradition, and assuming that meanings are part of language- and mind-external reality, we will now ask what sort of thing a sentence-meaning is.

As English speakers, we know the meaning of the sentence:

The circle is inside the square.

With this knowledge, we can display a certain ability. If I show you the picture on the left in diagram 2, you can tell me that the sentence is true, and if I show you the one on the right, you can tell me it's false.

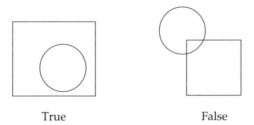

True   False

Diagram 2

More generally, provided with a range of scenarios, you can divide them into two classes. Calling these the "true set" and the "false set," you can draw a circle around the true set, as in diagram 3.

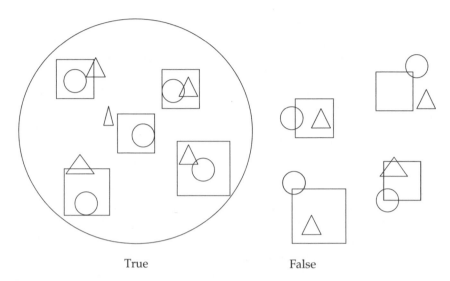

True   False

Diagram 3

One very important way of thinking about meaning is to take these kinds of abilities as crucial clues as to the nature of meaning. The knowledge of meaning involves (at least) the knowledge of the conditions under which a sentence is true, and those under which it's false. So let's begin our semantic investigation by focusing on this particular aspect of meaning as if it is all there is to the semantics of sentences. It's worth seeing where that gets us.[11] A theory which says that all there is to the meaning of a sentence is its truth-conditions is a *truth-conditional theory*. This might seem kind of odd, but I'll spend the rest of this chapter giving a number of reasons why this odd idea has a lot to recommend it. Perhaps it's even right – many formal semanticists think it is! But whether or not it's ultimately right, we'll see in this book that we can use it to understand many aspects of language better than we did before.

One common misunderstanding of truth-conditional semantics should be dealt with right away. Knowing the meaning of a sentence amounts to knowing its truth-*conditions*. It has nothing to do with knowing whether it is in fact true or false (what semanticists call its truth-*value*). You can know the meaning of a sentence without knowing whether it's true or false, or even having prospects for ever finding out. For example, you know what it would take for the sentence *The third closest star to earth has six planets, one of which is inhabited by intelligent creatures* to be true, but you'll probably never find out if it's actually true or not. Yet, what you know – just the truth-conditions, not the truth-value – seems sufficient to say you know what it means.

Next, some terminology: there is a family of theories of semantics which we can count as just one theory for the purpose of this book. These theories go by names like *truth-conditional semantics, formal semantics, model-theoretic semantics, possible worlds semantics,* and *situation semantics.* These theories can be combined to some extent, so that one can practice model-theoretic possible worlds semantics, for example. From the perspective of the professional semanticist, there are important differences among these theories, but for the purposes of this book, I will treat them all as one, since they share the same central intuition about the nature of sentence-meaning. Since "formal semantics" is the most general term among these, this book is best described as an introduction to formal semantics. My discussion will freely borrow from the terminology of all of them, as it is convenient for making clear what I'm trying to make clear, but for the most part my discussion will be given from the perspective of the most popular flavor of formal semantics, the one known as possible worlds semantics. By and large, the ideas about language which I'll be presenting are compatible with any of the other flavors as well.

The little scenarios represented in diagrams 2 and 3 are called, in the technical terminology of formal semantics, *possible worlds* or *possible situations* (just "worlds" or "situations" for short). In diagram 3, I've represented nine different possible worlds or situations. There are infinitely many other worlds or situations which I didn't draw, but you can intuitively tell how they would be added into a more complete diagram. The terms "world" and "situation" are typically used in somewhat different ways, with "situation" suggesting a very incomplete scenario, a part of the universe bounded in space and/or time. For example, everything which is enclosed within the room as you read this sentence is a situation, as is everything enclosed by the boundaries of the District of Columbia on March 29, 2002, at 10:15 a.m. The pictures in diagram 3 are representations of very little situations. The term "world" is used when people have in mind a complete way in which the world could be. A possible world is a possible history of the universe – the kind of thing that often comes up in science fiction. If the pictures in the diagrams are thought of as representing worlds, then each one represents only very impoverished worlds only inhabited by a few shapes, and with no change over time (or perhaps no time at all). Or you can think of them as being merely partial depictions of some more ordinary worlds, with lots of details left out, so that each actually corresponds to many different worlds (a different one on each way of filling in the details).

The notion of possible world or situation may seem metaphysical and so disconnected from reality as to be a pointless place to start a scientific investigation of anything. But really, it's quite simple and familiar. We think about possible worlds all the time. Suppose we are investigating a murder, and have two hypotheses about who did it. We first imagine the scenario in which suspect no. 1 is guilty, thinking through what would have happened in that case, and then looking for evidence of whether those things did in fact happen. Then we imagine the scenario in which suspect no. 2 is guilty, and go through the same process. Roughly speaking, each imagined scenario can be thought of as a possible world. This way of thinking about what might be or might have been is quite common, and so the story about the murder investigation makes clear why the notion of alternative possible worlds is not really all that unfamiliar or odd.

As a philosophical aside, it's worth pointing out that it's not entirely accurate to say that the imagined scenarios are simply examples of possible worlds. When we imagine a scenario, we don't bother to be specific about each and every detail. But possible worlds are specific in every detail. The real world is a possible world after all, and it is quite specific in details that we never even consider, like how many leaves are on a particular tree in a particular forest on a particular day. For this reason, a scenario like our murder scenario is better thought of as a set of possible worlds. For example, we may imagine suspect no. 1 committing the crime at *about* 10 a.m., but what we imagine isn't specific as to whether it's *exactly* 9:59, 10:00, or 10:01. Suppose that these differences in the time of the murder are not significant to our investigation. What we imagine is compatible with a possible world where the murder happened at 9:59, and with one where it happened at 10:00, and with one where it happened at 10:01 (as well as all the ones with times in between). We don't care about the differences among these possibilities, and our imagination doesn't distinguish them. So, a scenario is more like a set of possible worlds such that the differences among the worlds is unimportant to whoever is imagining the scenario. End of aside.

On to the next piece of terminology. The meaning of a sentence is called a *proposition*. We say that a sentence *expresses* or *denotes* a proposition.[12] According to the truth-conditional view of meaning, the proposition expressed by a sentence amounts simply to its truth-conditions. The proposition denoted by *The circle is inside the square* is the one indicated in diagram 3 (relative to my laziness in just drawing nine scenarios, when in reality there are of course many more true and false possibilities). Within the terminology of possible worlds, a proposition is a set of possible worlds, in diagram 3 the set indicated by the big circle on the left. Thinking of propositions as sets of possible worlds captures the idea that the meaning of a sentence is its truth-conditions, since knowledge of what it takes to make a sentence true is exactly what you need in order to decide if a given possible world is in the "true set." Informally, we can think of the meaning of a sentence as parallel to the meaning of a common noun, in the following way: The noun *dog* describes certain things (the dogs) and not others, and so we can explain the meaning of *dog* by saying it denotes the set of dogs. Likewise, a sentence describes certain possible worlds (those in which it's true) and not others, and so we can explain its meaning by saying it denotes the set of possible worlds in which it's true.

1.3.1 Three reasons why truth-conditions are a central part of meaning

As promised above, our next task is to bring out some reasons why this weird truth-conditional view of meaning is worth pursuing.

1.3.1.1   *Reason 1: The semantics of logical words*

Thinking of meaning as truth-conditions lets us give a pretty good semantics for logical words like *and*, *or*, and *not*. These are called "logical words because of the important role they play in determining what patterns of reasoning are valid, the traditional concern of logic. If you know that a sentence of the form *p and q* is true, you also know that *p* is true – this is a logical fact. For example, the following sentence is made up of two sentences joined by *and* (so it is of the form *p and q*). If we know that it is true, we can conclude that the circle is inside the square (i.e., that *p* is true).

(4)   [*The circle is inside the square*] <u>*and*</u> [*the circle is dark*].

Suppose we indicate the truth-conditional meaning of each of the two component sentences in a possible-worlds diagram like the kind we've seen above. In diagram 4, the proposition expressed by each component sentence is indicated by a dotted circle. Then, it's easy to see what the truth-conditional meaning of the whole sentence is, in terms of the meanings of the two sub-sentences: the overlap between the two dotted circles. (The overlap between two sets is called the *intersection* of those two sets.)

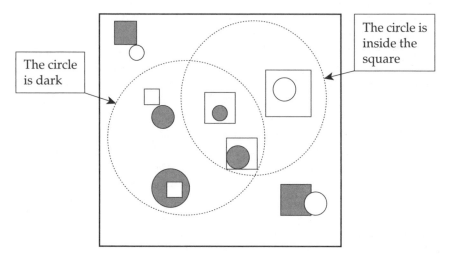

The circle is dark

The circle is inside the square

Diagram 4

From this diagram, you can easily see why (4) implies that the circle is inside the square, and that the circle is dark. In general, a sentence of the form *p and q*, where *p* and *q* are any sentences, describes the worlds in the intersection of the worlds described by *p* and the worlds described by *q*. In our example, *p = The circle is inside the square* and *q = The circle is dark*.

> Give a semantics for sentences of the form *p or q* and *It is not the case that p*. What you come up with should look a lot like what we've just seen for sentences of the form *p and q*. As you think about this exercise, work with particular sentences for *p* and *q*, e.g. *The circle is inside the square* and *the circle is dark*. But make sure that your answer would work for any sentences you could fill in for *p* and *q*, not just these particular ones.
>
> This exercise has an answer, no. 1, in the appendix.

At this point, most books on formal semantics would begin to get more formal, indicating the meanings of *and*, *or*, and *not* with symbols.

Right now we're focusing on the meaning of sentences. As an aside, though, notice that thinking of the meaning of *and* as intersection works for phrases other than sentences. Consider the following:

Mary is [*a student*] *and* [*a baseball fan*].

Let's assume that *a student* describes the set of students, and that *a baseball fan* describes the set of baseball fans. Then, what does *a student and a baseball fan* describe? Answer: the set of things which are both, that is, the intersection of the two sets. Saying that Mary is a student and a baseball fan therefore says that she is in the intersection of the set of students and the set of baseball fans, which implies that she is a student and that she is a baseball fan. Since this is exactly what the sentence should imply, it looks good for our idea that *and* means intersection.

There are problems, though. We can use *and* to combine words which don't intuitively describe sets, as in [*Mary*] *and* [*John*] *bought a dog*. If it is combining things which aren't sets, *and* can't mean intersection (since intersection is a way of combining sets and nothing else). Some semanticists think that *and* is ambiguous, sometimes meaning intersection and sometimes meaning something else more appropriate for *Mary and John*; others think that, contrary to naïve appearances, *Mary* and *John* do describe sets; still others think that *and* is, contrary to naïve appearances, not joining together *Mary* and *John*. We'll drop this issue for the time being, but you might want to think a bit about how each of these ideas would work before your thinking is corrupted by more education.

Maybe *Mary* and *John* do denote sets in the following way: *Mary* denotes the set containing only Mary, i.e., {Mary}, and *John* denotes the set containing only John, {John}. Explain why this does not solve the problem posed by our desire to understand the *and* in *Mary and John* as intersection.

1.3.1.2   Reason 2: Definitions of intuitive semantic relationships

Thinking of meaning as truth-conditions lets us define some basic semantic concepts: synonymy, contrariety, entailment, contradiction, tautology.

Two sentences are *synonymous* if they have the same meaning. Intuitively, (5) and (6) are synonymous:

(5)   The square is bigger than the circle.

(6)   The circle is smaller than the square.

Suppose we draw a box to indicate the set of all possible worlds (diagram 5). Call this box "W". (Semanticists often use "w" to stand for a single possible world, and "W" to stand for the set of all possible worlds, as here.) Then we draw a circle within the box W to indicate those possible worlds in which (5) is true. Call this "5." Then draw another circle to indicate those in which (6) is true, called "6." Circles 5 and 6 are the same, showing that the truth-conditional view of meaning can capture the sense in which (5) and (6) are synonymous.

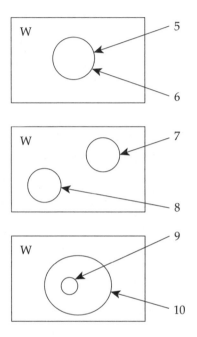

Diagram 5

Two sentences are *contrary* if both can't be true:

(7) The square is bigger than the circle.

(8) The circle is bigger than the square.

In terms of truth-conditions, these are contrary because the set of worlds in which (7) is true is completely disjoint from the set where (8) is true. A stronger notion than contrariety is *contradictoriness*. Two sentences are contradictory if they can't both be true and they can't both be false. (Since sentences (7)–(8) are clearly contrary, they are contradictory if it's impossible for both to be false as well. It may be that they can both be false in a situation in which there is no circle or no square, or it may be that they are neither true nor false in that kind of situation. See chapter 5 for more details on the meaning of phrases introduced by *the*.)

A sentence *p entails* another sentence *q* if the truth of *p* guarantees the truth of *q*:

(9)   The circle is inside the square.

(10)   The square is bigger than the circle.

As seen in diagram 5, (9) guarantees the truth of (10) because the set of worlds in which the former is true is completely contained within (a subset of) the set where the latter is true. That is, if a situation is in the (9)-set, it's guaranteed to be in the (10)-set too.

(a)   A sentence is a *contradiction* if, based on its meaning, it can never be true. A sentence is a *tautology* if, based on its meaning, it must be true. Two sentences are *compatible* if they are not contradictory. How would these terms be explicated in a possible worlds Venn (set) diagram?

(b)   In terms of your semantic analysis for sentences of the form *p and q*, *p or q* and *It is not the case that p*, show that:

- *p* entails *p or q*.
- *p* and *It is not the case that p* are contradictory.
- *p and q* entails *p*.
- If *p* entails *q*, and *q* and *r* are contradictory, then *p* and *r* are contradictory.

One way to do this is to work with Venn diagrams, which let you represent the relations among *p*, *q*, and *r* pictorially.

This exercise has an answer, no. 2, in the appendix.

Possible worlds also let us define some fancier semantic properties in a way quite similar to synonymy, entailment, and the like. For instance, as we'll see in chapter 8, they come in very handy when we try to understand *modality*, the semantics of words like *must*, *may*, *can*, *necessary*, and *possible*.

1.3.1.3   Reason 3: Meaning and action

Thinking of meaning as truth-conditions fits into a plausible story about the usefulness of language in daily life.[13] Why do we talk to one another, anyway? One simple, intuitive answer to this question is that language lets us pass on information about the world, so that we can benefit from the each other's experiences. This brings up another question: how do we benefit from information which comes from the experiences of others? An answer: by using that information to help determine which actions are most likely to lead to outcomes we desire.

Put a little bit more precisely, we can say that communication helps us refine our beliefs about what the world is like, and this lets us choose our actions in a rational way. An action is rational to the extent that it tends to maximize the satisfaction of our desires, given our beliefs. (Note that talking about desire here doesn't imply selfishness. One may have altruistic desires.) This may sound very philosophical, but the idea is quite simple. John tells Mary that it is raining outside, and so now she believes something about the world that she did not believe before. This belief helps her determine that it's a good idea to take an umbrella when she goes out, since this will maximize the chance that she'll stay dry (which she desires) given that she now believes it is raining.

We can describe this situation in terms of possible worlds, illustrated in diagram 6 (p. 22). Let's begin by thinking about her desires. Throughout, she wants to stay dry. This is indicated by the dashed line in the diagrams, which only contains worlds where she can avoid getting wet, either because it's sunny out or because she has an umbrella. (Notice that she doesn't desire all sunny worlds or all umbrella worlds, simply because some of these worlds may have other problems. For example, I believe that in the uppermost sunny world, she gets stung by a bee – we can't be bothered to put every detail of the world in our pictures, can we? – so she doesn't desire that world at all.)

Next consider Mary's beliefs. Before the weather report, she believes it will be sunny. This is indicated by the solid line, which on the left-hand diagram only contains sunny worlds. However, on the weather report John says "It will rain today," and this sentence denotes the set of possible worlds indicated by the dotted line. Since Mary believes John, she needs to shift her beliefs to a set which only contains worlds in the proposition expressed by *It will rain today*. This gets us to the right-hand diagram. As you can see in the right-hand diagram, the only worlds which match both Mary's beliefs and her desires are ones where she takes an umbrella. So she'll take an umbrella.

This little story helps support the idea that the meaning of a sentence should be thought of in terms of its truth-conditions because of the role played by John's sentence *It will rain today*. What John said was useful to Mary because it helped her decide to take an umbrella. The

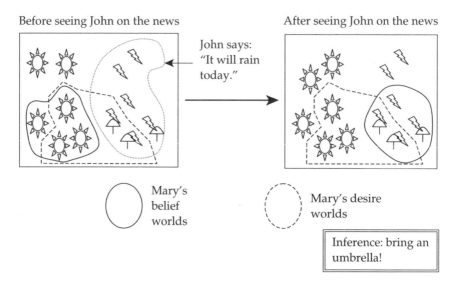

Before seeing John on the news

John says: "It will rain today."

After seeing John on the news

Mary's belief worlds

Mary's desire worlds

Inference: bring an umbrella!

Diagram 6

truth-conditional aspect of its meaning was precisely what was needed to explain how it helped her in this way. If we think that the fundamental function of language is to help us share information and so make better decisions about what actions to take, it seems that truth-conditional meaning is the kind of meaning which underlies language's fundamental function. And if this is so, it makes sense that it is considered to be the first kind of meaning to study!

To think about: many linguists would argue that this function of language is by no means the only one, and even that it's not fundamental. For example, a lot of small talk seems useless from the perspective of facilitating rational action, and might better be described as designed to build or maintain social relationships. The truth-conditional view of meaning sees that function of language as secondary, arising not from the meaning of what is said, but rather from the higher-level awareness of the conversation which is taking place. What do you think?

It can be an interesting exercise to select random things you say during the day (say, by having an alarm go off at hourly intervals), and then try to categorize each as to whether it's basic function is social, informational, or a combination of the two.

1.3.2 Non-declarative sentence types: interrogatives and imperatives

If the meaning of sentences is to be understood in terms of their truth-conditions, what of sentences which can't intuitively be described as true or false? It doesn't make sense to say that an interrogative sentence like (11), or an imperative sentence like (12), is true (or that it's false).

(11)   Who did Sylvia visit?

(12)   Draw a circle inside a square.

While they require us to expand our horizons a little bit, these non-declarative sentences nevertheless can fit naturally into the truth-conditional view of meaning.

First, interrogatives: a question is a request for information, and what the form of the question does is tell the hearer what sort of information is being looked for. In the case of (11), the speaker desires the kind of information that can be expressed with a sentence of the form "Sylvia visited person x." We might say that the fundamental role of a question is to tell the hearer what kind of answer is being sought. This has led to the major approach to understanding the meaning of questions in truth-conditional terms: the meaning of a question is defined in terms of its possible answers.[14] This can be made more precise in various ways, and the debates concerning them aren't important for us here. Hamblin, for example, says that the meaning of a question is the set of propositions which are possible answers to it. For example, suppose the only people relevant to the conversation are Lucia and Linna. (How it is determined that they are the only ones relevant is an important question, and clearly involves thinking about the situation in which (11) is used.) If only Lucia and Linna are relevant, and we assume Sylvia visited only one, the meaning of (11) would be the set of the following two propositions: the proposition that she visited Lucia and the proposition that she visited Linna (diagram 7, p. 24). In terms of this meaning, the function of a question is to provoke the hearer into picking the true answer(s) from this set.

Imperatives are a bit easier. Imperative sentences, like declarative sentences, categorize worlds into two kinds. Just as *The circle is inside the square* categorizes worlds in the way illustrated in diagram 3, sentence (12) categorizes worlds in a similar way. It's just that in the case of (12), we don't naturally call these the "true" situations and the "false" worlds. Rather, we might call them the "satisfactory" worlds and the "unsatisfactory" ones.

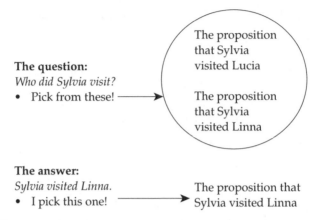

The question:
Who did Sylvia visit?
- Pick from these! ⟶

The proposition
that Sylvia
visited Lucia

The proposition
that Sylvia
visited Linna

The answer:
Sylvia visited Linna.
- I pick this one! ⟶ The proposition that
Sylvia visited Linna

Diagram 7

Worlds in which the addressee draws a circle inside the square are satisfactory, and other kinds are not. Therefore, imperative sentences teach us something more terminological than substantive: we would be better off if we do not describe sentence meaning in terms of "true" vs. "false" worlds, but rather we should use a more general term. We might call them the "yes" worlds vs. the "no" worlds. In the case of a declarative, "yes" is understood to mean "true," while with imperatives, it's understood to mean "satisfactory."

1.3.3   Semantic meaning vs. speaker's meaning

The following conversation takes place at a party:[15]

A: Most of the people here seem pretty glum.
B: Not everybody. The man drinking champagne is happy.
A: Where?
B: That guy! (pointing)
A: He's not drinking champagne. He's drinking sparkling water. The only person drinking champagne is crying on the couch. See?
B: Well, what I meant was that the first guy is happy.

The last thing B says is an explanation of what he meant when he said "The man drinking champagne is happy." He meant that the guy drinking sparkling water is happy. This points out the need to distinguish what a person means from what the words uttered by that person mean.

In saying "The man drinking champagne is happy," B meant that the guy drinking sparkling water is happy. And he meant something true. Nevertheless, what he said, "The man drinking champagne is happy," was false.

The *semantic meaning* of a sentence is its literal meaning, based on what the words individually mean and the grammar of the language. The *speaker's meaning* of a sentence is what the speaker intends to communicate by uttering it. Often these two coincide, but in the party scenario they did not, due to a mistake of speaker B. Sometimes they might fail to coincide for other reasons. Irony, for one (the semantic meaning is the opposite of my speaker's meaning). Convenience, for another (I know that the woman in a queen-costume at a costume party is not a queen, but say "The queen is quite beautiful." Even though my sentence is literally false, I'm confident you'll understand what I mean).

> What other situations can you think of where speaker's and semantic meaning would differ?

When we do semantics, we try to understand – no surprise here – semantic meaning. Speaker's meaning will become more of a direct concern in chapters 10 and 11, when we discuss the sister-field of semantics known as pragmatics. For now, we will try to put speaker's meaning aside, and concentrate on semantic meaning. But we'll have to work hard at this, because it is not always so easy to do. In some cases, it's not easy to figure out whether the meaning we see for a sentence is its literal (semantic) meaning, or a speaker's meaning. For example, a newscaster says "The people remember Tiananmen Square." Of course what she means is that the people remember certain events which took place in Tiananmen Square (and maybe other events which took place around the same time). Does the sentence also literally mean this, or is its literal meaning just that the people remember the physical square itself? It's hard to say. Until we know more basics of semantics, it's best to avoid examples of this kind, even though this means we have to avoid some aspects of how people actually talk. (Is it a problem that we avoid some aspects of how people actually talk? I think it's OK. We're doing science after all. Science typically steers clear of the complexities of our daily world in the hopes that from simplicity will come deeper truths. But science can often return to the daily world and be applied to real situations, and we must try to make sure that semantics eventually can do the same.)

NOTES

1   Quine (1953; 1960).
2   See Fodor and Lepore (1992). Some holists certainly think that holism is com-
     patible with semantics as it is practiced by linguists: see Block (forthcoming).
     Donald Davidson's approach to meaning is holistic, and he and his fol-
     lowers not only believe a scientific approach is possible, but have developed
     a formal semantic theory (see chapter 12 for more discussion). A recent paper
     interesting for linguists is Dresner (2002).
          This little book doesn't pretend to offer a substantial discussion of the debates
     among foundational theories of meaning, and indeed you don't have to know
     much to understand what linguists who practice formal semantics do. I just
     hope to explain in a pretty intuitive way the formal semanticist's perspect-
     ive on matters. The references in the notes to this chapter should provide the
     reader who has both linguistic and philosophical interests with some place
     to start. Other introductions to semantics would be useful too: Heim and Kratzer
     (1997); Chierchia and McConnell-Ginet (2000); Larson and Siegel (1995);
     Saeed (2003).
          I thank Steve Kuhn for discussion of the material in this section.
3   I like this terminology from Martin (1987), which discusses many of these
     philosophical issues in a very clear way. Some starter references on versions
     of the idea theory are: Jackendoff (1992; 1990). On the theory known as cog-
     nitive linguistics, see: Lakoff and Johnson (1980); Lakoff (1987); Fauconnier
     (1985).
4   See Fodor (1975) on the idea of a language of thought. Steven Pinker (1994)
     makes the claim that language understanding is the translation of regular lan-
     guage into the language of thought.
5   On Twin Earth, see for example: Putnam (1975); Burge (1979; 1982).
6   There are ideas about semantics which have something in common with the
     idea theory, but which don't identify meanings with ideas. We might say,
     for example, that meanings are ideas plus something else which makes up
     for the deficiency of the idea theory. See for example Field (1977); Block (1986);
     Harman (1987). Some of these theories are functional, holistic views about
     the nature of meaning in the sense we discussed earlier, so whatever is added
     to the hypothesis that meanings are ideas would need to make up for the
     problems we identified with holism as well.
7   This idea originates with Wittgenstein (1953). For a recent development, see
     Brandom (1983; 1994; 2000). Thanks to Mark Lance for discussion of these
     paragraphs.
8   This point does not seem clear to many linguists, who have the feeling that
     a social practice theory of meaning necessarily undermines formal semantics.
9   This way of thinking is consistent with the possibility that what counts as a
     dog is socially constructed, rather than a natural category. The category "office

worker" is socially constructed. Still, I would say that the term *office worker* describes all the members of this category. Perhaps all categories are like "office worker." This would have nothing to do with the point that meanings are in the world.

10 One shouldn't be thrown off the track by thinking about words like *idea* or *concept* themselves. One might think: if meanings are parts of mind-external reality, wouldn't the word *idea* show that ideas themselves are part of mind-external reality? But then wouldn't the idea theory simply be one version of the theory that meanings are out in the world? The difference is that the idea theory takes all meanings to be ideas, while this argument simply shows that some meanings are ideas. The perspective that meanings are out in the world puts ideas on a par with dogs and ancient Chinese philosophers as far as their ability to serve as meanings goes, and, in contrast to the idea theory, doesn't give them a paramount role to play.

11 On this strategy, see for example: Davidson (1967a); Lewis (1970); Field (1977); Lycan (1984).

12 I will use these terms interchangeably, but sometimes they are used differently. Some scholars would say that a word, phrase, or sentence expresses its sense, and denotes its reference. See chapter 5 for an explanation of the difference between sense and reference.

13 See Lewis (1986) and Stalnaker (1984), for two good examples.

14 Hamblin (1973); Karttunen (1977); Groenendijk and Stokhof (1982; 1984).

15 This example is based on Kripke (1977).

2 Putting a Meaning Together from Pieces

We now have some idea of what sort of thing the meaning of a sentence is. The meaning of a sentence is its truth-conditions. *The square is inside the circle* denotes the set of situations where it is true. So, knowing the meaning of a sentence amounts to knowing what it would take for it to be true.

Let's take an even simpler example: knowing the meaning of *Shelby barks* amounts to knowing that it's true if (and only if) Shelby barks. You might say: "This is silly! I bother to study semantics, and all you can tell me is that *Shelby barks* is true if and only if Shelby barks. This is trivial!" This is a natural reaction, one that almost every student of semantics has. But it's not trivial, for two reasons.

First, think about what happens when you don't know a foreign language. Suppose that I tell you in Chinese *Xaiobi jiao*, and you have the impression I'm telling you something important. But since you can't speak Chinese, you begin to get worried. "What is Paul telling me?" you wonder. It would be useful to you to know that what I said is true if and only if Shelby barks.

The statement "*Shelby barks* is true if and only if Shelby barks" seems trivial because I'm using English in two ways. I am using English to talk about English. The italicized *Shelby barks* is the piece of language I'm talking about; we say that it is an expression in the *object language*. It is a piece of the English language, but it could just as well have been Chinese. In contrast, the rest of what I say ". . . is true if and only if Shelby barks" is being used to say something about the object language; it is an expression in the *metalanguage*. The metalanguage is also English, because that's the language I know best and can write a book in. If I use English to talk about Chinese, or Chinese to talk about English, a lot of the appearance of triviality disperses. But it's most convenient for me to use English to talk about English.

The second reason that a statement like "*Shelby barks* is true if and only if Shelby barks" is not trivial is that it opens up another question: how does the sentence get precisely those truth-conditions? What contribution does each word make? Each makes a crucial contribution, since exchanging *Hobo* for *Shelby* or *sleeps* for *barks* would make a big difference. And what role does the grammar of English play? Consider a three-word sentence like *Shelby bit Hobo*. This does not mean the same thing as *Hobo bit Shelby*, so grammar is crucial too. We're not so much interested in the fact that *Shelby barks* is true if and only if Shelby barks, since any English speaker can tell us that; we're more interested in figuring out how it gets to mean what it does.

More fundamentally, the issue is that, because we intuitively know the meaning of *Shelby barks* or *Hobo bit Shelby*, it seems trivial to report on those meanings. But it only seems trivial. Just because something is intuitive and easy, this doesn't mean that it's simple. There are savants who know the answers to complex mathematical equations just by looking at them. But the fact that they find it easy doesn't mean that the math is simple; it only means that somehow their brains let them do complex problem solving effortlessly. You could say that we're all semantics-savants (or language-savants more generally), effortlessly solving complex meaning-problems. As semanticists come to understand the complexity of meaning, we can all appreciate just how amazing our effortless skill in creating meaningful language is.

In this chapter, we'll focus obsessively on the most simple English sentences possible, two-word sentences like *Shelby barks*, and try to develop an idea about how they get to mean what they do. This may sound like it's going to be pretty dull, but in fact there's a lot to learn from two-word sentences. Moreover, it will lay the foundation for studying more complex sentences in subsequent chapters.

2.1   Names Refer

Shelby barks has two words in it, so let's focus first on the first word. What contribution does *Shelby* make to the sentence's meaning? We have already discussed the meaning of names in the last chapter, and concluded that their meaning is their reference.[1] *Confucius* refers to a particular ancient Chinese philosopher; *Shelby* refers to my dog. This is at least a major portion of their meaning, and perhaps all there is to their meaning. Their reference is what they contribute to the meaning of a sentence in which they occur.

If I am walking with Shelby and wish to tell you that he barks, I could just point at him and say "Barks." By pointing at him, I would make clear that he's the thing which I am describing with my verb. If language had predicates but no names, we would need to keep around us everything we might want to talk about – we'd point to a thing and use a predicate to describe it.[2] Fortunately language gives us the flexibility to avoid this. We have names for things, and the name brings the thing into a statement without the need to have the thing itself at hand.

2.2   Incomplete Propositions

Diagram 8 is a new way of representing a proposition. Within the big oval, we indicate that if the dog (that's Shelby) makes noises like "Woof!" we have a true sentence, and if he doesn't we have a false one. (This is equivalent to the way we've indicated the meaning of a sentence before, drawing a bunch of situations, then indicating some as the TRUE set and the rest as the FALSE set.) Obviously, I intend this diagram to represent the meaning of the sentence *Shelby barks*.

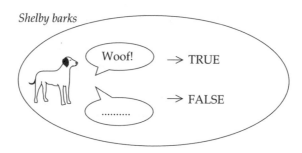

Diagram 8

Suppose we want the meaning of *barks* alone. One way to get at it is by subtraction: take the meaning of *Shelby barks*, and then remove the meaning of *Shelby*. What's left should be the meaning of *barks*. Doing that to diagram 8, we get diagram 9. This is the same picture as in diagram 8, except that there is a hole where we've cut out Shelby. (This can be a fun game if you don't mind cutting up the book, or making some copies. As you go through this book, you can create your own set of toy semantics building-blocks.)

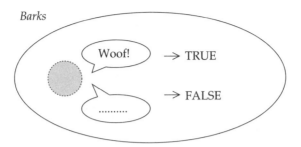

Diagram 9

The meaning of *barks* in diagram 9 is an incomplete proposition, a proposition with a piece missing. This is the basic idea behind the semantics of predicates: they are sentence meanings minus the contribution of the sentence's subject. Following the philosopher Gottlob Frege, semanticists frequently use the term *unsaturated*. A predicate is an unsaturated proposition. Another common term is *property*. A property is an unsaturated proposition, the kind of thing denoted by a predicate. This view of properties takes them to be the semantic core of the sentence, as can be seen by the fact that diagram 9 contains almost everything in diagram 8, minus only one little bit.

2.3   Predication is Saturation

Now that we've figured out what *Shelby* means and what *barks* means, we can work backwards and see what happens when someone takes a name and puts it together with a predicate to make a sentence. Somebody says *Shelby barks* to you. You think, "I know that first word. They are referring to Shelby." (This is indicated by the little circle in diagram 10.) Then you think, "I know that second word, they are denoting that property I am familiar with, the one from diagram 9." Finally you think, "The person talking to me put these two words together, so I suppose I'm supposed to put Shelby together with the property; I will saturate the unsaturated, letting Shelby fill in the missing piece of the property." The result is the proposition we saw earlier in diagram 8.

If we had another name instead of *Shelby*, the process would have been parallel, but the result is somewhat different. Suppose I had said *Bach barks*. Then instead of referring to Shelby, I would have referred to a particular composer. This might be represented by having the little circle picture

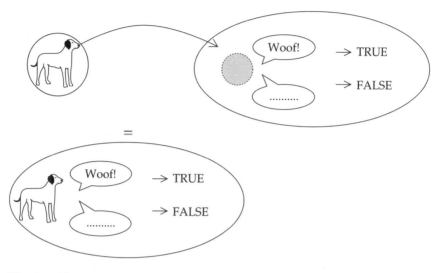

=

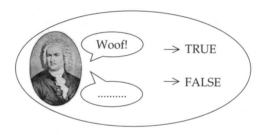

Diagram 10

Diagram 11

Bach, rather than a dog. This guy would saturate the property, and we'd end up with the proposition indicated in diagram 11.

The relationship between a predicate and its subject is called *predication*. We say that *barks* "is predicated of" *Shelby*. As we've seen, the semantics of a predicate is a property, or unsaturated proposition; the semantics of a subject (at least when that subject is a name) is a thing referred to. The semantics of predication is saturation, as the property receives its missing piece from the thing referred to. The phrase which saturates a predicate is known as an *argument* of the predicate. *Shelby* is an argument of *barks*.

There's a lot of terminology flying around how. Let me summarize how I'm using some words. Terms which pertain to the form of a sentence (in linguistics, what we call morphology and syntax) are in **bold**. Terms which describe the meanings (or semantics) of words or phrases are <u>underlined</u>.

- **Predicate** A kind of grammatical unit. *Barks* is an example. If you need more details, check out any grammar, or better yet syntax, book.
- **Name** Another kind of grammatical unit. *Shelby* is an example.
- **Noun phrase** A kind of grammatical unit centered on a noun. A name is a kind of noun phrase.
- **Subject** A grammatical function which a name or other noun phrase can have in a sentence. In English, it's typically the noun phrase which comes before the predicate.
- <u>Property</u> A semantic object. The sort of thing which a predicate denotes. An unsaturated proposition. The property of being something which barks is an example.
- <u>Referent</u> A thing, in a very broad sense, which serves as the semantic meaning of a name (and certain other kinds of noun phrases). My dog Shelby, for example, is the referent of *Shelby* when it is used in this book.
- **Predication** The grammatical relationship between a predicate and a subject.
- <u>Saturation</u> Making an incomplete semantic object (like a property) more complete by filling in a missing part. Predication brings about the saturation of a property.
- **Argument** A word or phrase whose referent saturates a predicate. A subject is an example.

2.4 Compositionality

A language is an infinite collection of phrases, sentences, and discourses. This can be easily seen from the fact that any sentence can be made longer by combining it with another sentence – in fact, it's possible to do this in very many different ways. (1) becomes (2) by adding another sentence using *and*. (2) becomes (3) by adding a relative clause *which is fat*. It's not hard to see that with tricks like this, there is no longest sentence.

(1)   The cat ate the rat.

(2)   The cat ate the rat and the bat ate the cat.

(3)   The cat which is fat ate the rat and the bat ate the cat.

Since humans are finite creatures, one of the main tasks of linguistic theory is to understand how their minds can give rise to the infinity of language. This is one of the main reasons for the linguistics industry known as syntax (the field which studies how words are combined into phrases and sentences), but the infinity of language is equally an issue for semantics. Each of those infinite number of pieces of language has meaning, and the theory of semantics must somehow be able to link each one to the right meaning.

Apart from the issue of infinity, semanticists (like other linguists) also have to consider the fact that language is creative. We are constantly hearing new phrases and sentences, ones we've never heard before, and yet we somehow manage to figure out what they mean. Semantic theory, considered from a psychological perspective, has to provide an account of the knowledge of meaning which language users have, and which allows for their ability to quickly and easily understand novel pieces of language.

Semanticists seek to bring the infinity and creativity of language within the capacity of human minds by appealing to the *principle of compositionality*. In its simplest form, the principle says that the meaning of a piece of language is based solely on the meanings of its (linguistically relevant) parts, and the way they are put together. With the principle of compositionality, the infinity and creativity of language are comprehensible, since it means that we only have to know a finite number of basic things (the meanings of the smallest pieces of language and the methods of combining them), and this gives us enough knowledge to associate the right meaning with every bigger piece of language.

We've seen the principle of compositionality applied to simple subject–predicate sentences like *Shelby barks*. The meaning of this sentence is based on the meanings of the parts *Shelby* and *barks*, and the way in which they are combined, by predication: in the sentence *Shelby barks*, *Shelby* is the subject and *barks* is the predicate. *Shelby* refers to a thing, Shelby; *barks* gives us the property of barking; and predication tells us to saturate that property with that thing. The rest of our discussion of semantics is essentially about fleshing out this picture. We'll need to understand what each basic language-piece means (adjectives, determiners, various sorts of verbs, conjunctions, . . .), and what each way of combining pieces of languages says about how to combine those meanings.

2.5   Syntax and Semantics

The principle of compositionality tells us that semantics is always going to have a close relationship with the field of syntax. As mentioned above, syntax is about how sentences are constructed. The internal structure of a sentence arises from how it is constructed, and this structure can be represented with a *phrase structure tree*, a kind of diagram like (4) which indicates the internal structure of the sentence:

(4)

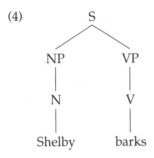

In (4), S stands for "sentence," NP for "noun phrase," VP for "verb phrase," N for "noun," and V for "verb." The lines show how the phrases higher in the tree are composed of the pieces lower in the tree. The individual points in the tree connected by lines are known as "nodes," so that S, NP, N, etc. are all nodes. When two nodes are connected by a line, the lower one is known as a "daughter" of the higher one, its "mother."

Looking at the tree in (4), the principle of compositionality says that the meaning of S is derived from the meaning of the NP, the meaning of VP, and the method of combining NP and VP to make S. It says that the meaning of the NP is based on the meaning of the N and the method of construction ("make an NP from an N, if that N is a name"), and that the meaning of this N is based on the meaning of *Shelby* ("make an N from a word, if that word is a noun"), and so forth.

The principle of compositionality leaves a lot of leeway in terms of precisely how we see the relationship between syntax and semantics, and because of this leeway, many different technical theories have been developed. One major division among the ways of thinking about the issue is between what are called *rule-by-rule theories* and *interpretive theories*.

A rule-by-rule theory sees the meaning of a sentence as being built up in parallel with its structure. It suggests a method like the following for building up the meaning of our simplest sentence, *Shelby barks*:

(5) • Take the noun *Shelby* from the lexicon (= the storage space for words), and also take its meaning (let's call that meaning **s**).
    • Take the verb *barks* from the lexicon, and also take its meaning **b** (a property).
    • Assign *Shelby* to the category N, and assign this N the meaning **s**.

- Assign *barks* to the category V, and assign this V the meaning **b**.
- Assign *Shelby* to the category NP, and assign this NP the meaning **s**.
- Assign *barks* to the category VP, and assign this VP the meaning **b**.
- Combine the NP and the VP into an S, and assign this S the meaning you get by saturating **b** with **s**.

Notice how the rule-by-rule theory makes semantics operate in tandem with syntax, in that the meaning of the sentence is built up as the sentence itself is built up. The theory is called "rule-by-rule" because as each syntactic rule is brought to bear (e.g. "combine the NP and the VP into an S"), so is a corresponding semantic rule ("saturate **b** with **s**").

An interpretive theory has all of syntax happen first, and then has semantics work on a tree like (4) which is the output of syntax. The semanticist needn't worry about all the details of syntactic theory. All she needs to know is that the result is (4). Then, a series of semantic rules applies to this tree, determining the meaning of the S in terms of the meanings of its parts in a compositional way. For example, the procedure might look like the following, starting at the bottom of the tree in (4):

(6)
- Look up the meaning of *Shelby* in the lexicon (again, let's call this meaning **s**).
- Look up the meaning of *barks* in the lexicon (= **b**).
- Because *Shelby* is the sole daughter of N, assign **s** as the meaning of N.
- Because *barks* is the sole daughter of V, assign **b** as the meaning of V.
- Because N is the sole daughter of NP, assign **s** as the meaning of NP.
- Because V is the sole daughter of VP, assign **b** as the meaning of VP.
- Because NP and VP are the two components of S, and one of their meanings is a property **b**, while the other's meaning is a thing **s**, let **s** saturate **b** and assign the result as the meaning of S.

To a considerable extent, an idea which can be presented in terms of a rule-by-rule theory can also be presented within an interpretive theory, and vice versa. The fundamental difference between them has to do with whether every syntactic process corresponds to a something semantic.

The interpretive theory requires that the final tree derived by syntactic processes be given a meaning, but it doesn't require that every syntactic step along the way has semantic relevance. For instance, if during the process of building up a sentence, some phrase can be created and then destroyed, the interpretive theory doesn't require that the destroyed phrase have a meaning. The rule-by-rule, instead, requires that every syntactic step correspond to a semantic step.

Here's an analogy: suppose that business X wants a new office, and orders that a skyscraper be built. Let's consider two ways X could be charged for this building:

- The price could be based on the cost of each activity which takes place during construction: $40 for each hour of worker time, the actual cost of all materials used by the construction company plus 10 percent, $100,000 for design work, and so forth. Suppose that as it builds the office tower, the construction company puts up and later removes some scaffolding. According to this pricing scheme, business X will be billed for the scaffolding, and the time it takes to put it up and take it down.
- The price could be based on the specifications of the final building: $100 for each square foot of floor space, for example. According to this pricing scheme, business X will not be directly charged for scaffolding. Its cost must be factored into the price of the final building.

The first scheme is analogous to a rule-by-rule theory, and the second to an interpretive theory.

A real linguistic example might be a sentence like (7):

(7)   What did John sit on?

Many syntactic theories would propose that *what* is originally combined with *on* to form a prepositional phrase *on what* (parallel to *on the chair*), and that *what* is then moved away to the beginning of the sentence. If this is right, the rule-by-rule theory would say that *on what* should have a meaning, and that this meaning contributes to the meaning of the whole sentence, while the interpretive theory would not need to claim such a thing. The interpretive theory would just base its explanation of the meaning of (7) on the final structure, with *what* at the beginning of the sentence. We would require more detailed technical knowledge than we're going for in this book to pursue the question of which approach is better. I'll frame the discussion in this book mostly in terms of the interpretive theory.

Let's put aside the distinction between the rule-by-rule theory and interpretive theory. Another goal which motivates how semanticists talk about the relationship between syntax and semantics is to simplify the format of the rules as much as possible. For example, looking at the procedures in (5) and (6), we can see the following pattern:

(8)   If a node has a single daughter, the meaning of that node equals the meaning of the daughter.

It's better to have a single general-purpose rule like (8) rather than a collection of more specific rules like "if an NP has a single daughter N, the meaning of the NP equals the meaning of N," "if a VP has a single daughter V, the meaning of the VP equals the meaning of the V," and so forth.

One important issue in the relationship between syntax and semantic is whether semantic rules ever need to pay attention to syntactic relationships other than what is the daughter of what. Consider the process of combining the NP and the VP to make an S, and the corresponding semantic operation of predication. Should this rule be stated as in (9) or (10)?

(9)   If an S has two daughters, one an NP and the other a VP, the meaning of the S equals the result of allowing the meaning of the NP to saturate the meaning of the VP.

(10)   If a node has two daughters, and the meaning of one of the daughters is a thing and the meaning of the other is a property, the meaning of the mother equals the result of allowing the thing to saturate the property.

In (9), we need to know that we have an S, an NP, and a VP in order to trigger the semantic process of saturation. In (10), we need to know that we have one daughter whose meaning is a thing and another whose meaning is a property. That is, in (9) we focus heavily on syntactic facts, while in (10) we focus primarily on semantic facts. Semanticists these days typically strive for rules like (10), and the resulting theories are known as *type-driven theories*.[3] (They are called "type-driven" basically because it is the types of meanings at hand which determine how semantics works, not the syntactic categories like NP and VP.) Type-driven theories may be either of the rule-by-rule sort or the interpretive sort. If we're working with a type-driven interpretive theory, one nice feature is that it makes the node labels S, NP, VP, etc. in the syntactic tree irrelevant to how the meaning is arrived at. So, we can drop all those labels and use a simplified tree like (11) instead of (4):

(11)

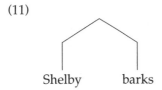

Shelby   barks

NOTES

1   There are other views on the semantics of names. See chapters 5 and 6 below for discussion.
2   If we had enough predicates, we could be creative and get away without having names. Instead of saying *Shelby barks*, we could say *There is something which shelbies, and it barks* (by definition, Shelby is the only thing that "shelbies"). So the point made in the text is meant as a statement about how language actually works, not how it must work on basic logical principles.
3   Klein and Sag (1985).

3   More about Predicates

This chapter and the following ones will elaborate upon the fundamental ideas concerning sentence meaning introduced in the previous chapters. So far, we can explain how the meaning of a simple sentence like *Shelby barks* works. This sentence has a single noun (a name) and a single verb. We will slowly work toward incorporating more and more complex sentence types, and along the way will improve our understanding of simple names and predicates as well. In this chapter, we'll go into more detail concerning the semantics of predicates.

3.1   Other Types of Predicates: Adjectives, Predicate Nominals

Sentences (1) and (2) are name+predicate sentences like *Shelby barks*, but seem a bit more complex.

(1)   Shelby is small.

(2)   Shelby is a dog.

The main predicate in (1) is *small* and the main predicate in (2) is *dog*. For example, we could represent the meaning of *small* as in diagram 12, and Shelby could saturate this property in the way we're familiar with. But then, what about the extra words in (1) and (2): *is* and *a*?[1]

Let's focus on *is* in (1). This word seems to have no semantic function at all (apart from the fact that it indicates present tense – let's put tense aside for now, and come back to it in chapter 8). *Is* is just getting in the way of letting *small* be the predicate of *Shelby*. How can we get it out of the way? One possibility is to simply say that it is meaningless. Then, we

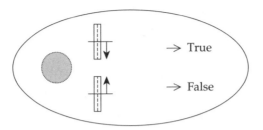

Diagram 12

might think that it's invisible to the understanding of meaning, so that when we try to go through a procedure like (5) or (6) in the last chapter, *is* is simply ignored. We might think of this as taking the syntactic tree for (1) and erasing *is* before we think about the sentence's meaning. This way of thinking about *is* says that, while it may have an important grammatical role to play, that role is purely syntactic – having to do with sentence form – and not at all semantic. It would be a kind of grammatical matchmaker, bringing two words together and then disappearing as the love affair develops.

There are many languages which would not use (the word corresponding to) *is* in a sentence like (1). Does this support the idea that *is* is erased for semantic purposes? Another possibility would be that *is* is needed in English because *small* has a different meaning in English than in languages which wouldn't use *is*. Can you think of a way to make sense of this idea?

Another possibility is to give *is* a meaning, but one which doesn't interfere with the combination of the words on either side of it. What we want is a kind of property which dissolves into nothing once it combines with another, more contentful property. More precisely, we want a property which is not saturated until it combines with another property, and the result of combining the two is equivalent to that other property. We could indicate this meaning in terms of our cut-out pictures as in diagram 13. Just as a regular property has a hole in it that's the right size for filling in a thing like Shelby, this diagram has a bigger hole which is the right size for filling in a whole regular property like *small* or *barks*. This diagram indicates an empty shell of a property, a property with a property-sized hole in it, so that once you insert a property into this hole, the resulting property is just the same as the property you inserted. Pictorially, diagram 13 would combine with the property we saw in diagram 12 as in

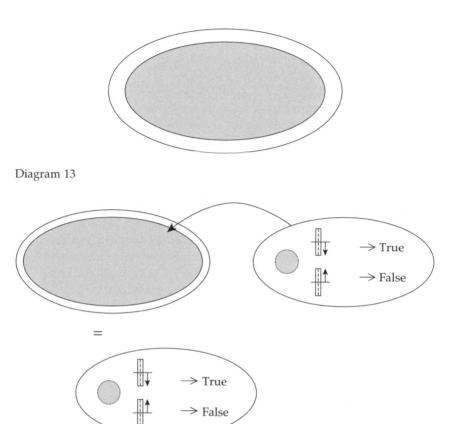

Diagram 13

Diagram 14

diagram 14, and the result is just the same as diagram 12. (Ignore the extra width added by the outer shell of diagram 13. This extra width is only present because I can't draw an oval with zero width.)

Metaphorically speaking, the meaning for *is* indicated by diagram 13 is something like a politician with no ideas of his own. Whoever pays the most money is allowed to feed the politician the words of her choosing, and the politician gratefully speaks out exactly the words that are put in.

What we have seen is that we can deal with the semantic non-contribution of *is* in either of two ways: by giving it no meaning at all, or by giving it a trivial meaning, one which makes no difference to the sentence. Now, how about the other little word in our current examples, *a* in (2)? A noun phrase introduced by *a(n)* is known as an indefinite noun phrase, and *a(n)* itself is called the indefinite article (or indefinite determiner). The semantics of indefinite noun phrases is something we'll come back to several times (especially in chapters 5 and 6), but in the current example (2) we find that *a*, like *is*, seems to be getting in the way of the predication between *Shelby* and *dog*. Many semanticists would handle it in the same way as *is*. So, for example, if we take the view that meaningless words are erased for semantic purposes, sentence (2) would have two words erased, and semantically speaking we'd just be dealing with *Shelby dog*.

> Stop for a moment and see if you can come up with any reasons why it makes sense (or doesn't) to think of (2) as being reduced to *Shelby dog* for semantic purposes. What do you think is the role of *a*? What do other languages tell you about this situation?

The idea that *a* is meaningless in *Shelby is a dog* is a bit more difficult to accept than the corresponding hypothesis concerning *is*. One reason for this is that we find *a* in other types of sentences, for example in (3) below. Here, *a* is not part of the sentence's predicate, and intuitively has meaning, a meaning of the same general type as other words like *the*, *one*, or *every* which can fit into the same slot, as in (4).

(3)   A dog bit me.

(4)   The/One/Every dog bit me.

Given these complexities, there are several alternative ways to think about *a*:

  i   We might say that we are dealing with two different versions of *a*, so that it has no meaning in (2) but has a meaning in (3).
  ii   We might say that *a* is indeed meaningless in (3), just like in (2). This would mean that *a* is very different from *the*, *one*, and *every*, since they clearly have a meaning.[2] The real job of *a*, we might say, is to indicate the absence of *the*, *one*, *every*, etc.
  iii We might say that we've been wrong about *a*, and that it has a meaning in all cases. This would force us to answer the question of how *a* and *dog* get together to express a property.

I personally think option (ii) is the best. However, it's clear that we can't resolve this unless we can think in detail about the meaning of (3).

Unfortunately, we have so far only considered sentences whose subjects are simple names, and so a two-word subject like *a dog* is beyond our understanding at present. (Plenty on this in chapters 5 and 6!)

3.2   Transitive Verbs

In example (5), the phrase *saw Hannibal* is a predicate. This predicate is different from the simple one-word predicate *barks*. It is also different from the multi-word *is cute* and *is a dog*, since these – though they contain two and three words – have just one meaningful word in them. *Saw Hannibal* is a two-word predicate where both words count.

(5)   Shelby *saw Hannibal*.

Within *Shelby saw Hannibal*, the name *Hannibal* makes a contribution similar to the one *Shelby* makes: it refers to a particular dog (the neighbor's). Both *Hannibal* and *Shelby* are arguments of *saw*. We can factor the contribution of the object argument *Hannibal* out of sentence (5) via "subtraction" in the same way as we previously factored the subject argument *Shelby* out of the meaning of *Shelby barks*. The result can be represented as in diagram 15. Diagram 15 shows how we can think of the meaning of *saw* as a similar sort of thing to *barks*, but missing two parts instead of just one, "doubly unsaturated," we might say. Each of the missing parts corresponds to one of the verb's arguments. Doubly unsaturated

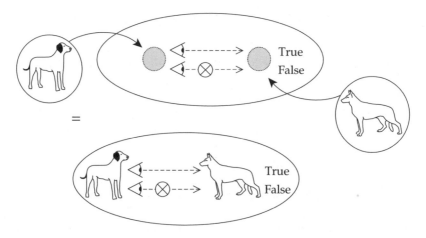

Diagram 15

propositions are known as *relations*. As the diagram shows, once the two missing parts are added into the relation, the result is a complete proposition.

According to the principle of compositionality, the "hole" in the relation which is to be saturated by Hannibal must be filled in before the hole which is to be saturated by Shelby. This is because the syntactic structure of the sentence is as in (6), where the object is closer to the verb than the subject is.

(6)

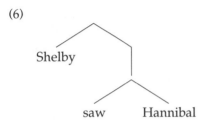

Because the verb and object are brought together first in terms of structure, the verb's meaning (the seeing relation) and the object's meaning (Hannibal) must be brought together first as we build up the meaning. The subject's meaning (Shelby) is added second, giving us a complete proposition. The formal devices which semanticists use to represent meanings can express the fact that there is an order to how things are combined with the relation, but our informal pictorial representations of meaning can't. And we're just not going to worry about this deficiency in the picture-language too much; just keep in mind the fact that things must be put together in the right order.

3.3   Relative Clauses

A relative clause is a phrase like the one within brackets in example (7) below. It is rather similar to a regular sentence, but one of the verb's arguments (in this case, the object) is replaced by a special word (*who*, called by linguists a "wh word" and by traditional grammarians a "relative pronoun") and moved to the beginning of the phrase. Though (8) seems pretty complex, it is actually just a simple subject-predicate sentence. The subject is *Hannibal*, the predicate is *who Shelby saw*, and *is* joins the two together just like in (1).

(7)   Hannibal is [who Shelby saw].

The only thing special about this sentence is that the predicate *who Shelby saw* is itself internally complex, but just like any predicate, this one denotes an unsaturated proposition.

We can figure out the meaning of the relative clause through the process of subtraction. The whole sentence (7) expresses the proposition that Shelby saw Hannibal, i.e. the proposition represented in diagram 16. To get the meaning for *who Shelby saw*, we need to factor out the contribution of *Hannibal*, putting a hole where Hannibal used to be. The result is diagram 17, which represents the meaning of the relative clause in (7). Note that both *saw Hannibal* and *who Shelby saw* express properties. However, whereas the simpler *saw Hannibal* has a "missing piece" corresponding to the "seer," *who Shelby saw* has a missing piece corresponding to the "seen." This implies, by the way, that the passive phrase *was seen by Shelby* expresses the same property as *who Shelby saw*.

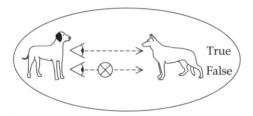

Diagram 16

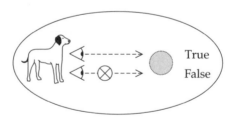

Diagram 17

The predicate in diagram 17 can combine with a subject via predication just like any other predicate can. In (7), *Hannibal* is the subject of the sentence, and so fills in this empty slot. The result is diagram 16.

Now that we've seen what the relative clause means, we can turn to a trickier question: how does it come to mean that? What is the compositional process which takes the relative clause, with a structure like (8), and interprets it like diagram 17?

(8)

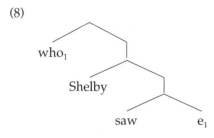

In (8), notice the node labeled "e_1." This e is there because I've drawn the tree in accord with a certain very popular type of syntactic theory. This theory tries to take account of the idea that *who* represents the direct object of *saw* (so that in prescriptively correct English, I ought to have written *whom*) by saying that at one level, it really is the object of *saw*. A more basic structure for the sentence is *Shelby saw who(m)*. However, the rules of English require us to pronounce *who* at the beginning of the clause, and so *who* is moved to a position in front of *Shelby*. The "trace" e occupies the original position as the object of *saw*, and the connection between e and *who* is represented by giving the two the same numerical subscript "1."

It is possible to compositionally interpret the structure in (8) so as to give the property in diagram 17. The details become pretty technical, but the idea is that e_1 helps to temporarily saturate *saw*, but that it does so in a way which is easy to "unsaturate." *Shelby saw e_1* is a complete proposition, built up in the same way as *Shelby saw Hannibal*. (You can think of e as like a pronoun, so this says something like "Shelby saw it.") Then *who*$_1$ tells us that some special semantic process needs to take place in order to unsaturate this proposition, giving us a property. Specifically, *who*$_1$ instructs us to unsaturate this proposition by factoring out the contribution of e_1. The result is what we see in diagram 17.

This process of creating unsaturated propositions from saturated ones is admittedly pretty complicated, but because the same sort of process is used a great deal by human language, it's important to understand the essential idea. You can think of the process of building up a property with a relative clause as parallel to building an arch on a support. As one constructs an arch, there's no way for it to stand up until the keystone is in place. So, first one builds a support on which the stones of the arch may rest. Once the keystone is in place, the support can be pulled away and the result is a free-standing arch – a wall with a hole in it. In building up a property with a relative clause, the e plays the role of the support, temporarily saturating the verb's relation until the clause is completed. Then, the *who* tells us to pull that temporary piece of meaning away, leaving the finished meaning, a property.

Another way of thinking of it can be motivated by remembering that the meaning of a transitive verb like *saw* is order-sensitive. The first argument that *saw* combines with is understood as the "seen," and the second argument as the "seer." If we were to just let the words of our relative clause combine by simple saturation, *Shelby* + *saw* would be interpreted, incorrectly, with Shelby as the "seen." The trace in (8) is a place-holder for the first argument of *saw*. This lets *Shelby* count as *saw*'s second argument, and be correctly interpreted as the "seer." Then, the relative pronoun instructs the place-holder to fall away, leaving the "seen" argument unsaturated until Hannibal comes in and saturates it.

3.4 Topicalization

One use to which we can put the technology of creating predicates from sentences is to help us understand the semantics of word-order variation. In many cases languages put the words of a sentence together in ways which don't match the basic grammar of the language. Some languages are known as "free word-order languages" because of their tendency to scramble their words in many different ways, and though English doesn't do too much of this, we do have sentences like (9):

(9) Shelby, Mary saw (but Hannibal, she didn't).

This will sound more natural if you pronounce it with stress on *Shelby* and *Hannibal*. With *Shelby* at the beginning of the sentence, despite the fact that an object should usually follow the verb, we have to wonder how the mind determines that this sentence means that Mary saw Shelby, and not for example that Shelby saw Mary. How do we associate this out-of-order sentence with the right meaning?

One way to think of (9) is involving a structure similar to (7). It's as if we had *Shelby is who Mary saw*, but with *is who* left out:

(10)

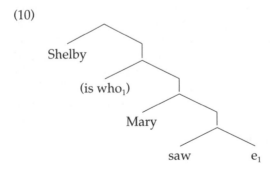

(I don't mean to argue that (9) is literally made up of *is* plus a relative clause with *is* and the relative pronoun dropped out, but I do think that the semantics of this construction is essentially the same as if it was, and thinking about it in terms of a relative clause is a concrete way of seeing the fundamental idea.)

The original structure of sentence (9) was *Mary saw Shelby*, but then *Shelby* was placed at the beginning of the sentence (for a reason having to do with pragmatics which we'll discuss in chapter 10). This leaves the piece *Mary saw e* behind, and it can be turned into a predicate, just like a relative clause. Its meaning is a property, the unsaturated proposition which when saturated by some X expresses the proposition that Mary saw X.

Sentence (9) combines the predicate *Mary saw e* with *Shelby*. Shelby saturates the property and the whole sentence expresses the proposition that Mary saw Shelby. This proves that thinking of *Mary saw* in (9) as semantically parallel to a relative clause is a workable hypothesis, and more generally that changes in word order can be seen as dependent on the process of creating predicates from clauses.

3.5   Sub-atomic Semantics

From a traditional perspective, words are the basic unit of meaning.[3] We have implicitly followed this way of looking at meaning, asking what the meanings of individual words are and then how they are combined into the meanings of complex phrases. There are many reasons to believe, though, that there are important components of meaning which are assembled below the level of the word. Terence Parsons has coined the term "sub-atomic semantics" to describe these aspects of meaning. We'll discuss two types of sub-atomic meaning which, according to many linguists, are relevant to predicates.

3.5.1   Events

Sentence (5) describes an event of Shelby seeing Hannibal.[4] Many linguists believe that thinking of the meaning of *saw* merely in terms of the relation seen in diagram 15 is insufficient, and the fact that the sentence describes an event should be made explicit. The meaning of *saw* should not be seen as a relation between two things, the seer and the seen, but rather as a relation among three things: seer, seen, and event of seeing. At first glance, this might seem to be an unnecessary complexification, but events turn out to provide an interesting and potentially useful way of thinking about many diverse aspects of meaning. We'll return to the idea of events as a component of sub-atomic semantics repeatedly in this book, and by the end you'll be able to think for yourself about whether bringing them into our understanding of the meaning of predicates is justified.

3.5.2 Thematic roles

One area of semantics where the concept of event might prove itself useful concerns the types of arguments which predicates have. In English, we have the verb *pet* used in sentences like (11). This sentence is true if Sylvia gently stroked Shelby's fur. However, in English we don't have what we might call the "reverse verb" *spet* which could be used to express the same thing as (11), only with the two names in the reverse order, as in (12):

(11)   Sylvia petted Shelby.

(12)   *Not English:* Shelby spetted Sylvia.

Another way to think of this point is to note that we don't have a verb *spet* which is synonymous with *was petted by*. Is this just an accidental fact – we have the verb *pet*, and so there's no reason to have *spet* as well? The answer is that it's not accidental. In English, if a verb has one argument which expresses an individual who actively does something, and another which expresses an individual to whom that thing is done, the doer will get to be the subject of the sentence rather than the done-to one. (Other languages seem to follow this pattern too, when expressed in a more subtle form, though human languages are so diverse that the comparison isn't always very straightforward.) The official terms here are *agent* for the individual who does something, and *patient* for the one to whom something is done. The categories of agent and patient are known as *thematic roles*, and there are more than just these two: we also have *locations, experiencers, themes* (things which move), and various other thematic roles. These thematic roles help linguists to categorize the arguments of verbs and other predicates in ways that let them express patterns in how the arguments are combined with the predicate. An axiom of thematic role theories is that the roles are unique, in that each clause has at most one agent, at most one patient, and so forth.

With the concept of thematic role, we can postulate principles of language like the following:

(13)   If a sentence has an agent, the agent will be the subject of the sentence.

(14)   If a sentence has a patient and no agent, the patient will be the subject of the sentence.

(15)   If a sentence has an agent and a patient, the patient will be the object of the sentence.

Discovering and explaining patterns like this are certainly among the things that semanticists ought to try to do.

> Come up with a bunch of simple sentences of the form NAME VERB and NAME VERB NAME, and think about how well the principles in (13)–(15) apply.

While the concept of thematic role seems fairly intuitive and useful as applied to (11), if we are to consider ourselves true scientists of language, we have to be concerned to be precise and explicit about just what thematic roles are. So, what is an agent? We said that it's the "doer" in a sentence, but that doesn't really get us anywhere since we then have to ask what a doer is. We need to find a way to give a precise explanation which is more than just a paraphrase. One idea which many linguists have pursued is that the notion of thematic role is closely related to that of event. We can paraphrase sentence (11) in the following way:

(16)   There is an event of petting, and this event's agent is Sylvia, and its patient is Shelby.

Now we're making some progress: a thematic role is a relation between events and individuals. The "agent relation" holds between an event and an individual whenever that individual undertakes willful activity as part of the event, and without that activity the event would not occur. (Something like that.) In (11), Sylvia willfully moves her hand, and if she hadn't moved her hand in this way, we wouldn't say that an event of petting occurred. Thus, Sylvia is the agent of the event (and we could then say that the noun *Sylvia* is the agent argument of the predicate). The patient thematic role might be defined like this: the patient relation holds between an event and an individual whenever that individual is affected as part of that event. In this case, Shelby has his fur pressed in a certain way and (presumably) enjoys the feeling that Sylvia has affection for him.

If this way of looking at thematic roles is satisfactory, and thematic roles are the best way to explain patterns like those in (13)–(15), we seem to have a good initial argument that events (and thematic roles) really are part of sub-atomic semantics.

I should mention that some linguists have questioned whether this is the best way to look at thematic roles. I'll focus especially on the critique by David Dowty.[5] He argues that it is impossible to give precise definitions of particular thematic roles which are useful for explaining patterns in how arguments are expressed. Consider the pair in (17):

(17) a. Joe hit the table with a hammer.
      b. Joe hit the hammer against the table.

Each sentence involves reference to three things: Joe, table, and hammer; moreover, the event described is the same in the two cases. Now, the events may not *seem* the same. We have the feeling that (17a) involves doing something to the table, and (17b) doing something to the hammer. But the question is what exactly this feeling arises from. Once we think objectively about what kind of event could be described by (17a) – go ahead, imagine one – it's hard to deny that the same event could be described with (17b). So whatever the difference between the two is, it doesn't seem possible to capture the difference with the notion of event. As for the question of thematic roles, principle (15) would force us to say that *the table* is the patient in (17a) and that *the hammer* is the patient in (17b). However, if the two sentences describe the same event, and thematic roles are unique relations between events and individuals, this is impossible.[6]

> Can you think of a definition of "patient" which would let this difference between (17a) and (17b) make sense? Also, think again about (11) in a critical spirit: We said that the patient is affected within the event. Is it really essential to petting that the thing referred to by the object be affected? Could one pet a diamond, and not affect it in any way? Is there a definition of "patient" that would make sense for all the cases you've seen so far?

Because of many cases like these, Dowty concludes that the notion of thematic role is too rigid, and rather opts for a more graded approach. With regard to (17), he says that we need to acknowledge that *Joe* is more agent-like than the other arguments, and that *the table* and *the hammer* are both more patient-like than *Joe*; however, *the table* and *the hammer* are more or less equally patient-like, and it would be wrong to force ourselves to call one of them "THE patient" while categorizing the other one as "NOT the patient."

Dowty's perspective also calls into question whether events are a crucial part of how we should define thematic roles. Instead, we can look at thematic roles simply in terms of entailments. An argument is agent-like to the extent that certain facts are entailed about it by all propositions expressed using the verb in question. Dowty lists the following:

- **Proto-agent entailments:** volitionality, sentience, causer, movement (relative to other participants), exists independently.

In (11), Sylvia is entailed to be volitional, to be sentient, and to cause something (movement in Shelby's fur, for example), and to exist independently. Moreover, in any sentence of the form *x petted y*, the thing referred to by *x* is entailed to have these properties. Shelby is only entailed to exist independently, and this is true in general for any thing referred to by *y*. So, based on the proto-agent entailments, Sylvia is more of an agent. Because Sylvia is the more agent-like, the name *Sylvia* should be the subject of the sentence. Dowty also lists a set of entailments which make for an argument being patient-like:

- **Proto-patient entailments:** undergoes change, changes portion by portion, causally affected, stationary (relative to other participants), doesn't exist independently.

(The entailment "changes portion by portion," what Dowty calls "incremental theme," is useful for cases like *Mary filled the bucket*. Here, the bucket is filled portion by portion as the event progresses. Mary is half-done filling the bucket when the bucket is half-full, three-quarters done when it's three-quarters full, and completely done when it's completely full.) According to these entailments, Shelby is more of a patient than Sylvia (check for yourself), and so *Shelby* is the sentence's object.

Notice that Dowty's perspective doesn't necessarily require any reference to events. When we encounter a new verb – say, *eat* – we can figure out what should be its subject and object without ever mentioning events. We want to express the thought that Klaus ate the noodles, and we know we're going to use the phrases *Klaus*, *the noodles*, and *ate* to do so. It turns out Klaus is more agent-like than the noodles, so *Klaus* (and any other corresponding phrase which represents the eater) will be the subject of that sentence. Similarly, *the noodles*, and in general the thing eaten, will be the object. If Dowty's ideas about thematic roles are correct, thematic roles don't give us a good reason to believe in events as part of sub-atomic semantics.

3.6   Modeling Properties with Sets and Functions

Here are two things we've learned:

i   Propositions are truth-conditions, expressed as a division of possible worlds into a "true" set and a "false" set (remember diagram 3).
ii   A property is a proposition missing a part.

Unfortunately, if we want to be picky (i.e. rigorous) these two things don't go together. The only "parts" of propositions which it really makes sense to talk about are the possible worlds, and yet the "parts" which are missing in properties are not worlds, but rather dogs, people, and other objects, as indicated by diagrams 9 and 12. My metaphorical way of explaining properties has led to an inaccuracy someplace, and though I don't think this is too bad a thing in an informal book of this kind, it will be worthwhile to see more exactly how the concepts of proposition and property relate to one another. In the next two short sections, I'll present two alternative ways of understanding what properties are. Both are more accurate than the diagrams we've been using. Thinking them through will give you a deeper understanding of properties. However, these sections are more technical than the rest of the book, and they may be skipped if the technical details aren't useful to you.[7]

3.6.1   Modeling properties with sets

Let me elaborate upon our old example *The circle is inside the square*. Just focusing on the worlds in diagram 18 (where each world is enclosed in a dotted circle), the proposition expressed by this sentence is indicated by the bold circle. Now, the meaning of *is inside the square* can be thought of as in diagram 19; this diagram shows, for each world, the set of things which are inside the square. For example, the top-right world has only a triangle inside the square (see diagram 18) and so in the corresponding part of diagram 19 only the triangle is presented as part of the predicate's meaning. In general, a property – the meaning of a predicate – indicates, for each world, those entities – animal, vegetable, or mineral – which are described by the predicate in that world.

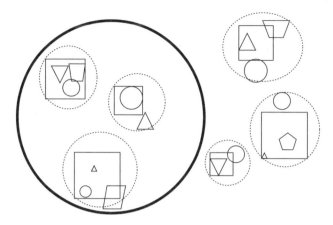

Diagram 18

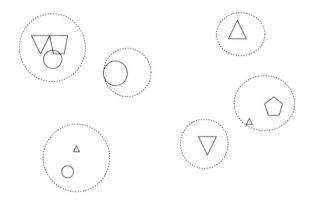

Diagram 19

To compositionally determine whether *The circle is inside the square* is true in a given world, we first identify the meaning of the subject and the predicate as applied to that world. Let's focus on the top-right world. The subject, *the circle*, refers to the circle which we see in diagram 18. Let's call that circle **c**. The predicate, *is inside the square*, describes the set of things indicated in the top-right dotted circle of diagram 19. The sentence is true if **c** is in that set. It's not, so the sentence is false in this world. We can go through the same procedure for each world, and prove that the sentence is true in the three worlds on the left, and false in the three on the right.

To sum up, this discussion shows that a property can be thought of as an association between worlds and sets – it provides, for each world, a set of things. Predication then amounts to figuring out, for each world, whether the object referred to by the subject is in the set which the predicate associates with that world. This way of thinking of properties and predication is more accurate than speaking of "propositions missing a part," and more precise than pictures like diagrams 9 and 12, but of course it's a bit more abstract as well. From now on, if you want to be very right-thinking, you may keep in mind that a picture like diagram 9 is only a convenience, and that diagrams like 18 and 19 are ultimately more accurate.

3.6.2   Modeling properties with functions

If you are currently taking a hard-core class in formal semantics, there is a good chance you're learning about such concepts as "functions'" and a system called the λ calculus (λ is the Greek letter lambda). It may be helpful to see the connection between the intuitive way of understanding properties used in this book and these more precise, but technical, notions. Notice once again the representation in diagram 3 of the proposition expressed by *The circle is inside the square* (p. 13). Now think about how we would indicate the proposition expressed by *The triangle is inside the square*. That sentence describes four worlds in the central area of diagram 3. As we create different sentences based on the predicate *is inside the square*, we find that these sentences describe different sets of possible worlds. This gives a clue as to another way to think about the meaning of the predicate. It can be something like diagram 20. (Notice that the right-hand part of this diagram is the same as diagram 3 turned on its side.) This diagram indicates in a new way the idea that the predicate's meaning is an incomplete proposition. The predicate's meaning needs to combine with a particular thing, in this diagram either the circle or the triangle, and then it will denote the appropriate proposition, indicated on the right-hand side. In principle, of course, all of the possible referents of the predicate's subject should appear on the left, and all of the resulting propositions should appear on the right.

The kind of object pictured in diagram 20 is known as a "function." A function is a mathematical object which has a set of possible "inputs," and for each input designates an "output." The input to a function is known as its *argument*, and the output is known as its *value*. The set of possible inputs (here, the circle and the triangle) is known as its *domain*, and the set of possible outputs (here, the two propositions) is known as its *range*.

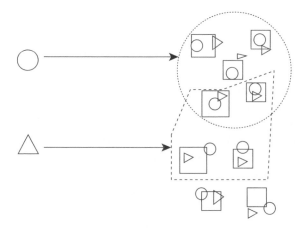

Diagram 20

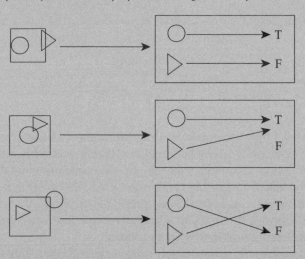

There are other possible ways of thinking of properties in terms of functions. For example, we can use functions to say approximately the same thing as we said with sets using diagram 19 by letting the domain be the set of possible worlds, and the range be a set of functions. These range functions will have as domain the set of things in that world, and as range the truth values "True" and "False." Here is a partial picture of the properties in diagram 20 represented this way:

Complete this picture in a way that represents the same property as we've been discussing in the text.

The exercise has an answer, no. 3, in the appendix.

3.6.2.1   A formal system: the λ calculus

The λ calculus is a system for expressing functions in a neat and compact way. This means that if we want to pursue a semantic system like the one indicated by diagrams 19 and 20, the λ calculus will be a convenient thing to use. Suppose that we indicate the proposition that Shelby barks by writing **Shelby barks** (I'll use bold face to make clear that we're dealing with λ calculus), and so **Shelby barks** = diagram 8. Functions are indicated by manipulating such representations of the saturated meaning. For example, the property denoted by *barks*, which is pictured metaphorically in diagram 9, is symbolized this way: put a single letter (called a *variable*) in the position of the sentence which indicates the "place" in which the proposition is unsaturated: *x* **barks**. This *x* stands for the argument of the function. Next, prefix to this *x* **barks** a λ plus the variable you used plus a period: λ*x*.*x* **barks**. The λ and associated variable are there to announce that this formula indicates a function, and to tell you that *x* stands for the argument of the function. To keep things orderly, enclose the whole thing in brackets (though sometimes we don't bother). This formula **[λ*x*.*x* barks]** indicates in semanticist-speak the property of being a thing which barks. This is the same property we have seen previously in diagram 9.

More examples:

Diagram 12	**[λ*x*.*x* is small]**
Diagram 13	**[λ*f*.*f*]**
Diagram 15 (upper oval)	**[λ*x*.[λ*y*.*y* saw *x*]]**

Notice that the formula corresponding to diagram 15 has two λ's at the beginning, because it needs to announce that it is doubly unsaturated, missing two parts. Also notice that the first variable mentioned, *x*, corresponds to the object of *saw*. That is, it represents what is seen, not the seer. The second variable, *y*, indicates the seer. This ordering of λ's is how the λ calculus indicates the fact that a transitive verb like *saw* combines with its object before it combines with its subject.

The saturation of unsaturated propositions (what I've drawn in pictures with arrows and pictures of dogs and such in little circles) is indicated as follows: write down your unsaturated meaning, then note within parentheses the thing which will saturate it. So if we're going to saturate the property of barking with Shelby, this would look like (18):

(18)   Unsaturated property   Thing that saturates it

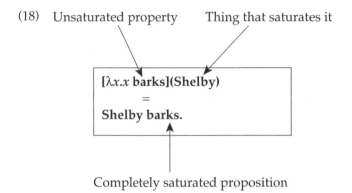

Completely saturated proposition

This is the λ calculus representation of what we drew with pictures in diagram 10.

> Indicate the functions in diagram 20 and the immediately preceding exercise using the λ calculus.
>
> This exercise has an answer, no. 4, in the appendix.

NOTES

1   The discussion here is based on that of Heim and Kratzer (1997).
2   This hypothesis would only imply a lack of semantic meaning. A could still make a contribution to pragmatic meaning.
3   Actually, linguists would say that the basic meaningful unit of language is the *morpheme*. Several morphemes may make up a word; for example, *cats* has two morphemes (*cat* and *-s*). From this slightly more sophisticated perspective, sub-atomic semantics would refer to complexities of meaning that occur within the morpheme.
4   Events were introduced into the linguistics literature via Davidson (1967b).
5   Dowty (1990).
6   The original idea of uniqueness of thematic roles implied that each clause has at most one patient. Since (17a) and (17b) are different clauses, there's no conflict with that kind of uniqueness. However, once thematic roles are defined in terms of events, we end up with the requirement that each event has at most one patient (likewise for other roles), and this requirement is in conflict with the examples. It would be possible to have a kind of intermediate view, where thematic roles are connected to events, but not define the thematic roles in

terms of events. Instead, we could say that *hit* can assign the patient role to either the argument represented by *the table* or the one represented by *the hammer*, and that whichever one it is, this is understood as the one affected by the event. There's no real problem with this way of thinking, but it is crucial to notice that events don't play a fundamental role in explaining what thematic roles are any more. The thematic roles come from verbs first and foremost. Thus, this way of thinking fails to provide an argument for events in sub-atomic semantics. If you believe in events for other reasons, it's fair to use them in this way; but if you don't, you won't lose much by foregoing them here.

7 The discussion in section 3.6.1, "Modeling properties with sets," will be referred to in chapter 7, but not in much detail.

4 Modifiers

The single semantic process which we have employed so far is saturation, the "filling in" of a missing piece of a property or relation. The paradigm case of this is predication. So far, the property or relation which gets saturated has always come from the main predicate of the sentence: a verb, predicate nominal, or predicate adjective. The element saturating it has always been a simple referring phrase, a name. (Though I also used definite noun phases like *the circle*, this was a bit dishonest, since we haven't discussed the meaning of *the* yet.)

In traditional grammar, another basic semantic relation is that of modification. We say that an adjective modifies a noun and that an adverb modifies a verb or sentence. The goal of this chapter is to discuss the nature of modification. An important issue will be whether modification is a completely new type of semantic process or whether it is just another case of saturation, different only in minor ways from predication.

4.1 Adjective + N Combination

As we learned in chapter 3, the italicized words in sentences (1) and (2) are predicates:

(1) Ossie is a *bird*.

(2) Ossie is *tall*.

The meaning of each can be represented by a picture like the kind in diagram 12 (p. 41). However, *tall* and *bird* can come together in a sentence like (3):

(3)   Ossie is a *tall bird*.

The phrase *tall bird* is itself a predicate, with *Ossie* as its subject, so what we appear to have here is two predicates being joined to create a new, grander predicate. An *attributive adjective* is one which modifies a noun, as in example (3), while a *predicate adjective* functions as the main predicate in a sentence like (2).

We can visualize the meanings of *tall* and *bird* as in diagram 21. As is clear from the shapes, neither of these properties can saturate the other. Each wants to be saturated by an individual like Shelby or Ossie. Neither can be saturated by another property – metaphorically, neither will fit into the "hole" in the other; they're just too big. We must find some other way to combine them.

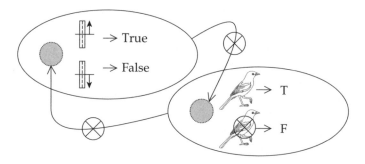

Diagram 21

Sentence (3) tells us that Ossie is a bird, and that Ossie is tall. This tells us that (3) in effect predicates both *bird* and *tall* of *Ossie*. The combined predicate *tall bird* has a meaning which simultaneously allows the subject of the sentence to saturate both of the component properties, those of the adjective and the noun. This can be visualized as in diagram 22. What this diagram shows is that the two original properties are overlaid, one on top of the other, so that their holes are in the same position. This ensures that when an individual (Ossie) is used to saturate one of them, it will simultaneously saturate the other. As a result, we'll have a proposition which is true if both Ossie is tall and Ossie is a bird. Diagram 22 represents in an intuitive and simple way our intuitions about the meaning of the modifier+noun combination *tall bird*.

There is a cost, however, to thinking of modification in this way, at least from the perspective of the formal theory of semantics. The two subpredicates are not brought together by one saturating the other; instead,

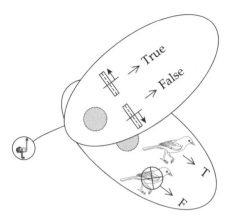

Diagram 22

they are "overlaid," and this is an entirely new process of semantic combination. We might call this new process of combination *modification*.[1] Having two semantic combination processes instead of just one is a major increase in complexity, and before we accept it, we should be quite certain that the extra complexity is justified. In other words, we should ask again whether it might be possible to explain the relationship between an adjective and noun as a case of saturation.

Suppose that instead of thinking of the meaning of *tall* as we have been, we visualize it as something like diagram 23. Here, *tall*'s meaning is a property with a property-sized hole in it. It's a property which can only be saturated by another property. In this case, the property expressed by *bird* is used to saturate it, giving the result in the lower part of the diagram. This combined property still has a hole in it, but this is a small object-sized hole originating with *bird*. Ossie can saturate this combined property, and the resulting diagram then indicates both that Ossie is tall and that Ossie is a bird.

The process pictured in diagram 23 only makes use of saturation as a method of combining meanings. We have both a higher-order saturation, where a property saturates another property, and a regular case of saturation (predication), where an individual saturates a property. There is an advantage here in terms of how we think about compositional meaning, since we can maintain that there is just one means of combining meanings – saturation. However, there are disadvantages as well. For one, the meaning of *tall* as a property which is saturated by another property is now rather more complex and less intuitive than in diagram 22. For another, and more importantly, the meaning of *tall* indicated here would not serve

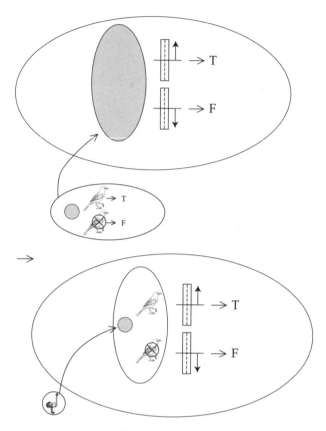

Diagram 23

well for a simple case where it is a predicate adjective, as in (2). In (2), we want to saturate the property indicated by *tall* with Ossie, but if *tall* has the meaning in diagram 23, the two pieces of the puzzle won't fit together. Ossie, the individual, is too "small" to saturate the big hole in *tall*'s property. This means we have three choices:

i   Go back to diagram 22 as our way of thinking about modification.
ii   Conclude that *tall* is ambiguous, in (2) denoting a regular property, and in (3) denoting a higher-order property.
iii Rethink (2), trying to find a way to let the higher-order version of *tall* work in this case as well. This would mean that the sentence is not a simple combination of subject *Ossie* with predicate *tall*.

> The more complex property for *tall* can be made to work in sentence (2) if *is* is given a meaning. What would that be? Does this make sense as a meaning for *is*? Is it worthwhile to overturn the idea that *is* is meaningless?

Sometimes as one studies linguistics, it is easy to get involved in a theoretical debate and lose track of what is precisely at issue. Ultimately it's pointless to think about whether *tall* is a regular property, or a property which can be saturated only by another property, unless we focus on what is significant about this debate from the perspective of what we want to learn about language. There are two important questions to keep in mind here. First, does the choice between approaches have any empirical consequences? In other words, does one approach lead us to expect anything about what sorts of words and constructions human languages will use that the other does not? We'll touch on this in section 4.2, "More Issues with Adjectives." And second, does one approach provide a more intuitively satisfying understanding for how language works than the other? It seems to me that in the present case, the model of diagram 22 is more satisfying; however, this bias could certainly change as we learn more about semantics. If we find lots of other aspects of language that remind us of diagram 23, and very few that remind us of diagram 22, we might well conclude that diagram 22 is a pretty odd way of thinking about adjectives.

4.2   More Issues with Adjectives[2]

Sentence (3) entails both (1) and (2). Because a tall bird is both tall and a bird, the adjective *tall* is known as an *intersective adjective*. The term "intersective" comes from modeling the meaning of predicates as sets. Recall that a predicate can be seen as determining a set for each possible world; just as *is inside the square* picks out a set of things in each possible world (diagram 19), the predicates *tall* and *bird* can each be seen as picking out a set of things in each possible world (the set of tall things and the set of birds, respectively). If we think of the meaning of *tall bird* in the same way, what set will it pick out in each possible world? Answer: the set of tall birds. This is the set of things which are in both the tall-set and the bird-set, in other words the *intersection* of the two sets. (There are also non-intersective adjectives. For example, *Mary is a former teacher* does not imply that Mary is a former, and a teacher. It doesn't even make sense to say that she's a "former.")

Many adjectives are *vague*. For example, we say that Ossie the Ostrich is a tall bird, and that he's tall, and that he's a bird. But we wouldn't necessarily call him tall in all situations. For example, if Ossie is standing among a herd of giraffes, we might find it strange to say that he's tall. Or, if he is tall compared to birds in general, but is the runt of his flock and much smaller than all the other ostriches, we might rather call him short than tall when we're comparing him with his fellow ostriches. But we'd still call him tall when comparing him with other birds. What counts as tall depends what you're comparing with.

When *tall* is combined with *bird* to make *tall bird*, it seems that the preferred comparison is with birds in general. Given this comparison, *tall* describes all things which are taller than the average bird, and its intersective meaning implies that a tall bird is both taller than the average bird and a bird. In principle it should be possible for attributive *tall* to be understood as involving comparison with something other than the set of birds, but it's not clear to me that this is really the case: suppose that Pauline is a horse, shorter than the average horse, and that in order to boost her self-esteem she hangs out with a group of ponies, smaller animals than her. Could I then say (4) to mean that Pauline is a horse, and taller than the ponies she's with?

(4)   Pauline is a tall horse.

It doesn't seem so (though it may have yet another meaning: Pauline is a horse, and horses in general are tall). This indicates that when a vague adjective combines with a noun, it is required that the adjective be understood as involving comparison with the other things described by the noun, not with some other set relevant to the conversation. This makes it different from an adjective functioning as the main predicate in a sentence (like (2)), since there the comparison can be with any relevant set of things.

The fact that vague attributive adjectives must imply comparison with the set of things described by the noun they modify has been taken to argue that adjectives are higher-order predicates which can only be saturated by another predicate (diagram 23), rather than being simple predicates (diagram 22). The reason for this is that, if *tall* can mean "tall compared with the other things I am looking at" when it's used as a main predicate, and it is simply overlaid with the noun's property to give the meaning of *tall horse*, compositionality should imply that it can continue to mean "tall compared with the other things I am looking at." So *tall horse* should be able to mean "tall compared with the other things I am looking at, and a horse" – but, as we've seen, it seems it can't. In contrast, if *tall*'s meaning is a property which is saturated by another property, we have more flexibility. By itself, this meaning of *tall* can't function as the main predicate of a sentence, since it can only be saturated by a property, not by a simple individual like Pauline, Shelby, or Ossie. So, the meaning of *Pauline is tall* is not directly relevant to the meaning of *Pauline is a tall horse*. We can say that *tall* has a meaning which is saturated by a property P, and then means "is a P, and is taller than the average P." We might picture this as in diagram 24. When the property for *bird* is used to saturate this property, this says to select the average bird and make that your basis for determining what counts as tall. In light of this, *tall bird* describes anything which is a bird, and which is taller than that average bird.

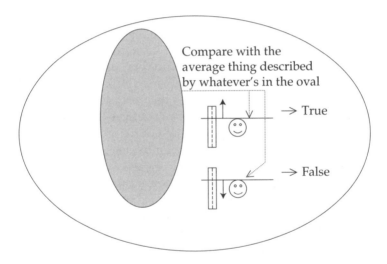

Diagram 24

Here are a few adjectives whose meanings are a bit more complex than those we're focusing on in the text: *possible* (as in *a possible solution to the problem*), *mere* (as in *a mere semanticist*), *former* (as in *a former teacher*), and *fake* (as in *a fake gun*). Do these adjectives tend to provide an argument for one of the two views about adjectives semantics (that they combine by modification or by saturation?

If vague attributive adjectives must be understood as having this kind of complex meaning, there are a few open questions. First, what about non-vague intersective adjectives like *dead*? It seems that what counts as dead doesn't depend on what you're comparing with. Thus, the argument that *tall* has a higher-order meaning doesn't apply to *dead*. As far as we can tell, it could have a simple predicate meaning, and could modify a noun by the overlaying strategy. However, do we want to say that *dead* and *tall* combine with nouns using totally different semantic processes? And second, how are we going to understand uses of *tall* as a predicate adjective, e.g. *Ossie is tall*? If *tall* can only be saturated by another property, how is it able to combine with *Ossie*? We must either say that *tall* is ambiguous, sometimes saturated by properties and sometimes by individuals, or that the structure of *Ossie is tall* is not what it seems. If it's ambiguous, we would hope to have some mechanism (in the semantics literature, called *type-shifting*)[3] for constructing one meaning from the other, rather than saying, implausibly, that the two meanings are totally unrelated; metaphorically speaking, we could imagine that we convert the basic picture for *tall* in diagram 21 into that in more complex one in diagram 23 or 24 whenever we find ourselves in need of the latter, fancier meaning. If we take the alternative approach and think that the structure is not what it seems, we might think that there is a hidden noun present, so that *Ossie is tall* should be thought of as *Ossie is (a) tall (thing)*. In that case, there would be no such thing as a predicative use of *tall*; what appears to be a predicative use is actually an attributive use with a hidden noun. Yet another possibility is that *is* isn't meaningless, contrary to what we've assumed so far. Rather, we could hypothesize that it has a meaning that allows *tall*'s property, which wants to be saturated by another property as in diagrams 23 and 24, to be combined with an individual, Ossie.

All of these possibilities are reasonable, and I can't tell you which one is right. More research among those semanticists who study adjectives is needed. As someone being introduced to semantics for the first time, you should think of the above discussion as showing you what an open issue in semantic theory looks like. Semantics, and linguistics more generally, are full of open issues like this one. If you are a young student, you needn't worry that the job of figuring out how linguistic meaning works is going to be all finished before you get to join the fun!

4.3   Relative Clauses as Modifiers

Relative clauses can function as modifiers in the same way as adjectives can. In example (5), *dog* and *which Shelby saw* are both predicates, and they are combined into a bigger predicate in the same way as an adjective+ noun:

(5)   Hannibal is a *dog which Shelby saw.*

Relative clauses and adjectives differ syntactically, in that a relative clause follows the noun it modifies, but adjectives typically precede the noun. This difference seems not to have a semantic effect; the combinations of meanings are processed in identical ways. Some semanticists think that cases like this show that the order in which phrases occur has no effect on their meaning (semantic meaning, that is); all that matters is what is combined with what, not what is placed before what as they are combined. (This is not to say that order has no effect on other sorts of meaning, such as speaker's meaning; as we will see in later chapters, there is reason to believe that order is relevant there.)

4.4   Adverbs

I'm sure your grammar teacher has told you that adjectives modify nouns and that adverbs modify verbs (and perhaps other things as well, like clauses). This leads us to expect that adverbs will have a meaning somewhat parallel to adjectives, though different to take account of the differences between nouns and verbs. As we'll see, such an intuition can be developed in two different ways. One of these takes up the idea that verbs describe events as part of their sub-atomic semantics in the way discussed in the previous chapter. This leads to a simple, intuitive theory, at least for certain types of adverbs. The other does not need to assume anything about events. It leads to a less intuitive theory, but one that can be readily applied to a wider variety of adverbs.

4.4.1   Adverbs with events

In sentence (6), what does the adverb *loudly* contribute to the meaning of the sentence? It says that Shelby's bark was loud. Shelby's bark is the event described by the verb *bark*.

(6)   Shelby barked loudly.

So, speaking in terms of events we can say that the meaning of (6) is "there was an event of barking, with Shelby as its agent, and it was a loud event."[4] We might say that the suffix *-ly* changes the adjective *loud*, which describes regular things (e.g. *Shelby is loud*), into something which can describe events.

This way of thinking about adverbs is parallel to what we've already seen with adjectives. According to the idea that verbs have events as part of their semantics, we can think of the meaning of a verb as a property of events. In other words, it describes a set of events (for each possible world). For example, *bark* in (6) describes barking events, and the subject specifies that the sentence describes barking events whose agent is Shelby.[5] The adverb *loudly* also is a property of events; more precisely, in each possible world, it describes the set of events which are loud in that world. If we "overlay" the two properties (as we did in diagram 22), this will imply that the sentence as a whole describes barking events which are loud and which have Shelby as their agent. Not only is this just right, but also the process is exactly parallel to the way in which an adjective modifies a noun.

Other adverbial expressions can be seen in a similar way. For example, in (7) *in the back yard* describes the place of the event of barking. *Yesterday* describes the time of the event:

(7)   Yesterday, Shelby barked in the back yard.

> Before reading on, come up with as many adverbs and other adverbial expressions as you can and see how well you can explain their meanings in terms of the idea that they describe the verb's event.

Adverbs and other adverbials provide one of the best reasons to think that events play an important role in semantics. *Manner adverbs* like *loudly* are naturally thought of as describing the manner of an event; *locatives* and *temporals* like *in the garden* and *yesterday* describe the time and place of an event. I don't think there's another way of thinking about these types of adverbials which so naturally reflects our intuitive ideas about their meaning.

Unfortunately, there are difficulties. Consider the adverbs in (8):

(8)   a.   John intentionally met Mary.
   b.   John chopped the onion finely.
   c.   Surprisingly, John cried.

We can't simply say that *intentionally* describes the event of meeting as intentional. Suppose that Mary intended for this event to happen, but John didn't. In this case, (8a) would be false. However, we'd have to say that the event was intentional (on Mary's part, but not on John's), so if all *intentionally* did was say that the event was intentional, it ought to be true. *Intentionally* describes events which were intended by the person referred to by the subject (here, John), not by other individuals. What this shows is that *intentionally* must have a special connection to the subject, and this goes beyond simply saying that it describes an event.

In (8b) it doesn't really make sense to say that *finely* describes the event as fine. Rather, what is fine are the pieces of onion after they are chopped. Here we have an adverb which has a special connection to the thing referred to by the object (the onion). Between them, (8a) and (8b) show that adverbial meanings may be closely linked to the things referred to by the verb's subject and object, not just the event.

Example (8c) is what is known as a *speaker-oriented adverb*. This sentence says that it's surprising to the speaker that John cried. It may not be surprising at all to John, or to anyone who knows John, that he cried. This shows that the meaning of adverbs may have a special relation to individuals not even mentioned in the sentence.

Given that the adverbs in (8) don't simply describe events, we should rethink whether adverbs give us a good reason to believe that events are part of semantics. One thing worth noting here is that, though each of the adverbs in (8) depends on more than just the event described, they still are all naturally understood as being partially about the event. (8a) says that John intended that the event of meeting occur. (8b) says that as a result of the event of chopping, the onion is in fine pieces. (8c) says, perhaps, that the speaker finds the event of crying surprising. So these cases don't prove that events are irrelevant to the semantics of adverbs, just that other things can be relevant too.

This way of thinking leads us to a perhaps surprising perspective on adverbs. It suggests that they are very similar to verbs. For example, *intentionally* in (8a) says something about the relation between Mary and an event: Mary did that event intentionally. Compare that to what an event-friendly semanticist would say about an intransitive verb like *cried*. In *John cried*, the verb describes a relation between John and an event: that was an event of John crying. A simple adverb like *loudly* only describes an event, not a relation between a person and an event. There are verbs like this too; think about *It rained*. Here, *it* doesn't refer to anything; it's called an *expletive* subject, one which fills the subject position (because every English sentence needs a subject) but which doesn't contribute anything to the sentence's meaning. Since *it* doesn't refer to anything, *rained* all by itself describes an event.[6] In this, it's similar to *loudly*. Comparing *loudly* to *rained* and *intentionally* to *cried*, we might say that the fundamental idea of this approach to adverbs is that they are semantically like verbs but syntactically unable to function as the main predicate of a sentence.

> How could it help our understanding of these issues to widen our perspective from English to other languages? If adverb meanings are similar to verb meanings, what would you expect to find if you examined adverbs from a random sample of fifty languages? Do languages that you know use adverbs differently from English in sentences like (6)–(8)? Are there differences which seem relevant to semantics?

4.4.2   Adverbs without events

We can also understand the meaning of adverbs without bringing events into the picture at all. If we forget about events, we'd just say that the verb *bark* in (6) is a regular property. It describes a set of individuals in each possible world. Specifically, it describes those individuals who bark. When *loudly* combines with *bark*, we don't describe quite so many individuals. Among the individuals who bark, we only describe those who do so loudly. That is, *loudly* combines with *bark* and restricts it to a smaller property; the set of things *bark loudly* describes (in each world) is a subset of the set which *bark* alone describes.

This way of thinking about adverbs can be modeled in parallel to the more complex perspective on adjectives (that pictured in diagram 24) which we discussed earlier in this chapter. *Loudly* is a property which is saturated by another property. It says: I am saturated by another property X, and together we'll be the property which describes an individual if that individual did X loudly. In the case of (6), *loudly* is saturated by *bark*, and together they form a complex property. This complex property describes an individual like Shelby if it barked loudly.

Perhaps needless to say, this way of thinking about *loudly* doesn't grab onto intuition as easily as describing it in terms of events did. But it does have something to recommend it. It is more general, and can be directly applied to example (8a). *Intentionally* combines with the predicate *met Mary*. Together, their meaning is a complex property which describes an individual which acted intentionally in meeting Mary. More generally, *intentionally* is saturated by a property X, and together they form a complex property which describes an individual y if y did X intentionally.[7]

This perspective on adverbs can't be directly applied to (8b), but if slightly modified it can. *Finely* is not saturated by another property. Rather, it is saturated by a relation. In (8b), *chop* is doubly unsaturated, and is first filled in by a choppee (the onion) and then by a chopper (John). Once *chop* is fully saturated, it makes a true proposition if the chopper chopped the choppee. *Finely* combines with the completely unsaturated *chop* and together they form a new, bigger relation, one which is still saturated by a choppee and a chopper. Once this new relation is saturated, the result is true if two things are true: (i) the chopper chopped the choppee, and (ii) the choppee is in fine pieces as a result. The difference between a subject-oriented adverb like *intentionally* and an object-oriented one like *finely* is that the subject-oriented one is saturated by a property and together they create a new, grand property, while the object-oriented one is saturated by a relation, and together they form a new, grand relation.

We can extend this perspective on *intentionally* and *finely* still further to capture *surprisingly*. This speaker-oriented adverb has a meaning which is saturated by a fully saturated proposition, and together the two form another proposition. *John cried* denotes a proposition, one which is true in a given world if John cried in that world. The meaning of *surprisingly* is saturated by this proposition. The resulting proposition is true in a given world if both John cried in that world and the speaker is surprised at this fact.

We can summarize the event-free view of four adverbs in the table below.

Loudly, intentionally	Saturated by a property, and results in a new, combined property: unsaturated → unsaturated.	
Finely	Saturated by a relation, and results in a new, combined relation: doubly unsaturated → doubly unsaturated.	
Surprisingly	Saturated by a proposition, and results in a new, combined proposition: saturated → saturated.	

It seems to me that, while this event-free way of looking at adverbs is more complex and less intuitive when it comes to describing particular adverbs' meanings, it gives a good perspective on what adverbs do *as a class*. In general, they combine with more-or-less unsaturated propositions, and as a result give us an equally (un)saturated proposition. Though this new proposition is just as (un)saturated as what we started with, it has been changed in some way. This perspective seems to capture the intuitive idea behind the traditional term "modifier": a modifier merely adds to what it modifies, without changing the type of meaning which is expressed.

4.5   The Form of Meanings and their World-describing Content

This is an opportune place to discuss the kinds of questions semanticists choose to ask about meaning, and the consequences of those choices. Much of this chapter has had to do with what we might call the *form* of meanings. For example, we have spent a lot of time considering whether attributive adjectives are saturated by ordinary things (like predicate adjectives) or by other predicates; we have considered whether adverbs describe events or modify predicates, relations, or propositions into other predicates, relations, or propositions. These questions are important from the perspective of a compositional theory, since we need to answer them in order to say how the meanings of individual words get put together. Because scholars working in the field of formal semantics take the commitment to compositionality as fundamental to what they're doing, questions like these tend to dominate the field.

There are other kinds of questions about meanings that we may want to ask. For example, a simple one is "What is the difference in meaning between *tall* and *long*?" In terms of the form of their meaning, they are probably alike. Look at diagram 21 again; there the oval on the left represents the meaning of *tall*. All that would change as we converted that oval into one for *long* would be that we'd put the "ruler" in the picture into a horizontal orientation. That's fine, but the orientation of a little piece of a picture doesn't really have any status within the theory we've developed. I've taken advantage of how I know you'll read these pictures to get you to think that a little picture of a ruler oriented a certain way really does represent the meaning of *tall*, but the picture isn't part of any theory I've presented to you. So all I've really done is tell you that *tall*, in its predicate use, represents a certain property – you know the one! – which is saturated by an individual to give a complete proposition. Likewise, *long* represents a different property – you know the one! – which is saturated by an individual to give a different complete proposition. All I've taught you is the "saturated by an individual to give a different complete proposition" part; the "you know the one!" part is just that, something about which you only know as much as you knew beforehand.

A linguist who tries to answer questions like "What is the meaning difference between *tall* and *long*?" is doing *lexical semantics*. One can do lexical semantics within formal semantics. For example, there is a tradition of studying the lexical semantics of verbs,[8] and there is also very interesting work on the semantics of adjectives within the formal semantics tradition.[9] However, semanticists who are not working within a formal semantics theory tend to focus a much higher percentage of their effort on lexical semantics than formal semanticists do.[10] Moreover, they say that formal semanticists miss out on what's really important about linguistic meaning by, relatively speaking, not paying much attention to lexical meaning. Formal semanticists reply that, lacking a precise understanding of compositionality, non-formal semanticists are ignoring a fundamental feature of language, the fact that meaningful words are used in combination with one another. Moreover, they say (rightly I believe) that not every difference in lexical meaning is a linguistic issue at all. Take, for example, the difference in meaning between *sparrow* and *quail*. *Sparrow* describes some birds and *quail* others. You just have to learn which ones are which when you learn those words, and there's not much else for a linguist to say – though there's something for a biologist and maybe a psychologist to say. (Another complaint lodged by many formal semanticists against their non-formal colleagues is that their theories are not precise enough. This book, being itself an informal presentation of formal semantics, is not the right place to take this issue up.)

There is something more fundamental at issue in the debate between formal semanticists and non-formal, lexically oriented semanticists. Most linguistically oriented semanticists who wouldn't call themselves "formal semanticists" subscribe to some form of the idea theory. But formal semanticists feel that the idea theory was long ago disproved by the considerations outlined in chapter 1.

My perspective is that a middle position is possible. As was stressed in chapter 1, the fact that meanings are not mental objects does not imply that how the mind works is irrelevant to semantics. A formal semanticist, who believes that meanings are in the mind-external world, would still agree that the question of which meanings out of all the possible ones are actually encoded in a language has to do with how our minds work (and perhaps other things too, like how our cultures work). The property of smiling has a verb to express it, *smile*. The property of touching your head with three fingers is equally out there in the world, and so it's a candidate for having a word to express it.[11] But no word does express it, in English or (as far as I know) any language. Perhaps our minds are so built that we don't think about three-fingered-head-touching in a way which induces us to assign a word to it (and if some language did have a word for it, this gesture would certainly have some special cultural significance among some speakers of the language). This doesn't imply that the meaning of *smile* is anything other than the mind-external property we've taken it to be; it just says that this mind-external property is one we have a word for because of how it is integrated into our mental lives. In this way – and this is a very oversimplified way of thinking about it, to be sure – it's possible to understand aspects of lexical meaning in terms of how we mentally represent concepts, without adopting the idea theory hypothesis that meanings and mental concepts are the same thing.

NOTES

1   Heim and Kratzer (1997), on whose discussion some of this section on adjectives is based, refer to this combination process as the rule of Predicate Modification.

2   This discussion follows that of Heim and Kratzer (1997) to a significant extent, though my ultimate conclusion is different.

3   See Partee (1986).

4   This way of thinking about adverbs is due to Donald Davidson. Though he didn't propose using thematic roles along with events, events and thematic roles often go together in contemporary work in semantics. (The reference again: Davidson 1967b.)

5   This makes more sense when we take advantage of the event argument and relate the subject of the sentence to the verb via a thematic role. Without thematic roles, we'd want to say that the subject+verb combination here expresses a property of events. In this case, it would describe, for each possible world, the set of events of Shelby barking.

6   According to a semantics for verbs which doesn't use events, we'd say that *rain* expresses a proposition all by itself. It isn't unsaturated like most other verbs.

7   You may wonder what it means to say that John acted intentionally in meeting Mary. One thing we might say it means is that the event of meeting was intentional for John. From an event-free perspective, though, this won't work. We rather need to say that the proposition that John met Mary was intentional; that is, *John met Mary intentionally* is true if John intended that

the proposition expressed by *John met Mary* be true, and it in fact did come true.

8   See Dowty (1979) and references therein.

9   See Kennedy (1999).

10 Some of the books mentioned earlier are relevant here: works by Jackendoff (1990; 1992), Lakoff, Johnson (Lakoff 1987; Lakoff and Johnson 1980), and Fauconnier (1985). Another important approach to lexical semantics is represented by Levin and Rappaport Hovav (1995), as well as other works by these authors and their associates.

11 More properly, the issue is whether there's a morpheme to express it.

5 Complexities of Referring Expressions

Names refer to things: people, dogs, cities, stars, . . . But names are not the only pieces of language that refer; nor are ordinary things all that get referred to. In this chapter we'll examine some of the varieties of reference, and will discuss the nature of reference a bit as well.

5.1 Definite NPs

Definite noun phrases are introduced by the definite article *the* followed by a noun plus associated words like modifiers. Some definite noun phrases: *the dog, the old man, the picture of Mary, the woman who Susan knows I met*.

If Shelby is the only dog which lives at Paul's house, in seems that sentences (1) and (2) have the same truth-conditions. That is, according to the definition of synonymy we're working with, they are synonymous.

(1)   Shelby is cute.

(2)   The dog which lives at Paul's house is cute.

A semantic theory ought to explain why these two sentences are synonymous. Given that they differ only in that one has *Shelby* where the other has *the dog which lives at Paul's house*, the principle of compositionality predicts that, if *Shelby* and *the dog which lives at Paul's house* refer to the same thing, (1) and (2) are synonymous. So a good hypothesis is that *Shelby* and *the dog which lives at Paul's house* refer to the same thing. Since *Shelby* refers to my dog, this would mean that *the dog which lives at Paul's house* does too.[1]

Notice that it's not a logical conclusion from the synonymy of (1) and (2) that *Shelby* and *the dog which lives at Paul's house* refer to the same thing.

They could refer to different things, or it could be that one refers (to Shelby) and the other has a kind of meaning which is not a simple reference (like a predicate of some sort); their meanings could differ in one of these ways but still just happen to give the same overall meaning when combined with the predicate *is cute*. Two different roads can reach the same destination. We'll touch on this possibility in chapter 7.

In order to get into the compositional process which lets language users understand the meaning of (2), let's think about it a bit in terms of a syntactic tree and cutout pictures of meanings. (I drop the relative clause to keep the tree simpler.)

(3)

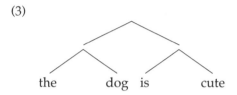

    the   dog is   cute

We know a bit about the meanings of the parts of this sentence already. *Cute* and *is cute* both express a property, i.e., an unsaturated proposition. So does *dog*, though of course it expresses a different property. We can picture the dog-property as in diagram 25 and the cute-property similarly. The dog-property can't saturate the cute-property, since the "hole" in the cute-property is just an ordinary-sized circle, to be saturated by an individual, and too "small" to fit another property into. This is why we can't say (in English) *Dog is cute*. Fortunately, we have *the* in the sentence, and *the* works with *dog* to come up with an individual (Shelby) which can saturate the cute-property. The meaning of *the* is combined with the dog-property, and together they refer to Shelby. How do they do that?

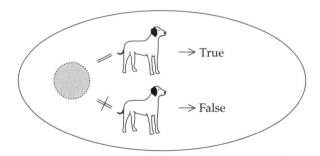

Diagram 25

The turns the predicate *dog* into a referring term. It tells us to find the thing which is described by the property expressed by the noun (or the rest of the noun phrase, when it contains other material like modifiers), and then consider this the reference for the definite noun phrase as a whole. In order for it to do this, there must be one and only one relevant individual described by the rest of the phrase – since otherwise, how would we know which thing described by the noun to use as the reference? (What do we mean by a "relevant individual"? It could be that there is just one thing described, as in the case where only one dog lives at Paul's house. In that case, it's obvious that *the dog which lives at Paul's house* refers to that dog. But with *the dog*, we all know of many dogs, and the referent will be a particular dog which can be identified within the situation at hand. We'll get into how this works in a bit more detail below.) According to this way of thinking, the meaning of *the* can be thought of as a kind of robot which takes a property and goes out into the situation to retrieve a thing which is described by that property (diagram 26). If our robot is given the property in diagram 25, it will find us the single relevant dog in the situation. In one situation, this might get us Shelby and in another it might get us Hannibal. Whatever dog it may bring us, in sentence (2) that dog is described as cute.

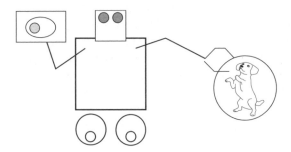

Diagram 26

5.2   Some Subtleties

When looked at in this general way, definite noun phrases seem quite simple. They just refer to something described by their descriptive part. However, the study of definites is a perilous field, and huge amounts have been written about *the* in the linguistics and philosophy literatures. I would like to mention of few of the many subtleties which arise as we think about definites in a bit more detail.

Assuming that *Shelby* and *the dog which lives at Paul's house* both refer to the same dog seems to give us a puzzle. After all, *the dog which lives at Paul's house* needn't refer to Shelby; if Paul had adopted a different dog, Hannibal, it would refer to Hannibal. But *Shelby* would still be unlikely to refer to Hannibal, even in that situation. That contradicts the assumption that *Shelby* and *the dog which lives at Paul's house* have the same meaning. The solution to this puzzle is to distinguish two kinds of meaning. Given the facts as they stand in the real world, *the dog which lives at Paul's house* refers to Shelby, and this is its meaning *in light of those facts*. But in a more general sense, its meaning is variable, letting it refer to different dogs given different facts. Following the philosopher Gottlob Frege, semanticists often use the term *sense* to describe the second kind of meaning, and use the term *reference* to describe the first. Roughly:

(4) a. The **sense** of *the dog which lives at Paul's house* tells us that, given the facts as they actually are, it refers to Shelby; but given the facts in the alternative scenario, it would refer to Hannibal.

   b. The **reference** of *the dog which lives at Paul's house* (given the facts as they actually are): Shelby.

There is more to say about both the sense and the reference here.

The reference is the compositionally relevant aspect of the meaning.[2] The compositional role of the subject of sentence (2) is to provide an individual which will saturate the property expressed by *is cute*. That which saturates the cute-property is the reference, not the sense. Whatever a sense is, it's not an individual, so it would not be suitable for saturating a property.

The sense is a rule or procedure which directs us to a particular reference in light of particular facts. The sense of *the dog which lives at Paul's house* identifies the appropriate reference (Shelby or Hannibal or another dog) given relevant information.

Therefore, (4a–b) lead to an equivocal answer to the question "Are *Shelby* and *the dog which lives at Paul's house* synonymous?" In terms of reference, they are synonymous in situations in which the latter refers to Shelby. In terms of sense, they are not synonymous, since *Shelby* would under no circumstances have referred to Hannibal, while *the dog which lives at Paul's house* might have.

What we have in (4) isn't much of an explanation of what a sense is. It only says that *the dog which lives at Paul's house* refers to different things in different situations. It doesn't tell us specifically what it refers to in a given situation. In order for people to productively use the phrase, the sense must be more informative. Fortunately, we know a few things about what *the dog which lives at Paul's house* refers to in various situations. For one, it must be a dog. And it has to live at Paul's house. If there is a kind of bear which I think is a dog, the phrase *the dog which lives at Paul's house* can't refer to it. (Of course, the speaker could refer to the bear using the phrase *the dog which lives at Paul's house*. But this has to do with speaker's meaning. Remember that here we're discussing semantic meaning.)

Another thing we know about the sense is that the dog which is referred to has to be the most prominent one at the time the words are used. Suppose that two dogs live at Paul's house; one is at home right now, while the other, Shelby, is playing with some other dogs in front of us. It's most likely that *the dog which lives at Paul's house* refers to Shelby. The reason for this is that the other dog is not prominent enough in our consciousness at the time the words are uttered; Shelby is the dog we have in mind. (This is not to say that you couldn't embellish the situation so that *the dog which lives at Paul's house* does refer to the other dog. But if you do come up with a situation like that, you'll see that you have found a way to make the other dog more prominent in the situation, and this just proves the point that *the dog which lives at Paul's house* refers to the most prominent one at the time the words are used.) Semanticists often use the term *salience* to describe the type of prominence necessary for a thing to be referred by a definite noun phrase. The exact nature of salience is a topic in its own right, but one we're not going to examine here. In a rough fashion we can just assume that whenever a phrase such as *the dog which lives at Paul's house* is used, certain things are salient and certain things aren't. Given this:

(5)   The **sense** of *the dog which lives at Paul's house* specifies that, in a world where there is a unique animal which is a dog living at Paul's house and which is salient in the situation of use, the phrase refers to this animal.

This is all there is to the sense of *the dog which lives at Paul's house*, so if there is not a unique salient dog living at Paul's house, then there is no guidance as to what it refers to.

Let's imagine a situation where there are two dogs in the group before us, both residing at Paul's house, and neither known to us or special to us in any way. In such a situation, sentence (2) would be confusing, and would not have a clear truth-condition. The fact that it lacks truth-conditions can be taken to mean that *the dog which lives at Paul's house* doesn't refer to anything in that situation. If it doesn't refer to anything, there won't be anything to saturate *is cute*, and so the sentence will not express a proposition. If the sentence doesn't express a proposition, this is a good reason to classify it as odd. We can describe this situation by saying that the phrase has a *presupposition* that there is a unique most salient dog which lives at Paul's house. See chapter 10 for more on presupposition.

Similarly, *the dog* could fail to refer because there is not even one salient dog in the situation – you can try making up a situation of this kind on your own. Does it seem right that *The dog is cute* lacks truth-conditions in this situation?

5.3   A Bit about Indefinite NPs

Previously I had suggested that the *a(n)* of an indefinite noun phrase doesn't contribute to its meaning. There are many ways in which this could be wrong, either for some examples or for all examples. We can consider some of the issues with indefinite noun phrases – and their relation to our main topic right now, definite noun phrases – by looking at the examples in (6):

(6)   a.   A dog came into the house. The dog wanted some water.
      b.   I had dinner with a (certain) woman last night – you know the one.

In (6a), we have an indefinite NP (*a dog*) and a definite one (*the dog*). The definite has a presupposition, as we've just noted: it presupposes that there is a unique most salient dog in the context. At the point at which you read *The dog* . . . , this presupposition is satisfied because the preceding sentence mentions a dog, making it salient, and so *the dog* can refer to it. Turning now to the indefinite, at the point at which you read *a dog*, there isn't a salient dog in the context, and this seems just right for an indefinite NP. A basic intuition about indefinites is that they presuppose that something new, not something familiar, is being mentioned.[3] Irene Heim presents this contrast as the *novelty–familiarity condition*, which essentially requires that indefinites introduce new entities into the discourse, while definites refer to existing ones. These requirements are presuppositions, so that, according to this way of thinking, the familiarity (or as we called it in the previous section, salience) presupposition of definites parallels a novelty presupposition of indefinites.

Example (6b) throws another wrench into our understanding, because this is a case in which an indefinite seems not to introduce an entity which is so novel. The sentence explicitly says that the woman is already known to the hearer, so how can this indefinite be "new"? Some linguists have taken this type of case to show that there is a special variety of *specific indefinite* which is exempt from the novelty condition, or at least is subject to a weaker novelty condition.[4]

In closing this section, I should mention that many linguists believe that indefinite NPs (and definite ones as well) are actually quantifiers, the kind of noun phrase to be discussed in the next chapter. If they are, then issues of novelty and familiarity will have to be approached from a somewhat different angle.

5.4   Theories of Reference

A definite description can refer to a particular object because it has a sense which, given the specifics of the situation in which it is used, identifies a unique object. *The dog* can refer to Shelby because its sense leads the "sense robot" to Shelby in certain circumstances. The sense creates the link between the words and the thing referred to.

We have previously discussed a simpler sort of noun phrase whose meaning is to refer to particular individuals, names. We say that *Shelby* refers to Shelby, *Confucius* to Confucius, and so forth. What creates the link between word and referent in this case?[5] Philosophers have spent a great deal of effort on this question, and though the topic is not strictly speaking part of formal semantics, it is highly relevant and one that everyone well versed in semantics knows something about. For this reason, the next few sections will be devoted to the nature of the relation between a name and the thing it refers to.

You may wonder why the nature of reference is thought of as a philosophical question, rather than a linguistic one. After all, linguistics is the science of language, and reference seems to be a pretty basic fact about language. Semanticists are largely content to take for granted that a relation of reference exists between names and things, and talk about how this relation contributes to the system of meaning, without taking on the basic issue of where the relation comes from. Semanticists are in a way like lawyers (sorry, fellow semanticists), who take for granted a system of right and wrong, without asking the deeper question of what makes certain things right and wrong. Philosophers get to ask that question. (Actually, some lawyers do relate the study of the law to the more basic moral and ethical issues relevant to the law, and some semanticists relate their linguistics to fundamental concerns like the nature of reference, but this boundary-crossing practice is hard to do well, not necessary for a thriving career, and despite all this probably quite a necessary precondition for really original work to be done.)

Probably the nature of reference is seen as a philosophical rather than a linguistic issue because it is currently seen as so difficult. We don't have any consensus on what is the right way to think about the question "What makes the name *Confucius* refer to Confucius?" and no generally accepted framework in which the answer can be worked out. That is, we don't have a theory of reference which the community of linguistics can generally agree upon, and which is useful for asking and answering detailed questions about specific pieces of language. Any area of inquiry which is in such a state of disarray (or fascinating openness, depending on your perspective) is generally part of philosophy. Once we have an organized way of seeking answers to questions about the nature of reference, this topic will become part of the science of linguistics.

There are many different ideas about reference in the philosophical literature, and of course they can't all be discussed in this book. There are two general *types* of ideas with which most linguists are familiar, though, and my aim will be to introduce them to you. The first idea is that names are very much like definite descriptions in how they refer, and the second idea is that they are not.

There is another very simple way of explaining how names refer to things. This is to say that there is some kind of natural fit between the name and the thing; for example, that the sound of the name connects it to the thing. This perspective is discussed at length in Plato's *Cratylus*. In this dialogue, the character Cratylus thinks that for a name *N* to refer to a thing *x*, the form of *N* has to have a natural fit with *x*; that is, either the sound or etymology of *N* has to be descriptive of the referent *x*. Perhaps Cratylus would say that the name *Shelby* refers to Shelby because the *sh* sound is evocative of the sound the wind makes in Shelby's long fur. What do you think of this idea? In the dialogue, two other characters, Socrates and Hermogenes, attack it in a way that seems pretty effective to me, but you might find it interesting to read the dialogue for yourself and decide. If you do this, don't be discouraged by the long section of made-up etymologies and keep in mind that Socrates is a tricky character who doesn't always say what he really means. As another fun exercise, you might also want to compare naming conventions for babies in various cultures; this won't say much about how reference really works, but it can be interesting to consider how people *think* reference works, or should work.

5.4.1   Names as concealed descriptions

One idea about names is that they are semantically the same as definite descriptions. So perhaps *Confucius* means "the most famous Chinese philosopher." In other words, the meaning of *Confucius* is the same as the meaning of *the most famous Chinese philosopher*. That doesn't seem right, because then (7a) and (7b, c) would mean the same thing, since they differ only in one phrase, *the most famous Chinese philosopher*, which has been replaced by another phrase that would be synonymous, *Confucius* (or vice versa):[6]

(7)   a.   Confucius is the most famous Chinese philosopher.
  b.   Confucius is Confucius.
  c.   The most famous Chinese philosopher is the most famous Chinese philosopher.

Sentence (7a) is true, and potentially informative for someone who doesn't know anything about Confucius. (7b) and (7c) are true but not informative. This difference suggests that the two don't mean the same thing. To put it more precisely, the hypothesis that the name *Confucius* is semantically identical to *the most famous Chinese philosopher* implies that the two have the same sense and the same reference, but the data in (7) seem to show that they differ on either sense or reference (or both).[7]

Another consideration arises from a hypothetical scenario. Suppose we discover that the actual Confucius was not a philosopher at all. Rather, the real philosopher was a shy fellow, and Confucius helped him out by publicizing his ideas to the rest of the world, but also allowing the world to believe that he (Confucius) was responsible for the ideas. To put in bluntly, Confucius stole the credit from somebody else. In such a situation, we'd intuitively say that (7a) is false, since Confucius would not be a philosopher at all. However, the hypothesis that *Confucius* means "the most famous Chinese philosopher" wrongly implies that, in the hypothetical scenario, *Confucius* refers to the guy from whom credit was stolen, and furthermore leads us to predict that (7a) is true, and in fact just as trivial as (7b, c).

Notice the role compositionality plays in this argument. As (7a) is built up, we combine *the most famous Chinese philosopher* with *is*; according to the principle of compositionality, the meaning of this predicate is determined only by the meanings of its parts, *the most famous Chinese philosopher* and *is*. If *the most famous Chinese philosopher* means the same thing as *Confucius*, then *is Confucius* (whose meaning depends only on the meanings of its parts) should mean the same thing as *is the most famous Chinese philosopher*. Without the principle of compositionality, there would be no basis for expecting that (7a) and (7b) mean the same thing. This might seem like a good thing, since in fact (7a) and (7b) don't mean the same thing. But the situation would really be dire: without compositionality, there would be no basis for understanding anything about how the meanings of sentences are derived and related to one another. Abandoning compositionality is too high a price to pay, so we'd better just give up on the idea that *Confucius* means the same as *the most famous Chinese philosopher*.

It seems pretty clear that *Confucius* is not synonymous with *the most famous Chinese philosopher*, but this doesn't prove that it isn't semantically a definite description. Perhaps it's synonymous with some other description. In order to conclusively show that the description theory of names is wrong, we have to find a way to systematically consider all possible descriptions. Here's how. Suppose that someone proposes that name *N* has the same meaning as *the X*. We consider two possibilities. First, if it's possible to suppose that the person named by *N* was not an *X*, we can rerun the two arguments we just gave for *Confucius*:

(8) *N is the X* doesn't mean the same thing as *N is N* or *the X is the X*.

(9) Supposing that *N* is not described by *X*, *N is the X* would intuitively be false, but it shouldn't be if *N* means *the X*.

> Come up with a variety of names, and consider descriptions which might be plausible meanings for them. Do the above arguments apply and convince you that the description is not their meaning?

The second possibility is that it's not possible to consider that *N* was not an *X*. That is, being *X* is an essential property of the thing named by *N*. Examples are hard to come up with in the case of personal names. Perhaps you can come up with essential properties for a few very special names, like *God* or *Barney the dinosaur* (a character on a children's TV show), but I personally don't know any essential properties of Confucius or Shakespeare or Nelson Mandela. Yet I can perfectly well use their names. This shows that it's not going to work to say that the meaning of a name is, in general, a description of the form *the X*, where *X* gives an essential property of the individual named.

We can conclude that the meaning of a name is not the same as that of any definite description. If the advocate of the description theory of names isn't ready to give up completely yet, she can pursue a more conservative approach. She can propose that names have description-*like* meanings, but that these meanings are not absolutely equivalent to anything that can be expressed by real description. Perhaps the descriptions which give the meanings of names are similar to those expressed by *the*, but have some special property which makes them only appropriate for names. This approach can be used to try to get round the second objection to the description theory from above, the one having to do with the hypothetical case that Confucius was not actually a philosopher. One can say that *Confucius* has a meaning similar to *the most famous Chinese philosopher*, but which is different from it in how it responds to the hypothetical situation. More specifically, *Confucius* refers to the person who is in fact the most famous Chinese philosopher (namely Confucius), and continues to refer to the same person even under the hypothesis that Confucius does not meet that description. In other words, we say that *Confucius* is like the description with respect to the way things actually are, but sticks stubbornly to its reference even if we consider alternative hypothetical possibilities. Diagram 27 shows the situation where *Confucius* refers to the same individual across different worlds, but *the most famous Chinese philosopher* refers to different people, because Confucius is not the most famous philosopher in every possible world. A word or phrase whose reference stays the same across all alternative possible worlds is known as a *rigid designator*. It could be that names are semantically like definite descriptions, except that they are rigid designators.

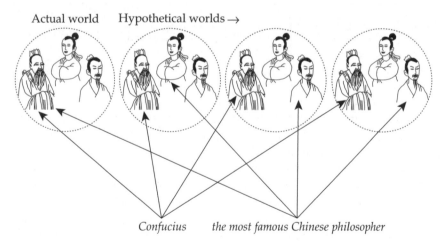

Diagram 27

The idea that names are like definite descriptions except that they are rigid designators is helpful as long we can base their meaning on a description that is, in fact, true (even if we can consider the possibility that it is not true). It will go wrong if the supposedly definitive property of the name's meaning turns out not to apply. So if the little story about Confucius stealing credit from the real philosopher actually is true, the name *Confucius* really refers to somebody else. This particular story is probably not true, but are we really so sure that our definitive information about all the people we can name is true? Do we feel totally confident that what we take to be our factual knowledge is accurate? If not, and we want to maintain the description theory of names, we have to admit that all our names might not be referring to the people we think they refer to. That sounds like an implausible thing to admit.

If names are not descriptive, the only bit of meaning we have left for them is their reference. Therefore we conclude that the reference of a name is all there is to its meaning.[8]

5.4.2   Names as directly referential: the causal chain theory

Saul Kripke, who criticized the description theory in ways similar to those in the last section, proposed that meanings of names are non-descriptive. Rather, the meaning of a name is nothing but its reference. But if a name lacks a descriptive sense, we have to come up with another way to explain the relation between the name and the thing it names. His explanation runs like this: when Confucius was born, his parents looked at him and said "We will call this baby 'Confucius.'" By virtue of their direct contact with him, and this act of naming, they were able to use the name *Confucius* to refer to the child. After that, various other people met baby Confucius, and they learned his name from the parents. As they did this, they borrowed the ability to refer to the baby with the name from his parents' original act of naming. In turn, other people learned the name from these people, and so on. When he was old enough, Confucius learned his own name, and hence borrowed the ability to use his name from his parents. Others could then acquire the ability to use his name from him. This chain of links from name-user to name-user ultimately extends from Confucius' parents down through history to us today, so that our use of the name is grounded in the original act of naming thousands of years ago. (Actually, his parents would have named him using the variety of Chinese spoken at that time. This theory will have to allow for the pronunciation of the name to change over time through processes of historical sound change, as well as through changes which accompany the borrowing of the name by speakers of one language from speakers of another.)

5.4.3   The role of the community in reference

There have been various reactions in the semantics and philosophy communities to Kripke's theory of names; I'm going to go into just one, a particularly interesting response by Gareth Evans.[9] Evans argues that Kripke fails to appreciate the importance of the social context of the use of a name in determining its referent. He points out that sometimes a person can use a name to refer to something even though he or she has no acquaintance with it, either directly or through a chain connecting him to someone who himself has a direct connection to it. For example, perhaps you have never been to New York City and have never heard anyone speak of 7th Avenue there. You have heard of 5th, 6th, and 8th Avenues, though, and so you surmise that there's a 7th Avenue between 6th and 8th. This is a perfectly good basis for referring to 7th Avenue when you say *I wonder what 7th Avenue is like.*

The ability of names to change their referent also argues against Kripke's theory. Evans tells us that *Madagascar* originally named part of the African mainland, but through a mistake by Marco Polo westerners started applying it to the island. For the first few people who made this mistake, we might say that the word *Madagascar* continued to refer to the original part of the mainland, and that they were wrong when they said things like *Madagascar is an island*. However, it would be ridiculous to say that such a statement is false still today. By now, *Madagascar* certainly refers to the island. Yet there is no causal chain tying our use of *Madagascar* to some initial speaker who had direct acquaintance with the island and named it.[10]

Evans argues that the semantic meaning of a name should be based on a conventional pattern of speaker's meaning. More specifically, a name *N* will refer to a thing *A* if it is common knowledge within the community that people use *N* to refer to *A*, and that their ability to use *N* to refer to *A* is based on the fact that other users have used *N* to refer to *A*. For example, I can use the name *Confucius* to refer to Confucius because people in the community typically use this name to refer to him, and their ability to use the name in this way is based on the common knowledge that people use the name to refer to him. This much seems unobjectionable – more or less, it says that *Confucius* refers to Confucius because the community as a whole uses it this way – but it leaves open the question of on what basis we say that the community has the practice of using a name to refer to a particular individual. Typically, Evans says, there is a causal link between the referent and the ideas that members of the community have associated with the name. Thus, *Confucius* refers to Confucius because our beliefs about Confucius originate in Confucius' own actions, mostly from the texts he authored. Even if he didn't author those texts, as on the hypothetical scenario we considered earlier, we believe he did, and our beliefs would originate in his actions (his publicizing those texts and philosophical ideas on behalf of the true author). Likewise, *Madagascar* refers to Madagascar because our most significant beliefs associated with the name originate from the island, not from the part of the mainland that originally bore the name.

Evans agrees with Kripke that names are unlike definite descriptions; they both propose that names refer directly, without any extra, hidden meaning which goes beyond their reference. The two differ in that Kripke thinks that the history of a name is responsible for its meaning, while Evans thinks that it's the practice and beliefs of the community which are crucial. Of course in many instances, the community finds the original use of the name to be extremely important in deciding how to use it today. For example, one could imagine the authorities in Madagascar deciding to change the name of the country because it reflects a historical mistake, and demanding that English speakers stop using the name. With prescriptive help from governments, map companies, and school teachers, in time the name might revert to its original reference. To my mind, this suggests that Kripke's ideas can be seen as an especially important specific case within Evans's more general theory.

5.4.4 Referential and attributive readings

The way of thinking about definite noun phrases which we have looked at earlier in this chapter says that their meaning is very similar to that of names. Their semantic role is to refer. Unlike with names, however, we have said that their descriptive quality is part of how they refer. Specifically, a definite refers to the most salient thing which its common noun-part describes: *the teacher* refers to the unique, most salient teacher in the situation in which it is used. This is a particular way of putting together the two aspects of a definite's meaning, the referring aspect and the describing aspect.

There are other important ideas in the philosophy and linguistics concerning the meaning of definite noun phrases. Bertrand Russell proposed that they do not refer at all. Instead, *the teacher* would have a meaning which fits into a sentence something like this:

(10) *The teacher is nice* is true if and only if (i) there is one and only one (relevant) teacher and (ii) everyone who is a (relevant) teacher is also nice.

This way of thinking about the meaning of a definite can be seen as taking its descriptive quality as the fundamental aspect of its meaning. The meaning in (10) never actually refers to a teacher; instead, it just says that one (relevant) teacher exists, and that any such is nice. Since part (i) of the meaning says that there is one and only one teacher, part (ii) will imply that this teacher is nice. Still, it never gets around to actually referring to this teacher.

Russell's way of thinking about definites treats them as a kind of *quantified noun phrase*. This can be seen in the fact that (10) needs to use words like *there is* and *everyone* to express the meaning of *the teacher*. Quantified noun phrases are the topic of the next chapter, so we'll leave off further discussion of the details of this idea for now.

In the years since Russell's work, there has been a lively debate about whether it is best to think (with Frege) that definites fundamentally refer or to think (with Russell) that they fundamentally describe. One famous contribution to this debate was made by Keith Donnellan.[11] He argued that both approaches are right: definite noun phrases have a *referential use* and an *attributive use*. On the referential use, the noun phrase refers to whatever the speaker can assume that the hearer will figure that she's trying to refer to. Donnellan gives a famous example:

Scenario #1

For example, suppose that Jones has been charged with Smith's murder and has been placed on trial. Imagine that there is a discussion of Jones's odd behavior at the trial. We might sum up our impressions of his behavior by saying, "Smith's murderer is insane." If someone asks to whom we are referring, by using this description, the answer here is "Jones." (Donnellan 1966: 286)

Note that as far as this story goes, *Smith's murderer* would refer to Jones here even if he is actually innocent. It doesn't matter whether the descriptive part of *Smith's murderer* actually describes Jones. All that matters is that the hearer figure out that that's who the speaker wants to talk about.

On the attributive use, a definite noun phrase doesn't refer at all. Here's Donnellan's story for that:

Scenario #2

. . . we come upon poor Smith foully murdered. From the brutal manner of the killing and the fact that Smith was the most lovable person in the world, we might exclaim "Smith's murderer was insane." I will assume, to make it a simpler case, that in a quite ordinary sense we do not know who murdered Smith (though this is not in the end essential to the case). (Donnellan 1966: 285)

In this situation, you might say that *Smith's murderer is insane* means the same thing as *Whoever murdered Smith is insane*, where *whoever murdered Smith* is a sort of descriptive-quantificational thing with a meaning along the same lines as what Russell proposed for definite noun phrases. The attributive meaning corresponds to Russell's analysis of definites.

Donnellan's conception of the referential use is different from the referential analysis for definites we worked out above. We said that a definite will refer to the unique thing its common noun-part describes, while Donnellan says that it refers to the individual which the hearer can determine that speaker wants to refer to. Because of this, contrary to what you might think, scenario no. 2 does not work against our Fregean referential analysis. According to our analysis, in scenario no. 2 the phrase *Smith's murderer* will refer to the unique individual who murdered Smith, despite the fact that we don't know who that is. That's great. Indeed, it's scenario no. 1 that gives trouble. Here, *Smith's murderer* will not refer to Jones if it so happens that Jones is innocent, and in this way our referential analysis doesn't make the predication in scenario no. 1 which Donnellan thinks it should.

5.4.5 Speaker's reference and semantic reference

One key question for understanding what Donnellan is trying to say concerns what he had in mind with the term *use*. We have the referential use and the attributive use. Are these uses actually different (semantic) meanings, or do they relate to some non-semantic distinction in meaning? Saul Kripke[12] notes that Donnellan doesn't give his readers any theory of what a use is, and so the only clear way to understand what he says is to consider a use to be a (semantic) meaning. That is, Kripke interprets Donnellan as proposing that definite noun phrases are ambiguous, and then criticizes this by saying that "it is very much the lazy man's approach in philosophy to posit ambiguities when in trouble." Let's put aside the issue of laziness and focus on the question of ambiguity; linguists have ways of evaluating a proposal that some word or phrase is ambiguous. For example, we can consider a variety of languages; if a word is truly ambiguous in one language, we would expect that the two meanings are expressed by different words in others. (This doesn't work the other way around: if a word in one language can be translated by two words in another, this doesn't mean it's ambiguous in the first. There's no reason to say that English *rice* is ambiguous just because it can be translated by *fan* 'rice grains for eating in the usual way' or *mi* 'rice for other purposes', like planting or making flour, in Chinese.) It seems that languages don't have two definite articles, one for a referential meaning and one for an attributive meaning. They just have one article (or none). This point tends to support Kripke. It doesn't seem right to analyze definite noun phrases as ambiguous.

> It's possible that Donnellan might be right because the referential/attributive contrast is a structural ambiguity (involving different grammatical structures for the sentence), not a lexical one (involving different meanings for *the*). How plausible does this seem to you?

As mentioned in chapter 1, Kripke's solution is to say that definites have a single semantic meaning, and he claims that this semantic meaning may as well be the one proposed by Russell. The ability of definites to refer can be seen not as part of their semantics, but as part of their pragmatics, that is their speaker's meaning. Speakers may use a definite to refer to something, but this does not mean that the definite itself refers to that thing by virtue of its semantics. The situation can be seen as similar to the kind of metaphor whereby we refer to a person by virtue of an incidental property of theirs. For instance, a flight attendant might say *14B wants a coffee*, meaning that the person in seat 14B wants the coffee. Though *14B* doesn't (semantically) refer to a person, but rather to a seat (so that, literally speaking, this sentence is nonsense), it's a concise way for the flight attendant to convey a clear message.

Kripke's explicit aim in his article is to show that Donnellan is wrong in saying that Russell's analysis is inadequate when it comes to scenario no. 1. Kripke basically makes a methodological point ("we need to keep in mind the distinction between semantic and speaker's meaning") and a negative point ("your criticism of Russell isn't convincing"). Though he seems to have made his methodological and negative points quite effectively, if you read the paper it is important to keep in mind that he has not provided a positive argument for Russell's theory. Because of this, we should not take Kripke's paper as arguing that Russell's theory is better than the Fregean referential theory we worked out earlier. Indeed, what Kripke says helps to save any theory which gets scenario no. 2 right from the troubles it faces from scenario no. 1.

5.5   Plurals and Mass Terms

So far we have spent quite a while discussing a narrow range of noun phrases: names, predicate nominals, and singular definites. The world of noun phrases is a diverse one, though, and we'll continue this chapter, as well as the next one, examining other interesting types. In this section we look at plural noun phrases (like *three horses*) and mass noun phrases (like *much milk*).

Godehard Link[13] has presented a very appealing theory of plural and mass noun phrases. He proposes that the set of individuals associated with a given noun has an internal structure which is relevant for how we talk about those individuals. As we've seen in chapter 3, the meaning of *horse* is a property, and this property can be modeled as an association between possible worlds and the set of horses in each world. This can be expressed as in (11):

(11)   w1 → {A, B}
        w2 → {B, C}
        w3 → {A, B, C}
        w4 → Ø

(In world 1, there are two horses, A and B. In world 2, there are also two, B and C. In world three, A, B, and C are all horses, and in world 4 there are no horses. Let's pretend that's all the worlds there are.)

To make things simpler, let's just focus on one world, w3, as we compare this meaning for *horse* to that of the plural *horses*. So (12) is the meaning for *horse*, modeled as a set, in world 3. To describe plural noun phrases, Godehard Link introduces the concept of a *sum* of individuals. Any two individuals A and B can be summed to make a plural individual A+B. This plural individual has A and B as *parts*. The meaning of the plural noun *horses* is then the set of plural individuals made up of horses, as in (13):

(12)   The meaning of *horse* in w3 = {A, B, C}

(13)   The meaning of *horses* in w3 = {A+B, B+C, A+C, A+B+C}

This meaning for plural *horses* can be used as a predicate nominal. (14) is true in w3 if the plural individual Silver+Trigger is in the set indicated in (13):

(14)   Silver and Trigger are horses.

The proper meaning of *horses* associates a set of plural individuals with each possible world. Convert the sample meaning for *horse* in (11) into a meaning for *horses*.

This exercise has an answer, no. 5, in the appendix.

The part–whole relations which relate *horse* and *horses* can be illustrated as in diagram 28 (ignore the part about Chinese for now). (Some technical terms: A, B, and C are the *atoms* of this part–whole structure, a *lattice*, while the rest are *plural individuals* or perhaps *groups*. We call A+B the *join* of A and B. A and B are *parts* of A+B. The parts of A+B+C are harder to describe; A, B, and C are all parts, as are the complex individuals A+B, B+C, and A+C. How many parts A+B+C has depends on how you look at it: three ({A, B, C}) or two ({A+B, C} or {A, B+C} or {A+C, B}).[14])

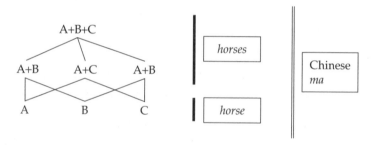

Diagram 28

Plural noun phrases are often modified by numerals, as in *the three horses*. We can make a good guess about the meaning of the numeral here based on our theory of plural noun phrases and what we know about the meaning of *the*. Recall that *the* combines with a predicate, and creates an expression which refers to the unique most salient thing described by that predicate. This tells us that *three horses* must be a predicate, since predicates are what *the* combines with. Therefore, *three* can be thought of as a kind of adjective, since as we saw earlier, adjectives combine with a noun predicate to form a larger combined predicate. More specifically, *three* combines with *horses*, and the resulting predicate describes any plural individual which is described by *horses* and which has three atomic parts. In other words, the meaning of *three horses* in world 3 is this set: {A+B+C}.

horse	*horses*	*three horses*	*the three horses*
A property which describes any individual horse	A property which describes any plural individual consisting of horses	A property which describes any plural individual described by *horses* with three atomic parts	Refers to the unique most salient thing described by *three horses*

In sets:

{A, B, C}	{A+B, B+C, A+C, A+B+C}	{A+B+C}	A+B+C

Diagram 29

The three horses refers to the unique most salient thing described by *three horses*. The plural individual A+B+C is the unique thing described by *three horses* (in w3), so *the three horses* refers to it. (See diagram 29.)

Many languages, like Chinese, don't distinguish singular from plural nouns. Emmon Bach suggests that nouns in these languages cover both atomic and non-atomic individuals, gathering together everything that in English is described by *horse* and *horses*.[15] That is, in Chinese the meaning of *horse* in world 3 would be {A, B, C, A+B, B+C, A+C, A+B+C}. If a language does not distinguish atomic from plural individuals, it is a bit of a mystery how a numeral like *three* would work, since the job of *three* is to count atomic individuals. Chinese, like many other languages, handles this by using *classifiers* (or *measure words*) which indicate the nature of the units that one counts by. Classifiers introduce into the semantic composition a specification of what the atoms are, allowing numerals to do their job. The measure word used with the word for horse, *ma*, is *pi*. So *three horses* is translated *san pi ma* 'three classifier horses'. Each of these words has a basic semantic function: *san* indicates we are counting three atoms, *pi* indicates that these atoms are large-animal-sized (in this case, A, B, and C), and *ma* indicates that their nature is that of horse-hood (that is, they are drawn from the set described by *horse*).

The comparison between Chinese and English reveals something about how languages express meaning that would not be clear by looking at either language alone. On the one hand, Chinese reveals that a simple phrase like *three horses* has three meaning components, not just two as English leads us to expect. In this respect, languages that use classifiers have a much more straightforward relationship between syntax and semantics than languages like English which do not. In English, two distinct semantic functions are condensed into nouns: *horse(s)* indicates both that we are talking about horse-sized things (corresponding to a classifier) and that the nature of these things is horse-hood (corresponding to the Chinese noun). On the other hand, English reveals that there is a fundamental difference between plural and atomic individuals, a point which is not clear in a language like Chinese which doesn't distinguish singular from plural. There is no sense in which either language's system is superior; there are simply different ways in which a given language can combine and express the deeper, fundamental components of meaning which all languages share.

Mass nouns (sometimes called "uncountable nouns") like *gold* present an interesting variation on this way of thinking about plurality. Mass nouns are associated with lattice structures like diagram 28. However, as far as our linguistic conception of things goes, one can always theoretically divide a piece of gold into two smaller pieces. There are no basic units, or atoms, of gold. (In reality, of course, there are atoms, but this knowledge isn't built into language.) Thus, the lattice has no bottom atomic layer, but goes on downward forever.

An English mass noun like *gold* is somewhat like the Chinese *ma*. The lattice for *gold*, like Chinese *ma*, does not categorize the totality of individuals in the lattice into atomic vs. non-atomic units. However, the two are not exactly the same, since the lattice for *ma* in Chinese does have atoms (it's not that the Chinese don't know that horses come in basic units – these atoms are simply not relevant to the meaning of *ma*). More similar to Chinese *ma* is a word like *furniture*, which is a mass noun even though we clearly understand what basic units of furniture are. This can be seen from the fact that combinations like *three furnitures* are obviously ungrammatical. To count furniture, we have to use a classifier-like word such as *piece*: *three pieces of furniture*.

There are relationships between the count and mass domains. Consider an example from Link's paper: the connections between *gold* and *ring*. Gold is a mass noun and *ring* is a count noun. Each gold ring is made up of some gold, so there is a connection, or "mapping," between the gold and the rings. This mapping preserves the internal structure of the ring domain, so that if we have two rings R1 and R2, made up of gold G1 and G2, the plural individual R1+R2 (i.e., *those rings*) is made up of G1+G2 (i.e., *that gold*). See diagram 30. As Link points out, it is necessary to distinguish the ring R1 from the gold G1, since the two have different properties – the ring can be new, but the gold old, for instance. But they have a very intimate relationship: the gold comprises the ring.

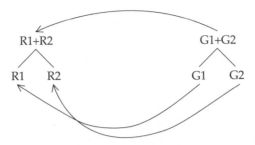

Diagram 30

> Think about the relationships between the count and mass domains suggested by *pig/pork*, *bottle (of beer)/beer*, *thing/stuff*, *(a) thought/(much) thought*.

5.6   Kinds

A bare plural noun phrase is a plural lacking a determiner like *the*, *all*, etc. Languages use bare plurals, and bare nouns more generally, to differing extents. English uses bare plurals pretty much, and they present a puzzle for semantic theory, since they appear to be radically ambiguous:

(15)   Horses are rare.   (= as a group)

(16)   Horses are mammals.   (= all)

(17)   Horses have tails.   (= almost all)

(18)   Horses give birth to their foals in the spring.
                                               (= many of the females)

(19)   Horses were galloping across the plain.   (= some)

But the thesis that the differences in meaning seen in (15)–(19) are due to an ambiguity of *horses* is a bad one. In the first place, it is hardly plausible that *horses* is five-ways ambiguous (at least), on some occasions meaning "all horses," on others meaning "some horses," and so forth. But more importantly, if *horses* were ambiguous, we would expect each sentence in (15)–(19) to be ambiguous. If *horses* can mean *all horses*, we'd expect (19) to be able to mean "all horses were galloping across the plain," (18) to mean "all horses give birth to their foals in the spring," and (15) to mean "all horses are rare" (something which doesn't even make sense). We don't find individual sentences to be radically ambiguous in this way, however. This suggests that the meaning differences in (15)–(19) don't arise from an ambiguity in the subject *horses*, but rather from differences between the predicates. In order to explain the pattern, then, we will embark on another foray into the sub-atomic semantics of predicates.

Greg Carlson[16] has proposed a theory of bare plurals which gives them a single meaning. But to accomplish this, he needs to think of the individuals which language talks about as having a certain kind of internal structure (this structure would be in addition to that proposed by Link). Carlson suggests that we distinguish the species of horse, an abstract entity which he calls the *kind*, from the regular *objects* typically known as horses. For Carlson, the term *individual* is a general term covering both kinds and objects. In addition to the distinction between kinds and objects, we have *stages*, or spatiotemporal "slices" of individual horses. For example, the horse Silver may have lived for 40 years, but we can focus on just the part of his existence which begins at 7:00 a.m. on a certain day, and ends at 7:00 p.m. that night. This 12-hour stage can be made more concrete by thinking of time as a spatial dimension. With Silver stretching for a 40-year length of this dimension, the stage is a 12-hour slice taken out of the overall length. Stages are not individuals, and we have no words to refer to them in natural language, but as we'll see below, according to Carlson they play an important hidden role in solving the puzzle of (15)–(19).

In diagram 31, S1 is a stage of the first horse H1; it also counts as a stage of the kind. We can say that S1 "realizes" H1 and K.

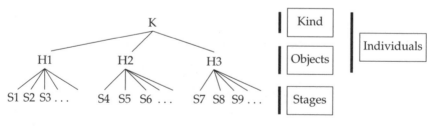

Diagram 31

The bare plurals *horses* always refers to the kind. However, predicates differ in whether they pertain to kinds, objects, or stages. A predicate like *rare* is naturally seen as kind-level; only kinds can be rare, single objects or stages cannot be. Thus the semantics of (15) is simple. The property of being rare is predicated of the kind "horses." We can symbolize this as follows:

(20)   rare(horses)

The predicate *have tails*, in contrast, is object-level. Kinds are abstract, and do not have tails. Object-level predicates express permanent, or nearly permanent, properties of things. Thus, they apply to objects, rather than stages, which are mere temporal segments. For this reason, we can straight-forwardly say something like (21):

(21)   Silver and Trigger have tails.
       have-tails(Silver+Triger) (ignoring the internal structure of *have tails*)

Since *have tails* is object-level, but *horses* refers to a kind, (17) above contains a mismatch. Carlson proposes that the species of horses can be said to have tails because, as a general rule, the individual horses do. This means that a basically object-level property like *have tails* can become kind-level. The operator Gn, for "generic," accomplishes this shift, as seen in diagram 32. If we start with an object-level predicate P, Gn(P) is a new property which is true of a kind k if (and only if) P is true of typical instances of k.

(22)   Gn(have-tail)(horses)

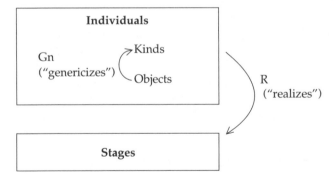

Diagram 32

The predicate *be galloping across the plain* is stage-level. Stage-level predicates express a temporary property of an individual. If we want to say something like *Silver was galloping across the plain*, we must turn this stage-level predicate into something that can apply to the individual Silver. Carlson shifts the predicate to an individual-level one that says something like "has a stage which is galloping across the plain."

(23)   Basic stage-level predicate:
Galloping-across-the-plain

Shifted individual-level predicate:
"has a stage x such that Galloping-across-the-plain(x)"

Silver was galloping across the plain. →
"Silver has a stage x such that Galloping-across-the-plain(x)"

This says that there is a stage of Silver that had the property of galloping across the plain; in other words, for some temporary period of time, Silver was doing that.

The individual-level predicate can also be applied to a kind, as in (19):

(24)   Horses were galloping across the plain. →
"The kind horses has a stage x such that x is Galloping-across-the-plain"

(24) says that there is a stage of the kind "horses" that had the property of galloping across the plain. Since any stage of a kind is a stage of one of the individuals which make up the kind, this correctly implies that some horses (not necessarily most or all) have stages which galloped. Notice the use of *some* in this paraphrase. We have explained why *horses* in (19) seems to mean "some horses."[17]

The overall picture here is that *horses* always refers to the same thing, the kind. It has a very simple semantics. The predicates that combine with it either directly describe the kind (*rare*), or indirectly use the kind to say something about the individuals or stages which realize it. The semantic complexity in the pattern (15)–(19) arises from different classes of predicates, not the bare plural.

5.7   Pronouns and Anaphora

Pronouns are another kind of word that can refer. For example, in the second sentence of (25), we would naturally say that *he* refers to Shelby, and therefore Shelby saturates the property described by *is a Keeshond*.

(25)   Shelby is cute. He is a Keeshond.

Pronouns are like definites in that they can refer to different things in different situations. In (25), *he* refers to Shelby, but if I had mentioned Bucky instead, it would have referred to Bucky. However, pronouns seem a bit different from definites in that it seems not enough just to say that *he* refers to the unique most salient individual which is described by its descriptive part. The only descriptive part of *he* is that we are talking about a male thing, and examples like (26) show that there need not be a unique most salient male thing for *he* to work:[18]

(26)   Shelby met Bucky. He sniffed him.

If Shelby is most salient, then both *he* and *him* should refer to Shelby – or if Bucky is most salient, to Bucky. It's not so clear how to work this out so that Shelby is most salient when *he* is read while *Bucky* is most salient when *him* is read. (Note that, for grammatical reasons, *he* and *him* cannot refer to the same thing.)

In fact the very same issue arises for definites, though it's a bit harder to see. For example:

(27)   Shelby met another male dog and a female cat. He sniffed the dog and bit the cat.

We can't really say that *the dog* refers to the unique most salient dog here, since Shelby is intuitively more salient than the other dog. So there are also problems for the semantics of definites we need to worry about, and what we say in this chapter about pronouns applies to definites as well. Nevertheless, much of the discussion of definites you'll find in linguistics and philosophy doesn't really get into these matters (although much of it does), and the way of thinking about definites discussed earlier in the chapter is good enough for many purposes.

The evidence from (26) and (27) shows that a simple notion like salience in combination with the obvious semantically descriptive quality of a pronoun does not give us enough information to resolve its reference. This means either that the situation of use provides us with richer information than just salience, or that the pronoun has more descriptive quality than it seems. Linguists have pursued both of these ideas.

5.7.1   The assignment function

The most common way of thinking about the meaning of pronouns says that context provides the pronoun's reference directly, only subject to the condition that the descriptive quality of the pronoun is respected. *How* the context provides references for the pronouns is then left for another day. The assumption is that it's not a problem for semantics, or indeed for pragmatics in the narrow sense of a component of linguistic theory. It is seen as an issue for a general psychological theory of language use. In these terms, the second sentence of (26) works like this:

(28)   He sniffed him.
            Context: *he*   → Shelby
                           him → Bucky

We interpret the sentence compositionally by saturating the doubly unsaturated proposition expressed by *sniffed* with Bucky and Shelby, the contextually determined referents of *him* and *he*.

Some terms: when thought of this way, pronouns are being understood as similar to logical *variables*. Variables are elements of formal logic which get their reference in a special way, from a *variable assignment function* (a mathematical object which associates a referent with any variable in a logical formula). For this reason, you may hear linguists calling pronouns "variables," and saying that they get their meaning from an "assignment function." As we will see below, it's actually a bit better to talk about an assignment function rather than a context as responsible for the meanings of pronouns, because not every pronoun gets its meaning from context. Rather, we should say that in simple cases the assignment function is determined by context, but in more complex cases, it's determined in other ways. However it's determined, the assignment function then gives meanings to the pronouns.

In examples (25)–(27), each pronoun seems to pick up its reference from a noun phrase which comes before it. For example, in (25) *he* refers to Shelby because it is, in some sense, linked to the preceding word *Shelby*. This relationship is called *anaphora*. The pronoun is an *anaphor* which is linked to *Shelby*, its *antecedent*. Our explanation of this link is that the relation between anaphor and antecedent is mediated by the context (or assignment function). Because of the first sentence *Shelby is cute*, the context comes to associate *he* with Shelby, and as a result when the second sentence is read, it means that Shelby is a Keeshond. This brings up the question of how the first sentence causes the association "*he* → Shelby" to be established. Is it a purely pragmatic phenomenon – mentioning Shelby makes him very salient, and so a reasonable hearer will figure out that *he* must be associated with Shelby – or a semantic one? While in (25)–(27) it may well be pragmatic, there is clear evidence that it is semantic in at least some cases.

Let's consider the examples in (29)–(30):

(29)   Only John loves his mother.

(30)   Every girl in the class loves the teacher who gave her a good grade.

In (29), we would naturally say that *his* refers to John, since the sentence means that John loves John's mother. But this is not all there is to its meaning. Because of *only*, the sentence also tells us something about who doesn't love whom. And the sentence is ambiguous. It can imply that nobody else loves John's mother, or that nobody else loves his or her own mother. On the first meaning, *his* remains simple; it just refers to John:

(31)   John loves his (=John's) mother, but
       Mary doesn't love his (=John's) mother, and
       Bob doesn't love his (=John's) mother, and . . .

However, on the second meaning, the reference of *his* seems to shift as we consider who doesn't love whom:

(32)   John loves his (=John's) mother, but
       Frank doesn't love his (=Frank's) mother, and
       Bob doesn't love his (=Bob's) mother, and . . .

(Notice by the way that this is a real ambiguity, not some kind of indeterminacy. The sentence can't mean that John loves John's mother, Frank doesn't love Frank's mother, Bob doesn't love John's mother, . . . That is, *his* either sticks firmly to John, or shifts every time. We can't get a mixture of (31) and (32).)

In order to understand how the meaning of (32) comes about, we need to invoke a process we last saw in the discussion of relative clauses (that's a surprise!). Here's the process: we begin by assigning the same numerical index to *only John* and *his*, to indicate the anaphoric link between them. We then move *only John* in a way very similar to how we moved *who*, leaving behind a co-indexed trace. At this point we have the structure given in (33b):

(33)   a.   Only John$_1$ loves his$_1$ mother →
       b.   Only John$_1$ [e$_1$ loves his$_1$ mother]

Though this movement is parallel to what we saw with relative clauses in chapter 3, there is a big difference. With relative clauses the movement converts a structure we don't see – *the boy Mary saw whom* – into one we do – *the boy whom Mary saw*. The movement in (33) converts a structure we do see, (33a), into one we don't, (33b). This new structure which we don't see but which is used for purposes of semantics is known as the *logical form* of the sentence. (Not all semanticists believe in logical form, and those who don't would find a way to give an analysis similar to the one I'm presenting without the movement represented in (33). I think the key ideas of how the relationship between *only John* and *his* works can be most easily seen by thinking about logical forms.)

Once we have the logical form (3b), it can help us out doing semantics. The part in brackets represents a property. A property is a proposition missing a part, and in this case, one could say that the missing part plays two separate roles in the property: it is both the one who loves, represented by the e_1 in subject position, and the person whose mother is loved, represented by the his_1. We might indicate this property as in diagram 33. (The heart symbolizes love. The person on the right is a mother, and the circle she's touching is her child. This circle is linked to the circle on the left, indicating that the two are filled in simultaneously. So, this property is only missing one piece, though this piece will play two roles in the ultimate proposition.)

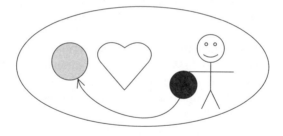

Diagram 33

This sort of pronoun, used to create an open position, or missing piece, in a proposition, is known as a *bound variable pronoun*. We call the element which turns it into an open position its *binder*. In this case, *only John* is the binder. When *only John* combines with a property, it says two things: when John saturates the property, you get a true proposition, and when anyone else saturates it, you get a false one. This gives us the meaning in (32).[19]

The point to notice now is that a bound variable pronoun does not get its meaning from context. Indeed, when (29) is interpreted as (32), it doesn't really make sense to say that *his* has a meaning at all. Rather, it enters into the semantic computation in a complex way that has nothing to do with the situation in which the sentence is used. With the technical concept of the variable assignment function, we can describe what's going on by looking at (33b). The phrase *only John* tells us the following two things. (i) We consider the assignment function which makes variables indexed "1" (i.e., t_1 and his_1) refer to John; then the part in brackets says something true. (ii) But then we consider any assignment function which makes t_1 and his_1 refer to anyone besides John; in that case, it says something false. As we see, in this situation the assignment function is under the control of *only John*, and not derived from the context.

Since we now know that in complex cases like (29) the pronoun is bound by its antecedent, and not dependent on context for its meaning, we may wonder whether the situation is the same in simpler cases like (25). Perhaps we should say that *he* is bound by *Shelby* in (25). This is a tricky issue. On the one hand, it would be nice to have a unified theory of anaphora, one that says that all anaphora involves variable binding. On the other, there are various problems. For example, we can't aspire to say that every single pronoun is bound, since not all pronouns have antecedents. We may say *He is tired*, referring to the baby crying before us, without having explicitly mentioned the baby previously. Moreover, binding between sentences is not in general possible:

(34)   Only John loves his mother. His father is bad.

Here *his father* simply refers to John's father; we don't have to consider whether other individuals have bad fathers. That is, (34) doesn't mean "Only John loves his mother and has a bad father." This shows that *his* is not bound by *only John*. So its antecedent has to be the sub-phrase *John*, not the whole phrase *only John*. Because of this, if we want to hypothesize that all anaphora involves binding, we would have to explain why names can bind across sentences, while phrases of the form *only X* cannot. Moreover, this is a general, headache-inducing problem: for example, indefinites (phrases of the form *an X*) would be like names in allowing binding across sentences, while certain quantifiers like *every X* would be like *only X* in not:

(35)   A dog_1 walked in. He_1 was cute.

(36)   Every dog_1 walked in. ??He_1 was cute.

Suffice it to say that there is much debate concerning these questions. (We'll discuss some additional theoretical ideas of relevance in chapter 10, under the label "dynamic semantics.") We have learned plenty, though: pronouns are interpreted by the assignment function, which is derived from context in some cases, and controlled by the semantics of the pronoun's binder in others. Pronouns are simple little words that gives rise to all kinds of semantic complexity.

5.7.2   E-type pronouns

We have been discussing using the notions of context and the variable assignment function to solve the problem of (25)–(27). I mentioned that there is another possibility, and it is the idea that pronouns have more descriptive content than they seem. We could see them as abbreviations for definite noun phrases. Sentence (26) might be really a terse version of (37):

(37)   Shelby met Bucky. The dog who is named "Shelby" sniffed the dog who is named "Bucky."

(Correspondingly, example (27) could show that definites also have more descriptive content than they seem, since *the dog* there doesn't have enough content to pick out the other dog over Shelby. It might be short for something like *the dog which Shelby met.*)

If pronouns are understood along these lines, we can call them *E-type pronouns* after the philosopher Gareth Evans.[20] He gives the following example:

(38)   Few politicians admire Kennedy, and they are very junior.

In example (38), *they* is not a bound variable. If it were, the sequence would mean "there are few politicians who admire Kennedy and who are very junior." This leaves open the possibility that there are other, senior, politicians who admire Kennedy too. But (38) means that all politicians who admire Kennedy are junior, and that there are few of them. A way to account for this is to take the pronoun *they* to mean *the politicians who admire Kennedy.*

Perhaps the E-type theory is correct about cases like (38). But one thing to be clear about is that it doesn't get rid of the need for variable binding – there's no way it can account for the meaning of (29) and (30) without variable binding. Since we need variable binding, we need the assignment function. With the assignment function, we can analyze pronouns

without antecedents in the way illustrated in (28); the assignment function will be specified by context to a sufficient degree to give meanings to
pronouns without antecedents. One may wonder, then, if (38) shouldn't
be handled in the same way. At the time when a hearer (or reader) tries
to understand *They are very junior*, couldn't the assignment function just
be seen as providing the group of politicians who admire Kennedy as the
referent of *they*? There's no reason it couldn't. The real issue will be to
explain why this particular referent for *they* is so obviously the right one
in this context. Just appealing to a variable assignment function leaves open
the whole question of how the context contributes to pronoun reference;
the move we have made amounts to saying it's not a semantic issue, but
rather a pragmatic one. This contrasts with the E-type theory's position,
which says that it is a semantic question to a significant extent, since *they*
is taken to mean (semantically) "the politicians who admire Kennedy,"
though this particular meaning for the pronoun is due to pragmatics; this
meaning is pragmatically available because of the preceding sentence *Few
politicians admire Kennedy*.

A semantic theory of E-type pronouns has been called upon to explain
such examples as the following:

(39)   The man who deposited his paycheck in his bank account is wiser
       than the one who invested it in Enron.[21]

(40)   Everyone who buys a sage plant here buys eight others along with
       it.[22]

In (39), *it* seems to mean "his paycheck." Since no particular man is being
described, there's no particular paycheck either. This means that the
variable assignment function can't provide a referent for *it* in any simple
contextually based way. Nor does *it* have a real antecedent, since *his paycheck* has to do with the paychecks of those who deposited their money
in a bank while *it* has to do with the paychecks of those who invested
in Enron. Likewise in (40), because we're talking about every sage plant
purchaser, *it* doesn't refer to any particular sage plant. So the variable
assignment function can't provide it with a reference in any simple way
based on context. One solution, the E-type solution, is to let *it* mean "the
sage plant he or she bought."[23] Notice that this explanation of the pronoun's
meaning itself contains a pronoun within it (that is, "he or she," which
I'd like to think of as one genderless pronoun). This pronoun itself is a
variable bound by *everyone*. That is, though the E-type theory denies that
pronouns are, in general, just variables, it has to allow them to contain

variables. A true bound variable pronoun, then, could be thought of as an E-type pronoun which contains a variable and nothing else.

To my mind, though, this rather messy situation shows that our understanding of pronouns, particularly cases like (38)–(40), isn't yet complete. It's an area of much vigorous research.

NOTES

1   A difference between *Shelby* and *the dog which lives at Paul's house* is that the latter is only likely to be used in a situation in which more than one dog is under discussion. This is because, if Shelby is the only relevant dog, we'll just say *the dog*. Moreover, if we know his name, we'll probably say *Shelby* instead of either *the dog* or *the dog which lives at Paul's house*. This is all due to some features of pragmatics (see chapter 11) which tell us to use shorter and less ambiguous phrasing whenever possible.

2   At least this is true in sentences that aren't too complex. Frege told us that sense is compositionally relevant in certain structures which we'll discuss in chapter 8.

3   A particularly clear presentation of this idea is given in Heim (1982), and that work can lead you into some of the older literature on the topic. An important issue is that the "newness" of *a dog* and the "familiarity" of *the dog* hold even if the sequence of sentences in (6a) is false because there was no dog who came into the house at all (it was a pig). Therefore, a sophisticated presentation of these ideas needs to distinguish *discourse referents* from real *referents*: referents must actually exist, because they are things in the world, while discourse referents are representations of things presented as existing by some linguistic unit which may or may not actually exist. On discourse referents, see Karttunen (2003). Heim's work and Kamp (1981) incorporate the concept of discourse referents into two different, but related, theoretical frameworks.

4   On specificity, see, for example: Fodor and Sag (1982); Abusch (1994); Reinhart (1997).

5   There is a question parallel to this one that arises in the case of a definite noun phrase like *the dog*: What links the word *dog* to the property of being a dog? See Kripke (1972). He has argued that this relation is like that between a name and its referent.

6   See Kripke (1972); Putnam (1975).

7   Another possibility is that they are the same in semantic meaning and differ only in speaker's meaning. This would imply that the sentences in (7) are all synonymous and semantically no more informative than (7b) or (7c). Chapter 9 contains relevant discussion and references.

8   Besides Kripke (1972) and Putnam (1975), book-length discussions of this idea include Salmon (1986); Soames (2002). A critical discussion of the idea that names are rigid designators can be found in Stanley (1997). There is a huge literature on these topics, which the works cited can help you get into.

9 Evans (1973). Evans (1982) is a good resource for thinking more about the issues in this chapter.

10 We do have connections to individuals who have direct acquaintance with Madagascar, and who have used the name *Madagascar* to refer to it. Perhaps this is enough to create a proper chain of reference. But we'd need to have an explanation of why our connections to these people override our connections to other people who used *Madagascar* to refer to part of the mainland, and what Evans says is just as pertinent to finding such an explanation.

11 Donnellan (1966).

12 Kripke (1977).

13 Link (1983). My way of presenting the material in the next two sections is inspired by Bach (1989).

14 We don't usually divide up things into overlapping parts, like {A+B, B+C}, both of which contain B.

15 Bach (1989).

16 Carlson (1977).

17 We haven't explained why *Horses were galloping across the plain* implies that there was more than one horse involved, but to keep things simpler it's probably best not to bring an analysis of plurality into this discussion of kind terms.

18 A good starting reference on this topic (which has generated a vast literature) is Heim (1985).

19 Some semantic theories would have an additional structure in (33b) attached to the bracketed material, so that *only John* would not technically be the binder. This hidden additional structure would be similar to the relative pronoun in a relative clause, or the "hidden" version of the relative pronoun which we discussed in connection with topicalization sentences in chapter 3, section 3.4. So the logical form would be something like the following (putting *who$_1$* in parentheses is meant to indicate that the element in that position is like a relative pronoun, but nobody is saying it's actually a relative pronoun):

Only John$_1$ (who$_1$) [e$_1$ loves his$_1$ mother]

Like a relative pronoun, the additional structure would create a property from the phrase it attaches to.

20 Evans (1980).

21 Modified from Karttunen (1969).

22 Example from Heim (1982).

23 Enron is a company which collapsed due to the corruption of its executives. As an aside, note that the meaning we assigned to definite noun phrases, complete with uniqueness requirement, would run into trouble with *the sage plant he or she bought*, since the sentence explicitly says that nobody bought a unique sage plant. So perhaps the E-type theory won't work here. If it will, it would imply some sort of change in our theory of definite noun phrases. See Heim (1982) and also Heim (1985) for discussion.

6 Quantifiers

In discussing the contribution of noun phrases to meaning, we have been trying to figure out how they manage to refer. But even putting aside those used as predicates, not all noun phrases can be thought of as referential.[1] For example, it seems obvious that *every child* (a noun phrase just like *Shelby* or *the dog*) doesn't refer to any particular thing. The same goes for *nobody*. It may seem less obvious that indefinite noun phrases, those introduced by *a(n)*, are not referential. For example, in (1), we might think that *a man* refers to John:

(1)   A man walked in. His name was John.

However, as Bertrand Russell noted,[2] we don't have to look hard to find cases of indefinites which clearly do not refer:

(2)   Nobody has seen *a unicorn*, because there aren't any.

Phrases of the sort *every child* and *nobody* are known as *quantifiers* – this term suggesting that they have to do with indicating the quantity of something. For example, in the context of (2), *nobody* tells us about the quantity of people who have seen unicorns, namely zero. Other examples of quantifiers are given in (3):

(3)   two dogs, several animals, a few pigs, between three and six women, most people, much mud, some sweat, exactly three hundred prisoners

      More controversially: the frog, a man, trees, John.

As you can see, many quantifiers are introduced by a determiner, a word of the class *two, some, much, every*, etc. Even those which are not, like *nobody* or *somebody*, often incorporate such a piece, that is *no-* or *some-*. These are the 100 percent clear quantifiers. Some scholars who study quantifiers believe that all noun phrases (perhaps other than those used as predicates) are quantifiers, including definites, indefinites, bare plurals, and even names. We'll see below what this initially odd-sounding idea has going for it.

Because they don't refer, quantifiers pose an initial puzzle for semantic theory: how do they contribute to the meaning of the sentences of which they are a part? In this chapter, we'll examine the most popular solution to this puzzle. Plus, we'll get into a number of interesting linguistic patterns which can be studied from the perspective of the theory of quantifiers.

6.1 Generalized Quantifiers: Predicates of Predicates, or Sets of Sets

To figure out how the semantics of quantifiers works, we will consider whole sentences in which quantifiers occur, and then figure out what kind of meaning for the quantifier would make sense in such sentences. A nice simple example is (4):

(4)   Every baby cried.

We want to understand how the meaning of *every baby* works in light of the other conclusions we have already drawn about semantics. One group of previous conclusions has to do with how the meanings of phrases combine with one another:

Semantic composition: When two phrases combine, their meanings may be combined in one of the following ways:

(S)   One meaning may saturate the other.
(M)   If both are predicates, one may modify the other to produce a new predicate.[3]

Another group of conclusions has to do with the meanings of various parts of (4):

Word or phrase	Meaning
cried	A property, i.e., unsaturated proposition
baby	A property, i.e., unsaturated proposition, as well
Complete sentence	A proposition

A third important piece of the puzzle concerns the syntactic structure of (4): *[[every baby] cried]*. Compositionality tells us that the meaning of *every* combines with that of *baby*, and the result of this combines with that of *cried*, to give the whole sentence's meaning.

Let's tackle this structure from the top down. What does all of this let us conclude about the meaning of *every baby*? If the principles of semantic composition mentioned above are right (and there aren't more principles waiting to be discovered – a distinct possibility), *every baby* must combine with the meaning of *cried* by saturation. One of the two meanings must saturate the other. It can't be that the meaning of the noun phrase saturates that of the predicate, because the kind of thing that saturates a predicate is an individual, and that would mean that *every baby* refers to an individual, and we just said it doesn't. So it must be that the meaning of *cried* saturates that of *every baby*. In other words, the quantifier is saturated by a property, resulting in a complete proposition. This means that the quantifier is, metaphorically, a proposition with a property-sized hole in it (see diagram 34). This implies that in sentences with quantifier subjects, the usual mechanism of saturation is reversed. Normally, the

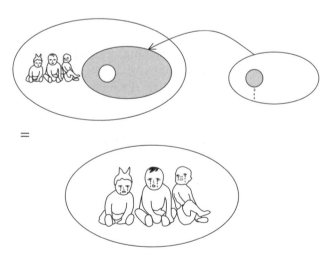

Diagram 34

subject is an argument of the predicate, and the referent of the subject saturates the denotation of the predicate; but here the denotation of the predicate saturates the denotation of the subject. A quantifier is a kind of second-order property, a property-of-properties.

If this idea that a quantifier is a property-of-properties is to be worth anything, we need to show that it actually makes sense to think of *every baby* that way. The idea would be that *every baby* describes the property expressed by *cried*. And indeed this does make sense: *every baby* tells us that the property it combines with describes all of the babies. Suppose that there are three babies, Noah, Merrill, and Dani. All three cried, while only Dani jumped and Noah and Dani swam. In this case, *every baby* describes the property of having cried, but not that of having jumped or swum.

This can be made more clear by comparing the following two tables, (5) and (6). The first table has nothing to do with quantifiers; it has to do with individuals and their properties, but is useful for setting up the point about quantifiers:

(5)

	Cried	Jumped	Swam
Noah	√		√
Merrill	√		
Dani	√	√	√

In (5), we see which individuals have which properties (in a particular possible world). If we have a sentence like *Dani cried*, we let the referent of *Dani* (taken from the left-hand column) saturate the property denoted by *cried* (taken from the top row); as we find a check where Dani's row and cried's column intersect, the proposition is true (in that world). Now we look at a table having to do with quantifiers:

(6)

	Every baby	Exactly one baby	Most babies
Cried	√		√
Jumped		√	
Swam			√

In (6), we see which properties are described by which quantifiers (in a particular possible world). Notice that, down the left-hand column, we now have properties. So in this table, properties play the role that individuals played in (5). Along the top row we have quantifiers; quantifiers play the role here that properties played in (5). We have the analogy "individuals are to properties as properties are to quantifiers." This analogy explains why we can call quantifiers "properties-of-properties." If we have a sentence like *Every baby cried*, we let the denotation of *cried* (taken from the left-hand column) saturate the quantifier denoted by *every baby* (taken from the top row); as we find a check where *cried*'s row and *every baby*'s column intersect, the proposition is true (in that world).

It can be helpful to think about quantifiers in terms of sets. In diagram 35, we see how a number of properties (the ovals) relate to the three babies. N, M, and D are the babies, and the x's are other individuals who are not babies. Each oval represents the individuals described by a particular property. The three properties mentioned in tables (5) and (6) are represented, as are a number of other properties. Some of them describe all of the babies, some describe two, or one, or none. Given what's in diagram 35, the dark circle in diagram 36 indicates the properties described by *every baby*. Diagram 36 shows why, if the property of having cried is used to saturate the quantifier which *every baby* expresses, the result will be a true sentence. But if the property of having jumped saturates it, the result will be false.

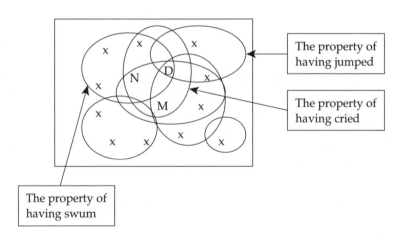

Diagram 35

The theory of noun phrases which takes up the ideas we've been talking about is *generalized quantifier theory*, and according to this, noun phrases (*every baby, nobody, some pigs*, etc.) are *generalized quantifiers*. This

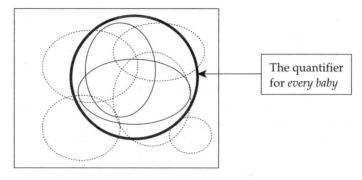

The quantifier
for *every baby*

Diagram 36

theory can actually be applied to all noun phrases, not just those which
are intuitively quantifiers. For example, a simple name like *Noah* can
be seen as a property-of-properties; this would imply that our simple
intuition from chapter 2, that names refer, is wrong. The idea works like
this: just as *every baby* denotes a property-of-properties which describes
those properties which describe all of the babies, so we can see *Noah* as
denoting a property-of-properties which describes those properties
which Noah has. Considering example (7), instead of saying that Noah
saturates the property expressed by *swam*, we would say that the property expressed by *swam* saturates the property-of-properties expressed
by *Noah*. In diagram 37, if the property of having swum saturates the
quantifier, the sentence will be true. However, if we let one of the dotted
properties do the saturating, it will be false.

(7)   Noah swam.

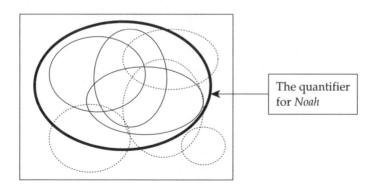

The quantifier
for *Noah*

Diagram 37

Notice how we have defined the complex, property-of-properties meaning for *Noah* in such a way that the result is identical to what we'd have if *Noah* simply referred (and the process of saturation worked as in chapter 2). In this sense, treating *Noah* as a generalized quantifier is inessential. Given that it's a complex idea, our first tendency may be to just forget about it. However, there may be some good arguments for this approach. The most simple argument, given by early formal semanticists like Richard Montague, is uniformity: since *Noah* and *every baby* are grammatically the same type of thing (they are both noun phrases), they ought to be the same type of thing semantically as well. This is an interesting argument, provided that by and large this kind of uniformity is respected in other areas of semantics. However, we may want an argument which is based more on data than on theoretical considerations, and we'll get one shortly (section 6.2 on "NP Conjunction").

Generalized quantifier theory also tells us what the meaning of determiners (words like *every, most, some*) must be. Let's focus on *every*. The quantifier for *every baby*, as we've seen, describes a property if that property is true of all the babies. Compare this to *every dog* – the quantifier for *every dog* describes a property if that property is true of all the dogs. And so forth for any noun: *every pig, every apple*, etc. In general, *every N* describes a property P if P is true of all the Ns.

We can think of "N" as representing an open slot in the meaning of a quantifier formed with *every*. In other words, *every* describes a quantifier missing a part, the part provided by the noun. When *every* and the noun combine, the noun fills in the missing part; in other words the noun saturates the incomplete quantifier represented by the determiner.

A determiner meaning is saturated by a property (from the noun) to become a quantifier. But remember that a quantifier is itself unsaturated; it combines with a predicate, and the property which is expressed by the predicate saturates the quantifier to make a complete proposition (diagram 34). So this means that the determiner itself is actually doubly unsaturated. In this respect it's like a transitive verb,[4] but while a transitive verb combines with two pieces which refer to individuals to form a complete sentence, a determiner combines with two pieces which express properties. These two pieces are the noun and the sentence's predicate:

(8) a. Every   baby   cried.
         unsaturated property   property
     b. Noah   saw   Shelby.
         individual unsaturated individual

This analogy between determiners and transitive verbs gives us another way to think about the meaning of determiners. The unsaturated meaning of *saw* combines with two individuals in (8b) and tells you something about the relation between them. It tells you that the one saw the other. Likewise, the unsaturated meaning of *every* combines with two properties and tells you something about the relation between them. It tells you that the baby-property describes a subset of the things described by the cried-property – in pictures, diagram 38.

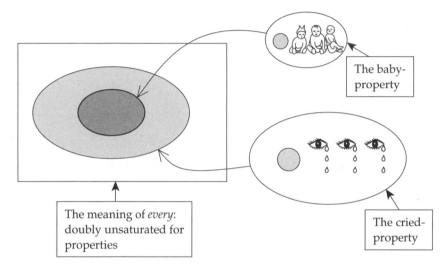

Diagram 38

Other determiners can be thought of in the same way. *Some* says that its noun-property and its predicate-property overlap; at least one thing is described by both. *No* says that the noun-property and the predicate-property don't overlap. *Most* says that its noun property describes more than half of the things described by its predicate-property. *Two* says that at least two things are described by both the noun-property and the predicate-property.[5] If indefinite noun phrases are quantifiers, then *a* has a meaning very similar to *some*'s.

Try to figure out the meanings of as many determiners as you can in generalized quantifier theory. Some tricky cases to think about are *both* and *the*. Generalized quantifier theory also works for complex determiners like *between two and ten*, *at least twenty*, and *an even number of*.

6.2   NP Conjunction

The idea that names are generalized quantifiers seems like a strange one. Why would we bother with the idea that a name denotes a property-of-properties, when it is so intuitive to think of them as simply referring to an individual? As mentioned above, one reason to give the idea a chance is the theoretical point that it would be nice to have all noun phrases be the same sort of thing, semantically speaking. But beyond this almost aesthetic perspective, there are concrete reasons to believe that all noun phrases can indeed be quantifiers. The clearest reason has to do with noun phrase conjunction, the joining together of two noun phrases with *and* or *or*.

(9)   a.   Noah and Shelby
      b.   Two babies and some dog
      c.   Noah or a cat

Notice that any two noun phrases can be conjoined, whether they are two names (as in (9a)), two quantifiers ((9b)) or a name and a quantifier ((9c)).

It is generally thought that conjunction can only join together two phrases which are syntactically and semantically of the same type. For example, if *or* joins together two predicates (adjectives), as in (10), it creates a new complex predicate:

(10)   The baby is **smart or happy**.

When *or* joins together two predicates, its semantics is very simple. In (10), the predicate *smart* describes a set of things, as does the predicate *happy*. Let's call *smart*'s set S and *happy*'s set H. The function of *or*, then, is to create a complex predicate which describes everything in S plus everything in H. In terms of set theory, we say that it describes the union of S and H, S ∪ H.

In a similar way, *smart and happy* is a complex predicate whose meaning is built out of S and H. It describes the intersection of S and H, S ∩ H; that is, the set of things which are in both. (There are examples where *and* doesn't seem to work this way. For example, the sentence *The flag is red and white* describes the flag as being partially red and partially white, but it does not imply that the flag is white. This differs from *the baby is smart and happy*, which implies that the baby is smart, and that he is happy. Let's leave these complexities aside.)

Returning to the topic of quantifiers, recall that they also describe things, namely properties. So we can talk about the set of properties that a given quantifier describes. If *or* works in the same way as with adjectives, two quantifiers joined with *or* should describe the union of the sets of things described by each individually, and two quantifiers joined should describe their intersection. This is exactly what happens.

(11)

	Every baby	Some dogs	Every baby and some dogs	Every baby or some dogs
Cute	√	√	√	√
Friendly	√	√	√	√
Happy		√		√
Smart				
Dumb		√		√
Furry		√		√
Human	√			√

Along the top row of (11), we have four quantifiers, two simple ones, *every baby* and *some dogs*, and two created by *and* and *or*. Down the left column we have seven properties which these quantifiers might describe. For example, the column below *every baby* indicates that every baby is cute, friendly, and human. In terms of compositional semantics, this means that if *every baby* is saturated by the property of being cute, or the property of being friendly, or the property of being human, the result will be a true proposition.

If you think through what checks should be in the columns below *every baby and some dogs* and *every baby or some dogs*, it will be clear that the former should get a check whenever there is a check in both the *every baby* column and the *some dogs* column, and the latter should get a check when there is a check in either the *every baby* or the *some dogs* column. That is, the *every baby and some dogs* column is the intersection of the *every baby* column and the *some dogs* column. Similarly, the *or*-quantifier gets the union of the checks from the *every baby* and *some dogs* columns. What this tells us is that when *and* and *or* apply to quantifiers, they can have the same meanings, intersection and union, as they have when they apply to ordinary predicates.

Finally, if we build a chart like (11) that includes names, it becomes clear why it's useful to think of names as generalized quantifiers. As a generalized quantifier, *Noah* describes all of those properties that

Noah has: in (12), the properties of being cute, friendly, and smart. This quantifier can be combined with a quantifier like *some dogs* using *and* and *or* using intersection and union in the same way as before.

(12)

	Noah	Some dogs	Noah and some dogs	Noah or some dogs
Cute	√	√	√	√
Friendly	√	√	√	√
Over 6 feet tall				
Smart	√			√
Yoga experts				
Furry		√		√
From Mars				

The semantic theory of generalized quantifiers fits into a simple, intuitive analysis of conjunction and disjunction, and the conjunction/ disjunction of names can be explained with no extra trouble if they are thought of as generalized quantifiers. This makes a strong argument that names can be quantifiers.[6]

> What does the word *not* do when it combines with a predicate (*not happy*) and when it combines with a quantifier (*not every dog*)?

6.3   Negative Polarity Items

The world of language contains a very strange species known as negative polarity item (NPIs). These creatures like the shade of negative sentences, those containing words like *not* or *nobody*, and dislike the full sun of positive sentences. *Ever* and *any* are examples of NPIs in English:

(13) a. Shelby won't <u>ever</u> bite you.
      b. Nobody has <u>any</u> money.

(14) a. *Shelby will <u>ever</u> bite you.
      b. *Noah has <u>any</u> money.

(The * in front of a sentence indicates that it is ungrammatical.) Before we go on to discuss NPIs, let me offer a few warnings: First, though many languages have NPIs, they aren't all exactly like those in English. Second, NPIs can even differ from one another within a given language. The discussion below will introduce you to some of the most important ideas which come out of research on NPIs, but be aware that the actual situation is more complex.

Despite their name, NPIs can be happy in certain sentences which are not obviously "negative" in meaning, including in questions, in clauses introduced by *if*, and inside certain quantifiers:

(15)   a.   Does Shelby <u>ever</u> bite?
       b.   Does Noah have <u>any</u> money?

(16)   a.   If Shelby <u>ever</u> bites you, I'll put him up for adoption.
       b.   If Noah has <u>any</u> money, he can buy some candy.

(17)   a.   Every dog which has <u>ever</u> bitten a cat feels the admiration of other dogs.
       b.   Every child who has <u>any</u> money is likely to waste it on candy.

But:

(18)   a.   *Some dog which has <u>ever</u> bitten a cat feels the admiration of other dogs.
       b.   *Some child who has <u>any</u> money is likely to waste it on candy.

In studying NPIs, the main questions are: what do the types of sentences which allow (semanticists say: "license") NPIs have in common? And what is it about NPIs that makes them require a licenser of that kind? We will focus here on how quantifiers fit into the picture.

To begin, we need to make a survey of quantifiers to determine which ones license NPIs and which ones don't. Let's look at a bunch of examples of the form

[DETERMINER NOUN MODIFIER] PREDICATE

The material inside the brackets forms the quantifier. As it turns out, we need to check separately whether an NPI can exist inside the quantifier and whether one can exist inside the predicate.

(19) **OK with NPI inside quantifier**
Every dog which has <u>ever</u> bitten a cat feels the admiration of other dogs.
No dog which has <u>ever</u> bitten a cat feels the admiration of other dogs.

(20) **Bad with NPI inside quantifier**
*Some dog which has <u>ever</u> bitten a cat feels the admiration of other dogs.
*Three dogs which have <u>ever</u> bitten a cat feel the admiration of other dogs.

(21) **OK with NPI inside predicate**
No dog has <u>ever</u> bitten a cat.

(22) **Bad with NPI inside predicate**
*Every dog has <u>ever</u> bitten a cat.
*Some dog has <u>ever</u> bitten a cat.
*Three dogs have <u>ever</u> bitten a cat.

It turns out that an NPI is acceptable inside the quantifier with *every* and *no*, and outside the quantifier (in the predicate) with *no*. An NPI is unacceptable outside the quantifier with *every*, and with *some* and *three* no matter what. What could explain this bizarre pattern?

Fauconnier[7] noticed that all of the cases which allow NPIs share a subtle logical property with the word *not*, considered by many to be the most basic of all the NPI licensers. For any piece of language which expresses a property, we compare it to words which describe a sub-property or a super-property. For example, the word *dog* expresses a sub-property of *animal*, since the set of dogs is a subset of the set of animals. (The technical terms are *hyponym* and *hypernym*. *Dog* is a hyponym of *animal*, and *animal* is a hypernym of *dog*.) Likewise, *Keeshond* expresses a sub-property of *dog*. A simple, non-negative, non-quantified sentence allows inferences from properties to super-properties, in the following way:

(23) a. I have a dog. **entails**
      b. I have an animal.

A logical feature of *not* is that it reverses this inference, creating entailments from properties to sub-properties:

(24) a. I don't have a dog. **entails**
     b. I don't have a Keeshond.

(24a) does not entail that I don't have an animal; I might have a horse, for example. The fact that *not* creates entailments from properties to sub-properties can be described by saying that it is *downward entailing* (with regard to its argument, the predicate). The opposite of downward entailing is *upward entailing*. The simple non-negative sentence (25a) is upward entailing.

A quantificational determiner's meaning is doubly unsaturated for properties. This means that it combines with two properties, those expressed by the noun phrase and the predicate, to form a complete proposition. Let's look at some determiners and see how they behave with respect to these downward and upward entailments

(Form: [DET PROPERTY NO. 1] PROPERTY NO. 2)

(25) a. Every dog barks.
     b. Every Keeshond barks.   (DE with respect to property no. 1)
     c. Every animal barks.
                         (Not UE with respect to property no. 1)
     d. Every dog barks loudly.
                         (Not DE with respect to property no. 2)
     e. Every dog makes noise.
                         (UE with respect to property no. 2)

Starting with the base sentence (25a), we can consider the entailments supported by *every* with regard to both of the properties it combines with. It combines first with the property of being a dog, then with the property of being something which barks, and says that the first describes a subset of the things described by the second. If we replace the first property with a sub-property, as in (25b), the result is entailed by the original sentence (25a). If every dog barks, then every Keeshond barks. This means that *every* is downward entailing with respect to the first property. If we replace the first property with a super-property, as in (25c), the result is not entailed. If every dog barks, this does not entail that every animal barks. This means that *every* is not upward entailing with respect to the first property. Turning to the second property, (25d) and (25e) show that *every* is not downward entailing, but rather upward entailing, with respect to the second property.

Take the time to run through the paradigm in (25) for the other determiners *no*, *some*, and *three*, and you'll find the following:

(26)

	First property		Second property	
	↓ entailing	↑ entailing	↓ entailing	↑ entailing
every	Yes	No	No	No
no	Yes	No	Yes	No
some	No	Yes	No	Yes
three[8]	No	Yes	No	Yes

The pattern of yeses in this chart exactly matches the distribution of NPIs observed in (19)–(22), as first noted by Ladusaw.[9] Combined with the fact that negation is downward entailing and licenses NPIs, it seems like a pretty good idea to hypothesize that downward-entailingness is precisely what allows a word to be a licensor.

> What about the determiners *most*, *few*, and *zero*? Determine the capacity of each to license the NPIs *any*, *ever*, *yet*, and *a bit* (as an adverbial, e.g. *I don't like this a bit*), and then see if each is up- or downward entailing. What do you conclude about the theory of NPI licensing? In fact, this entailment-based theory of NPI licensing continues to be developed and refined by semanticists. Another important thing for semanticists to think about is how NPIs work in languages other than English. You may want to give that a try in your spare time.

NPIs are licensed by a downward-entailing environment (or something along those lines). Why would this be? Why should a word care about an obscure logical property like that? Semanticists have had less luck in answering this question, but there is a basic intuition which is worth exploring. This intuition can be brought out by listing some NPIs:

(27)   ever, any, at all, the slightest difference, yet, a bit, a red cent (meaning "any money"), give a damn

Something common to many, and perhaps all, of these NPIs is the fact that they describe a very small, practically insignificant quantity of something. *Any money* has to do with even the smallest quantities of money; *the slightest difference* is obvious; *give a damn* has to do with only the smallest amount of concern. A word that describes an insignificant quantity of something won't exist very happily in an upward-entailing context, because it will barely make a difference to the sentence's meaning. For example, if it were grammatical, (14b) (*Noah has any money) would just mean "Noah has money." Given that *any* would not make a difference in this sentence, there seems to be no point in using it. Now, I'm not saying that this way of thinking is particularly precise, or that it works naturally for all NPIs, but many semanticists think that some idea along these lines is what's needed to explain why NPIs need to be licensed.

6.4 Quantifiers in Object Position

The idea that a quantifier is a property-of-properties works well when the quantifier is the subject of the sentence. The job of the quantifier is to describe a property. A predicate denotes a property (a singly unsaturated proposition) and since a sentence is made up of a subject plus a predicate, it has a property to describe right at hand. Things become more tricky when it comes to a quantifier that is not the subject of its sentence. For example, recall that a transitive verb denotes a relation (a doubly unsaturated proposition), not a property. So, a quantifier in object position is being combined with the wrong sort of thing.

For example, in (28), *every baby* is combined with *loves*, and *loves* is not a predicate:[10]

(28)

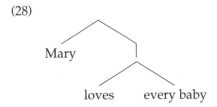

In semantic terms, what *every baby* wants to do is combine with a property and say that the set of babies is a subset of the set of things described by that property. The problem is that *loves* doesn't denote a property.

We have a few options for how to think about object quantifiers. It could be that the structure in (28) is wrong, and that the quantifier in fact combines with a predicate. Or it could be that *every baby* has a meaning different from what we think, and has no trouble combining with *loves*. Or, lastly, it could be that *loves* has a meaning different from what we think, and that meaning can be combined with *every baby*. There are many debates concerning this topic among semanticists, and to provide an idea of the issues involved, I will sketch two of the more popular alternatives for dealing with this problem.

The first alternative takes up the first approach mentioned: the structure of *Mary loves every baby* is not what it appears. Recall our discussion in chapter 5 concerning variable binding in *Only John loves his mother*. We raised *only John* in order to create a logical form with a bound variable where *only John* used to be:

(29)   a.   Only John$_1$ loves his$_1$ mother →
      b.   Only John$_1$ [t$_1$ loves his$_1$ mother]

What if the same movement occurs to the quantifier in (28)?

(30)   a.   Mary loves every baby$_1$ →
      b.   Every baby$_1$ [Mary loves t$_1$]

In both (29b) and (30b), the part in brackets is a lot like a relative clause, a sentence from which a part has been extracted. It is a sentence missing a part – in other words, a predicate. And its meaning is a proposition missing a part – that is, a property. In particular, it describes the property of being loved by Mary (the property of being an x such that Mary loves x). This means that in (30b) the quantifier is sitting next to a predicate, and so its role as denoting a property-of-properties can be fulfilled. In semantic terms, *every baby* can describe the property of being loved by Mary. The sentence says that the set of babies is a subset of the set of things loved by Mary. This result is accurate.

Another alternative for explaining the meaning of (28) begins with the assumption that the quantifier does not move at all. It remains in object position, but we hypothesize that its meaning is not the same as when it's in subject position. One way to look at a subject quantifier is as combining with a singly unsaturated thing (a predicate) and creating a fully saturated thing (a proposition). You could say that the level of unsaturation goes from one to zero. Diagram 34 gives a picture of that. We could then think of the quantifier in object position as doing something similar, but a bit different. It takes the level of saturation from two (*loves* is doubly unsaturated) to one (*loves every baby* is a predicate, so it's singly unsaturated). The idea of diagram 39 is that when the doubly unsaturated proposition on the right (the heart indicates that this is the meaning of *loves*) fills in the missing piece c of the quantifier on the left, one of its own missing pieces is filled in by the little white circle labeled a. This will leave the whole combined apparatus with a single piece waiting to be filled in, *b* in the picture. This will be saturated by the subject of the sentence, Mary in (28).

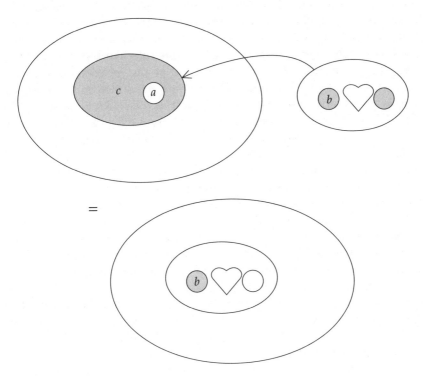

Diagram 39

As if this isn't complicated enough, we're only halfway to under-standing what the object quantifier does. Diagram 39 indicates that the quantifier is saturated by a doubly unsaturated proposition, and simul-taneously makes it become singly unsaturated. This only tells us the *form* of its meaning, and doesn't say anything precise about what *every baby*, as opposed to *every dog*, *two babies*, or *most people from Kansas*, means. In other words, any object quantifier will do this same trick, and we haven't yet looked at the meaning at a level of detail particular to *every baby*. We want to somehow hold on to the intuition gained from thinking about this quantifier in subject position: that it means "the set of babies is a subset of . . . ," where the ". . ." remains to be filled in by the rest of the sentence. Now, in (4) or (30b), there is a chunk of sentence which directly fills in the ". . . ." In (4), it's *cried*, giving us "the set of babies is a subset of the set of things that cried." In (30b), it's the material in brackets, which represents in a complex way the set of things Mary loves. But in (28), there is no piece of the sentence which represents the set of things Mary loves. You might think that initial piece of sentence *Mary loves* does that, but looking at (28), *Mary loves* doesn't form a unit. Since we are aiming for a compositional semantics, we must build up the meaning of the sentence in a way which respects its structure, and this rules out referring to *Mary loves*. (Fundamentally, this is the purpose of the movement approach represented by (30). This movement changes the structure so that *Mary loves* is a unit, giving us leave to refer to it in the semantic analysis.) In (28), the quantifier ("the set of babies is a subset of . . .") combines with *loves* alone. To solve this problem, *every baby* needs to perform a tricky maneuver. The technical details here are complex, but the idea is that *every baby* utilizes a slightly different meaning which we might indicate as "the set of babies is a subset of the set of things which *xxx* . . . ." There are two different unspecified pieces, represented by ". . ." and "*xxx*," and they are not filled in at the same time. When the quantifier combines with *loves*, the meaning of the verb fills in ". . . ," but the "*xxx*" remains unspecified for the time being. (In diagram 39, ". . ." is *c*, while "*xxx*" corresponds to *b*.) So we get "the set of babies is a subset of the set of things which *xxx* loves." This is the meaning of *loves every baby*, the sentence's predicate. When this predicate combines with the sentence's subject, *Mary*, Mary fills in the "*xxx*." In terms of diagram 39, the individual Mary saturates *b*. This gives us the right overall meaning, "the set of babies is a subset of the set of things which Mary loves."

A detailed comparison of these two approaches to object quantifiers would be too much for this small book. But some of the fundamental considerations are worth mentioning. In general, the movement approach can get by with much simpler semantic mechanisms; moreover, to a large extent, these mechanisms are ones we need anyway if we believe in logical form at all. But it pays the price with grammatical abstractness; it requires us to believe that the semantically relevant structure, the logical form, is significantly distinct from the apparent grammatical structure. In contrast, the no-movement approach reverses the costs and benefits. It requires a more complex semantics, one which distinguishes the meanings of quantifiers in object vs. subject positions. However, it uses a grammatical structure which has not been modified by any invisible movement. The choice between these approaches must ultimately be made in light of additional knowledge about the inner semantic workings of the worlds' languages.

NOTES

1   Heim and Kratzer (1997) provide arguments (in an easy-to-follow, textbook format) to prove this point.

2   Russell (1919).

3   We also considered the possibility that (M) is not needed, and (S) alone is sufficient.

4   This similarity between transitive verbs and quantifiers is expressed nicely in Larson and Segal (1995).

5   Note that this way of thinking of *two* as quantificational differs from the meaning we considered for *three* in *the three horses* (chapter 4). It could be that numerals sometimes have one sort of meaning and sometimes have the other, or it could be that one or the other idea is just wrong.

6   Another idea in the semantics literature (mentioned briefly earlier on in connection with adjective semantics) is *type-shifting*. The idea of type-shifting is that the semantic type of a given phrase may change, based on the environment it finds itself in. One application of this is to say that names sometimes refer to individuals, and sometimes are quantifiers. More specifically, in their basic meaning, they refer; in this regard, our original intuitions about their meanings are correct. However, if a name is conjoined with a quantifier, its meaning is shifted from referential to quantificational. This can be done through general, systematic rules (see Partee 1986).

7   Fauconnier (1975).

8   The pattern described in this chart for *three* assumes that it means "at least three." What would the pattern be if it means "exactly three"?

9   Ladusaw (2002). Some other ideas about negative polarity licensing are given by Linebarger (1987); Kadmon and Ladman (1993). Not all NPIs have the same pattern of distribution, and some of the differences are discussed by Zwarts (1998).

10 Sometimes a transitive verb is called a predicate, but this is always in a different sense of the term than the one we're using here. Since a transitive verb's meaning is doubly unsaturated, it is sometimes called a "two-place predicate." An ordinary predicate like *is tall* or *saw Mary* would then be called a "one-place predicate." In this chapter, when I say "predicate," I mean one-place predicate.

7 Extensional vs. Intensional Contexts

To compute the meaning of (1) or (2), we put together the meanings of their various parts according to the principles of semantic composition:

(1)   The circle is inside the square.

(2)   Mary loves every baby.

In (1) and (2), we have parts with a variety of kinds of meanings; among the noun phrases alone, we have definite noun phrases and names, which we take to be referential (though it's also possible they are quantifiers) as well as a clear quantifier, *every baby*. We also have a preposition and a transitive verb, both of which denote relations. But there's one important, yet very subtle, way in which the semantic contributions of all of these parts are similar. To see this, let's think about (1) in the context of diagram 18, repeated here, which we have used to represent the facts in various possible worlds relevant to whether (1) is true. Sentence (1) is true in the top left-hand world because the circle in that world is inside the square in that world. It is false in the top right-hand world because the circle in that world is not inside the square in that world. Notice that in both cases, whether (1) is true in a given world only depends on the circumstances in that very world. We could say that the truth-conditions only depend on *local* facts. Whether (1) is true in the top left-hand world does not depend on what the circle is doing in the top right-hand world.

In principle, we could have sentences whose truth in a given world depends on what's going on in various other worlds – there's nothing inherently wrong with *non-local* truth-conditions like the following:

(3)   a.   Sentence S is true in world w if the circle is inside the square in some world or another.

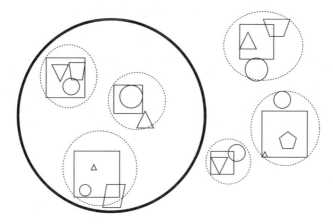

Diagram 18

    b.   Sentence S is true in world w if the circle is inside the square in all worlds.

    c.   Sentence S is true in world w if the circle is inside the square in all worlds which are similar to world w in terms of the type of triangle they contain.

And indeed, there really are sentences with truth conditions along these lines. For example, though it's not true that the circle is inside the square in the top right-hand world, if we lived in that world we could imagine the worlds on the left-hand side of the diagram and think "You know, though our circle is not inside the square, there's no reason it couldn't be. Perhaps we should move it, and make our world a little bit neater." That is, the sentences in (4) are true, even though sentence (1) is not:

(4)   a.   The circle could be inside the square.
       b.   Perhaps the circle should be inside the square.

This means that (3a) is a reasonable approximation of a truth-condition for (4a); more on sentences of this type, containing words like *could*, *perhaps*, and *should*, in chapter 8.

    Sentences which depend only on local facts for their truth-conditions are *extensional*. Up until this chapter, we have only analyzed extensional aspects of language. Sentences which are not extensional are *intensional*. *Could* in (4a) introduces intensionality into the sentence: it makes the meaning of the sentence depend on non-local facts in the sense that one has to look outside of a given situation to know whether it's true in that situation. We say that *could* has an "intensional meaning," and that it creates an "intensional construction."

Intensional constructions are more difficult for linguists to analyze than extensional ones, because – as we'll see – it takes some effort to make words like *could* sensitive to non-local facts. The complexity of intensional constructions is useful in a perverse way: it lets us create a test which can be used to detect intensionality. Take the following two phrases:

(5)   The tallest building in New York

(6)   The Empire State Building

Thinking about their meaning in a simple way, these two have the same meaning (at the time of my writing this book). They both refer to the same building. But obviously, from another perspective their meanings are different. They don't have to refer to the same building, and at one time they didn't, and at some point in the future they may again not. As mentioned in chapter 5, we call the simple variety of meaning, on which (5) and (6) have the same meaning, their reference, and we call the subtle variety of meaning, on which they differ, their sense. It's at least approximately true, and may be exactly true, that the reference of a name or definite is its extensional meaning, and its sense is its intensional meaning. That is, when a given sentence's meaning only depends on local facts, all a name contributes is its reference; and when a given sentence's meaning depends on non-local facts, its sense becomes relevant. Since *the tallest building in New York* and *the Empire State Building* have the same reference, it will not matter in an extensional construction which phrase we use. Extensionally, they are the same. But in an intensional construction, it will matter, since intensionally, they are not the same.

We can illustrate this point with (7) and (8):

(7)   a.   That tower is the tallest building in New York.
      b.   That tower is the Empire State Building.

(8)   a.   The new tower we are building will be the tallest building in New York.
      b.   The new tower we are building will be the Empire State Building.

Examples (7a) and (7b) have something in common semantically: if one is true, then so is the other. We say that the structure *That tower is* _____ passes the *substitutivity test*, in that we can substitute (6) for (5) within (7a), giving (7b), without affecting whether the sentence is true or not. However, the same relation doesn't hold between (8a) and (8b): *The new tower we are building will be* _____ fails the substitutivity test, since you can imagine a scenario in which (8a) is true, but (8b) is not. We can decide to build the tallest building in New York, with enough money and clout, but we can't build the Empire State Building since it's already been built.

This difference in substitutivity between (7) and (8) shows that (7) is an ordinary extensional construction, while (8) is an intensional one. The relevance of sense to (8), but only of reference to (7), is not surprising given what (7) and (8) mean. Only reference is relevant to (7) because, only looking at the world as it is right now, there is no way to distinguish the meanings of *the tallest building in New York* and *the Empire State Building*. The only thing we can point to in the world to indicate their meanings is that single building. Sense is relevant to (8), with its future tense, because if we compare the world as it was, is now, and will be in 20 years (see diagram 40), we can distinguish the meanings of *the tallest building in New York* and *the Empire State Building*. For all four times in the diagram, we would point at the gray building to indicate the meaning of *the Empire State Building*, but we would point to different buildings to indicate the meaning of *the tallest building in New York* (the twin towers in t1, the gray building in t2 and t3, and the tallest one on the right in t4). This is why intensional meaning, which depends on more than one situation at once (and here the "situations" represent different times), is sensitive to the difference between *the Empire State Building* and *the tallest building in New York*.

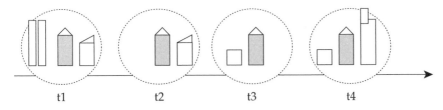

Diagram 40

Here are a few more intensional constructions and pairs of sentences showing that they fail the substitutivity test:

Modal verbs (verbs like *must, can, might*)
Assuming that Mary is the student council president:

(9)   a.   Mary should resign from being the student council president.
      b.   Mary should resign from being Mary.

Past tense

(10)   a.   One of the twin towers was the tallest building in New York.
       b.   One of the twin towers was the Empire State Building.

Sentence-embedding verbs (many of them: *think, believe, want, doubt*)
Mary is a 5-year-old, and she believes that her house (which seems huge to her) is the tallest building in New York, and she thinks that the second tallest building is the Empire State Building:

(11)   a.   Mary thinks that her house is the tallest building in New York.
       b.   Mary thinks that her house is the Empire State Building.

Be sure you see how the pairs in (9)–(11) exemplify the substitutivity test, and therefore provide evidence that the constructions are intensional.

8 Tense, Aspect, and Modality

Intensional constructions are some of the most intricate, interesting, and difficult areas of semantics. *Tense* concerns where something happens in time; for example, a past tense sentence would be used to describe an event which occurred before the present moment. *Aspect* covers a wide variety of topics having more or less to do with how an event unfolds in time. For example, one type of aspectual construction is the progressive: the progressive sentence (progressive refers to the *be+VERB-ing* form) in (1a) seems to differ from the non-progressive sentence in (1b) in that (1a) has to do with an event which was ongoing at the moment under consideration:

(1) a. Shelby was barking at the cat.
     b. Shelby barked at the cat.

Modality has to do with things which are true in other possible worlds, and how they relate to what's true in reality. For example, the modal sentence (2a) (the word *might* is a modal verb here) differs from the non-modal (2b) in that Noah's becoming a doctor is treated as a mere possibility in (2a), but is treated as a reality in (2b).

(2) a. Noah might be a doctor.
     b. Noah is a doctor.

In this chapter, we'll touch on some of the fundamental ideas concerning the semantics of tense, aspect, and modality.

It is definitely worth knowing that the ways in which tense, aspect, and modality are expressed differ from language to language in dramatic ways. For example, there are numerous languages which lack a direct expression of tense (for example, Chinese and Biblical Hebrew). Speakers of such languages nevertheless do not become confused about whether people are talking about the past, present, or future. This means that what one learns about tense from the study of English can only be extended to other languages with caution and sensitivity to the fact that each language needs to be studied in its own terms. An important task of semantic theory is then to relate what we learn about each individual language to an overall theory of language in general, but this is a difficult undertaking.

In this chapter I want to talk about tense, aspect, and modality in enough detail to see how semantic theory deals with these phenomena. In doing this, I'll have to focus on English alone, in order to keep the discussion brief enough.

8.1   Tense

As mentioned above, "tense" refers to the position of situations in time. There are many kinds of tense systems in the languages of the world. For example: some languages don't have any tense at all; some languages distinguish a past tense from a non-past (present or future) tense; and some languages have past, present, and future tenses. It's unclear and controversial what kind of system English has. It clearly has a past tense, since (3) tells us about Mary's past, not about her present or future. It also has what we typically call the "present" tense, as in (4):

(3)   Mary knew French.

(4)   Mary knows French.

However, the present tense can describe future time as well, making it plausible that this is really a non-past tense:

(5)   a.   Mary <u>leaves</u> for California tomorrow.
      b.   If that guy <u>wins</u> the election next year, we'll have to move to another state.

Moreover, what we call the "future" tense is grammatically very different from the past and present. Whereas the past and present are verb forms, the "future" is expressed with an auxiliary verb, *will*.

(6)   Mary will know French by the time the semester ends.

This auxiliary verb is of the same grammatical class as words like *must, can, might, may, should.* These are words that express modality, leading some to think that *will* is really a modal word, not a tense word. Another piece of evidence is the fact that *will* has a past tense form, *would.* Notice how the past tense verb *knew* in (7a) corresponds to *would* in (7b):

(7)   a.   A year ago, Mary said "I know French." →
            A year ago, Mary said that she *knew* French.
      b.   A year ago, Mary said "I will know French by the time the semester ends." →
            A year ago, Mary said that she *would* know French by the time the semester ended.

If *would* is the past tense form of *will*, then *will* is the present tense form of *would*. It's possible that *will* <u>is</u> present tense, but <u>indicates</u> future tense, but then we at least have to distinguish grammatical tense, of which English has only past and non-past, from semantic tense, of which English has past, present, and future. This should be enough to convince you that it is, indeed, unclear what kind of tense system English has!

How would you try to decide whether *will* is truly a marker of future tense, or whether it has some other meaning? Is the fact that the "present" tense can be used to express future facts (as in (5)) relevant? In what cases would comparison with other languages be relevant?

If *will* is indeed a marker of future tense, what can be said about the meaning of *would*? In light of any ideas you have about *would*, be sure to go back and reconsider *will*.

8.1.1   The theoretical framework

In order to explain the meaning of names, we had to assume that the world is populated with individuals. Likewise, in order to express the semantics of tense, we need to assume some notion of time. One way to do this is to bring back the concept of event initially brought up in chapter 3. We can assume that time is just a relation among events. So if (8a) is true because of one event e1, and (8b) is true because of another event e2, then e1 precedes e2.

(8)   a.   Sylvia went to California.
    b.   Noah will go to California.

We can indicate this relation with the symbol "$<$," so that $e1 < e2$. When somebody utters a sentence, this is of course an event in its own right. Let's use the symbol u_S to indicate the event of uttering sentence S. The simplest idea one might have about the past tense is that it indicates that the event described by the sentence precedes u_S. In chapter 3, we discussed example (9), and indicated its meaning as in (10):

(9)   Sylvia petted Shelby.

(10)   There is an event of petting, and this event's agent is Sylvia, and its patient is Shelby.

Incorporating the meaning of the past tense into (10) would give us (11):

(11)   There is an event of petting, and this event's agent is Sylvia, and its patient is Shelby, and this event precedes u_S.

Or more concisely:

(12)   There is an event e: e is a petting, and the agent of e is Sylvia, and the patient of e is Shelby, and $e < u_S$.

Events are a convenient way to indicate the semantics of tense.

It is also possible to develop a semantics for tense using an event-free framework. The idea is to incorporate times into the meaning of predicates in the same way as we have previously incorporated worlds (cf. diagrams 18–19). Let's consider a sentence that is easier to diagram than (8), namely (13):

(13)   The circle was inside the square.

The pictures in diagram 41 indicate, for each moment in time, what is happening in shape world.[1] (There are only four moments in this short-lived world.) Given the events in shape world, diagram 42 indicates the meaning of *is inside the square*, relativized to time. In t2, for instance, the right triangle and the circle are inside the square, so diagram 42 indicates these two shapes at t2, since these are the things described by the predicate at t2.

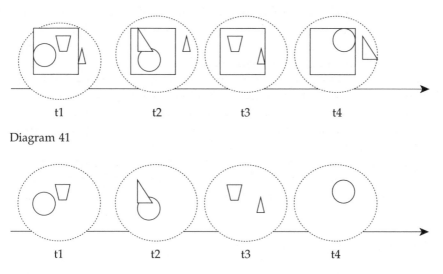

Diagram 41

Diagram 42

Since the meaning of a predicate is relativized to time, it isn't possible to say whether some object is described by a predicate unless an indication is given of what time or times are relevant. In the case of (13), the past tense indicates that a past time is relevant. Suppose that the sentence was uttered at t2. Then it will be true if at time t1 the circle has the property. In the diagramed world, the circle does have the property at t1. So the sentence is true in the world of the diagram. However, the present tense sentence *The small triangle is inside the square*, uttered at t1, would not be true, because – as diagram 42 indicates – the small triangle does not have the property at t1.

Events and predicates-relativized-to-times are two ways of thinking about how tense and time can be incorporated into our semantic system. The choice between these two ways probably comes down to overall decision about whether events are a necessary component of semantic theory. If we need them for thematic roles, adverbs, and such, we might as well use them for tense; if we don't, we shouldn't dream them up just to account for tense, since we can handle tense through the event-free method.

8.1.2 More details on the past and present tenses

8.1.2.1 *The past tense*

Apart from the issue of how, technically, we should incorporate time into our broader semantic system, there is much else to learn about the semantics of tense. So far I've assumed that a past tense sentence is true if there is a past time at which its content (minus tense) is true. So, *The circle was inside the square* is true if (and only if) the circle has the property "inside the square" at some past time. However, this is certainly too simplistic. One issue concerns how "definite" the past tense is. The semantics sketched above assumes that tense is completely indefinite; a past tense sentence is true when it describes a fact true at *some* past time. That time can be one minute or one million years ago. However, Barbara Partee[2] has pointed out that there are instances when the past tense seems to be definite, that is to refer to a particular past time. Her example is (14). Imagine you and a friend got up early to go on a long trip, cooked some eggs for breakfast, and then rushed off. Driving down the road, you say:

(14)   I didn't turn off the stove.

This does not mean that there is some time in the past at which you didn't turn off the stove (or that there is no time at which you turned off the stove). It means that you didn't turn it off between the time you finished cooking the eggs and the time you left the house.

On the basis of observations like this, Partee suggests that tense should be thought of as analogous to pronouns. The tense in (14) refers to some contextually relevant past time, just like the pronoun in *He is cute*. And indeed, tense shows other similarities to pronouns. For example, it can be bound by a quantificational element, as in (15):

(15)   Whenever you were late for work, you didn't turn off the stove.

Here, *whenever you were late for work* is a kind of quantifier over times, similar to a phrase introduced by *every*. That is, it means something like "every time you were late for work."

However, there are cases in which the idea that a tense is like a pronoun is a bit difficult to maintain. For example, I could start out a story with (16):

(16)   Last month, I went for a hike.

We can't really say that the past tense here refers to a particular, contextually specified past time, if this is taken to mean that the time of my hike itself is given by context. All that is given by context is an interval of time (last month) within which I took a hike. That's unlike what happens with a pronoun, where a non-bound pronoun needs to refer to a particular individual, not to some individual in a specified set. (Think about: *I have several Masters students. ??He got an A.*)

What (14) and (16) show us is that there is something definite and something indefinite about the past tense. One way to think of this situation was introduced by Hans Reichenbach.[3] So far we have been describing the meaning of tense in terms of two times: the time at which the sentence is used and the time at which something happened. (In the case of (16), we have the time at which I tell my story and the time I took the hike.) Reichenbach describes the semantics of tense in terms of *three* times. He calls these the *speech time* (S), the *event time* (E), and the *reference time* (R). In (16), S is the utterance time, E is the time of my hike, and R is a new time which is used to link S and E. The past tense in English must satisfy the following equations: $R < S$, $R = E$. Furthermore, *last month* in (16) gives some further information about the location of R, that R is during the month before S. This explanation lets us say that E is definite in that it corresponds precisely to R, but that R can be more or less precisely given. In the case of (16), it's known to be during last month. In (14), it's assumed to be during the stretch of time between when I finished cooking the eggs and when we left the house, and since this is a much shorter interval, we get a feeling that the time is more "definite." The difference is just a matter of degree, though; sometimes we know can pin E down pretty precisely, and sometimes we cannot.

Reichenbach's reference time is a very important contribution to our understanding of tense, but there are some conceptual difficulties with it as it stands. For one thing, it's not clearly doing a whole lot for us in the explanation of (14) and (16) – which isn't to say it's wrong to use it in this way, since it might do something for us in other cases like those we'll talk about below. It's not doing much for us because, since $E = R$, anything we say about R we could say about E directly. So why mention R at all? And more importantly, though Reichenbach explains what R *does*, he doesn't tell us what it *is*. And the term "reference time" isn't too helpful: reference to what? Or is it: made reference to by what? Most likely, help on this latter point – a better understanding of the intuitive nature of R – would help us understand better how it ought to be used.

Klein[4] helps us understand R a bit better. He renames it the *topic time*, telling us that it gives the time which the speaker is talking about. Though many semanticists will scream that nobody has explained to them what a topic is (this kind of pickiness is usually a good thing!), there is no doubt that the term "topic time" gives a more intuitive grasp of what the time is doing than "reference time" does. In this case of (16), we might say that the time we are talking about is last month. That's what the adverbial tells us. So the topic time equals last month (T = last month). The past tense tells us that T < S (something we knew based on the meaning of *last month* anyway, but redundancy is OK). I presumably didn't hike for the whole of last month (that is, it's not plausible that T = E, at least knowing me). Instead, it makes more sense to specify that E took place during T (E $\subseteq$ T; that is, E is included in T). In this way of looking at things, T is definite and "pronoun-like" in Partee's way of talking, while E is more or less definite, depending on how specific the information provided by the equation E $\subseteq$ T is in a specific case. If T is a short piece of time, E is relatively definite, while if T is long, it's relatively indefinite.

Another problem for understanding the past tense concerns the difference between examples like (16) and ones like (17):

(17)   Yesterday, Noah had a rash.

In this case, E is the situation of Noah having a rash and T equals yesterday. It's not really correct to say that (17) implies that E $\subseteq$ T, since Noah's rash may well have started before yesterday and lasted the whole day and beyond. That is, the time of the rash is not necessarily included within yesterday, as E $\subseteq$ T implies, but rather may be the other way around, T $\subseteq$ E.

Come up with a set of sentences which, like (16), have E $\subseteq$ T, and another set which, like (17), have T $\subseteq$ E.

This exercise has a sample answer, no. 6, in the appendix.

The difference between (16) and (17) is that in the former E is truly an *event*, something involving a change of some sort happening in time.[5] In contrast, in (17) E is a *state*, a situation in which something just is, with no essential change going on. To go for a hike, one has to move, so there must be change, but to have a rash is not like this. Once the rash is in place, a lack of change is what makes the rash persist. Let's write E_e to indicate an event time based on a true event, and E_s to indicate an event time (what we could call a "state time") based on a state. With E_e, the correct equation is $E_e \subseteq T$. With E_s, the opposite equation $T \subseteq E_s$ is also possible. Certain ways of specifying T virtually require that the relation be $T \subseteq E_s$. For example, in the context *When I came in, . . .* , if ". . ." is filled in by an event sentence, we understand this event as happening just after I came in: *When I came in, Mary rolled her eyes*. But if "..." is filled in with a state sentence, we may understand the state to have been in place before I came in, and to continue after I came in: *When I came in, Mary was unconscious*.

To summarize: the "Reichenbachian" theory tells us that understanding the past tense requires reference to three times, S, E, and T (or R). The following equations hold: $T < S$ and $E_e \subseteq T$ or $E_s \subseteq T$ or $T \subseteq E_s$. S and T are specified further by their nature, in that S is the time at which the sentence is used and T is the time the speaker is talking about.

> To the extent that the notions "the time at which the sentence is used" and "the time the speaker is talking about" are unclear, there's more work to be done. What situations can you think of in which these notions are not clear?
>
> The relation between E and T depends on understanding the difference between events and states. What types of situations can you think of where it's unclear whether there is "change" (an event) or "no change" (a state)?

8.1.2.2   The present tense

The "pastness" in our semantics for the past tense is encoded in the equation $T < S$, so we might expect that a semantics for the present tense could be had by just changing this to $T = S$. But while this might work for some languages, English is unusual among languages in not allowing a simple present tense sentence to be used to describe an ongoing event. We can't say (18a) when we mean (18b). A simple present tense sentence is fine if it describes a state, as with (18c).

(18)   a.   Mary runs.
       b.   Mary is running.
       c.   Noah has a rash.

Of course (18a) is meaningful; for example, it can mean that Mary runs regularly for exercise. But it does not mean what (18b) means (although many languages would use a sentence corresponding to (18a) to mean what (18b) means). We call (18a) the simple present tense, and (18b) the present progressive. Progressive, the form made by combining a form of the verb *be* with an *-ing* verb form, is an aspect, and we'll discuss it in the next section. For now, we want to understand the simple present tense better. The fact that the present tense is unremarkable with state sentences gives us a clue to understanding why (18a) means what it does. The meaning "Mary runs regularly for exercise" is really a state meaning; it doesn't describe a change, but rather tells us a persistent quality of Mary. (It's not so simple to explain, in compositional terms, how it comes to describe this persistent quality of Mary, but we won't go into that here.) In general, it seems that the English simple present tense can only be used with states. Nobody really knows why this is so, but that's how it works. Therefore we can specify the meaning of the simple present with the following equations: $T = S$ and $T \subseteq E_s$.

Come up with some more simple present tense sentences and evaluate the idea that they are always state sentences.

The present tense has other uses. We have the *historical present*, the present tense used to describe past situations, as in (19a). We can also use the present tense to describe an event concurrent with the speech time when the speaker is reporting events in real time, for example when a sportscaster describes a game for television or radio, as in (19b):

(19) a. This guy comes up to me, and he says, "give me your wallet"
. . .
b. She kicks the ball, and – it's a goal!

Both of the uses of the present tense illustrated in (19) give a greater sense of "immediacy" to the events being described than a past tense (*This guy came up to me . . .*) or a present progressive (*She is kicking the ball . . .*) would. It's important for semanticists studying the present tense to figure out what the nature of this "immediacy" is, and whether these uses belong to the same basic meaning of the present tense seen with state sentences in (18a) and (18c).

8.2   Aspect

Within a Reichenbachian theory, the primary function of tense – locating some situation that we want to talk about in time – corresponds to setting up a relation between S and T (or what's the same thing, S and R). With past tense, we have $T < S$, and with present tense, we have $T = S$. We have discussed the relation between T and E a bit as well, noting that we have E ⊆ T or T ⊆ E. In either case, though, E and T match up pretty well. We could say that E ≈ T; that is, E is approximately equal to T. You might wonder whether other relations between E and T are possible. They are, and the category of aspect is important for establishing those E/T relations.

8.2.1   Aspect vs. aspectual class

Before going into details on some of the aspectual constructions in English, it's worth pointing out a terminological issue. Words like "aspect" and "aspectual" are used in two different ways. One refers to particular grammatical forms which help determine the way in which a sentence describes an event as unfolding in time (the E/T relation is part of this). The other has to do generally with how a sentence describes an event as unfolding in time, whether this is marked by a particular grammatical form or not. This latter sense is more accurately described with the terms *aspectual class* or *aktionsart*. The difference between event sentences and state sentences is one of the most basic distinctions of aspectual class. Other more or less intuitive distinctions include one between events that are more-or-less instantaneous (often called *achievements*, e.g. (20a)) and those that inevitably take time ((20b–c)), and one between events that are associated with some state which determines that they are completed (*accomplishments*, e.g. (20b)) and those that are not (*activities*, e.g. (20c)).

(20)   a.   Shelby awoke.
         b.   Shelby ate the bone.
         c.   Shelby ran around in the yard.

An event described by (20b) is done once the bone is gone (there being no bone is the state marking the end of the event), but (20c) is not limited in this way.

> Make up some more examples of sentences in each class: states, achievements, accomplishments, activities.
>
> This exercise has an answer, no. 7, in the appendix.

Aspect in the sense of particular grammatical forms contributes to aspectual class, but aspectual class is also determined by the particular words which make up the sentence. For example, while (20b) is an accomplishment sentence, *Shelby had the bone* (differing only in one word) is stative.

Sometimes the term *eventuality* is used to describe all the sorts of events and states. So we end up with the following family tree:[6]

(21)

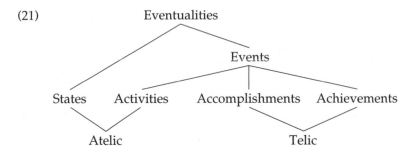

An important distinction among eventualities is that between *telic* eventualities, those with a predetermined endpoint (accomplishments, which end when the final state is reached, and achievements, which end the moment they begin), and the *atelic* ones, those without.

Usually people find the classification of aspectual classes to be pretty intuitive, but it can become confusing when one looks at a wide range of new examples. (This difficulty gets much worse as they look at other languages, but that's something we won't even go into here.) One reason for this is that a given sentence is often ambiguous between multiple aspectual classes. For example, (22) has an activity meaning similar to (20c), but it also has an accomplishment meaning (he ran one lap around the yard, and then was done):

(22)   Shelby ran around the yard.

The source of this type of ambiguity is unclear. Is the verb or some other word in the sentence ambiguous? Is there a hidden difference in grammatical structure? Is there some hidden force which can change a sentence's class – and if so, is this force semantic or pragmatic in nature? Linguists who study aspectual class have to work through all of these possibilities.

8.2.2 The perfect

As mentioned above, aspectual constructions concern the relation between E and T. This is easiest to see by looking at the English *perfect*.

The perfect is built up by the use of a form of the verb *have* plus a past participle; for example, *has eaten* or *had arrived*.

(23)   When I got there at 6 o'clock, Mary had arrived an hour before.

The main clause of (23), *Mary had arrived an hour before*, is past tense. According to Reichenbach's theory, this means that $T < S$. Thinking of T as the topic time (the time we are talking about), T is 6 o'clock. The fact that the sentence has perfect aspect tells us that $E < T$. In this case E, the time of Mary's arrival, is 5 o'clock.

(24)

E	T	S
Mary's arrival	My arrival	speech time
5 o'clock	6 o'clock	later than 6 o'clock

In the absence of any particular aspectual marking, as in examples (14)–(19), we can think of the sentence as having a kind of "non-aspect" which gives us the default relation $E \approx T$ (i.e., $E \subseteq T$ or $T \subseteq E$).

The Reichenbachian theory gives us a nice, neat picture of various temporal forms which can be summarized as follows:

(25)

		Non-perfect Default $E \approx T$ $(E_e \subseteq T$ or $T \subseteq E_s)$	Perfect $E < T$
Present	$T = S$	*speaks* $T = S$ and $E_e \subseteq T$ or $T \subseteq E_s$	*has spoken* $T = S$ and $E < T$
Past	$T < S$	*spoke* $T < S$ and $E_e \subseteq T$ or $T \subseteq E_s$	*had spoken* $T < S$ and $E < T$

Though this way of thinking about the perfect is intuitive and beautifully simple, it has some problems. In particular, though it tells us the right temporal relations in many cases, it fails in two major sorts of circumstances: First, sometimes the $E < T$ relation doesn't seem right; and second, certain cases in which the perfect cannot be used are unexplained.[7]

The $E < T$ relation doesn't seem correct with examples like (26):

(26)   Mary has been in Belmont for two days.

Actually, (26) is ambiguous, and one meaning fits the relations T = S & E < T indicated by the chart above. This meaning can be brought out by thinking of (26) in the context of (27):

(27)   *Has Mary ever been in Belmont for more than just one day?*
       Mary has been in Belmont for two days – *that was a year ago.*

Here E (the time when Mary was in Belmont) is before T (which = S). But this sort of meaning is not usually the first one that comes to mind. At first glance, many people interpret (26) to imply that Mary arrived in Belmont two days ago, and that she is still there. But if Mary is still in Belmont, this means that E is not entirely before S, and since S = T, E is not entirely before T either. Thus, it seems that the equation E < T is wrong.

This sort of case, in which E is not entirely before T, is known as a *continuative perfect*. Continuative perfects only arise when E is a state: *Mary has walked to the market*, which describes an event, is not ambiguous. In addition, other complex circumstances are involved. For instance, if you take the adverbial phrase *for two days* out of (26), it no longer has the continuative meaning. Semanticists have not figured out the whole picture here yet.[8]

The Reichenbachian analysis of the perfect also runs into trouble because it makes us expect that some sentences in the perfect form should make sense, but they actually don't:

(28)   ?Gutenberg has discovered the art of printing.[9]

(29)   ?Einstein has visited Princeton.[10]

(30)   *Mary has walked to the market yesterday.

(The question marks in (28) and (29) indicate that these sentences are odd, when you first encounter them.) In my opinion, (28) and (29) show that the perfect has some meaning beyond its temporal meaning, while (26) and (30) show that E < R is too simplistic a way of thinking about its temporal meaning.

8.2.3   The progressive

The progressive aspect is built out of a form of the verb *be* plus the present participle, as in (31):

(31)   Shelby is running in the street.

The most basic point to make about the meaning of the progressive is that it indicates than an event is ongoing at the time indicated by the tense. So, a present progressive sentence like (31) indicates that something is ongoing at the speech time, while a past progressive (*Shelby was running in the street*) would indicate something ongoing at a time before the speech time.

Using the Reichenbachian notation, we can say that the progressive indicates that $R \subseteq E$:

(32)   Time of Shelby running in the street

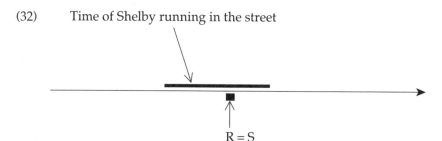

$$R = S$$

Since $R \subseteq E$ is exactly the relation we find in non-progressive sentences when E is a state, one way to think about the progressive is that it turns any kind of sentence into a state sentence.[11] That is, though intuitively running is an event, since it involves change, *is running* is treated as describing a state. This would also explain why the progressive can't be formed from sentences that already describe states (**Shelby is being a dog*) – the use of the progressive would have no point. Such a way of thinking about things has the merit of getting the temporal relations right (or more-or-less right, as we'll see below), but calls into question whether the terms "event" and "state" really have any content at all. How can running sometimes be an event and sometimes a state? Are we just attaching the terms "event" and "state" to sentences in order to describe the temporal relations we see, without really understanding what events and states are? That would not be a true semantic analysis, though it might be a useful exercise in classification.

Another possibility for explaining the progressive would not go quite so far as to say that progressive sentences describe states. We might say that they describe events which have something in common with states, and that this which they have in common with states explains the fact that they are like states in allowing the R ⊆ E relation. In other words R ⊆ E$_X$, where X includes both states and progressives.[12] But still, to have a true semantic analysis we'd need an independent understanding of what the members of X have in common.

It's possible that the R ⊆ E relation seen with the progressive has nothing to do with states, and that it's simply the meaning of the progressive that it expresses R ⊆ E for event sentences. But this wouldn't be the end of the story on progressives, since the progressive brings up other puzzles. The most famous other puzzle concerns the fact that the event described by a progressive sentence can remain forever incomplete:

(33)   Max was crossing the street, when he was hit by a bus.

As David Dowty pointed out,[13] examples like (33) make it clear that any variation on R ⊆ E as a way of describing the meaning of the progressive is insufficient. In (33), E should be an event of Max crossing the street. But Max never does cross the street in the situation described by (33). So it would appear there's no such E, and the sentence should be automatically false – which it isn't. Therefore something is wrong in how we're thinking about the semantics of (33).

Dowty's solution[14] is to say that the progressive involves not just a temporal relation (a relation between R and E in Reichenbach's terms, though this isn't how Dowty talked about it), but also a modal relation. As I mentioned above, modality involves paying attention to what occurs in non-actual possible worlds. Considering (33), even though Max didn't cross the street in the actual world (assuming that (33) is true), he did cross it in some non-actual possible worlds. And some of these possible worlds seem of special relevance to sentence (33). For example, in worlds in which Max's actions were not interrupted by the bus, he crossed the street. So, even though there's no E in the actual world in which Max did cross the street, there is an E in actual world which, in certain other possible worlds, was an event in which Max crossed the street. Look at diagram 43. In the actual world, Max's event stops at stage three. In possible world 1, the event starts out in the same way, but in this possible world the truck doesn't hit him. So in possible world 1, there is an event of Max crossing the street. (In possible world 2, the bus gets Max even earlier than it does in the real world.) Dowty calls worlds like possible world 1 "inertia worlds." Inertia worlds are worlds in which what was going on in a given world at a given time continues to its "normal completion."

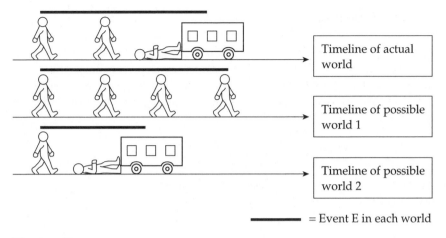

= Event E in each world

Diagram 43

Given the concept of inertia worlds, we can define the meaning of the progressive something like this: the progressive form of a sentence describes an event which, if it were to be completed normally, would be described by the simple non-progressive form of the sentence. More precisely:

(34)   The progressive sentence S describes an event E in world w if and only if the non-progressive sentence S' describes E in all inertia worlds (for E in w).

For example, the progressive sentence *Max be crossing the street*[15] describes an event E in the actual world if and only if the non-progressive sentence *Max cross the street* describes E in all of the inertia worlds for E in the actual world. As seen in the diagram, in inertia worlds like possible world 1, Max crosses the street in E, so in the actual world *Max is crossing the street* describes E.

According to this theory, the function of the progressive is to utilize modality to create a sentence (the progressive sentence) which describes an event which the non-progressive sentence would not itself describe. This can be useful, since we may want to describe Max's actions in terms of what he meant to do – cross the street – rather than what he actually did – get killed. That is, the progressive provides us with the ability to describe events in terms of what they would have been, rather than what they actually were. It's as if we had a way of describing people not in terms of their actual attributes, but in terms of the ones they would have had if things had gone in the expected or normal way.[16]

8.3   Modality

"Modality" refers to language whose meaning depends on alternate possible worlds. We have already seen some examples of this: the progressive, as analyzed by Dowty; and *could*, as described in chapter 7. Words of various grammatical categories involve modality in their meaning; for example:

Nouns	*possibility, necessity*
Adjectives	*possible, probably, necessary*
Adverbs	*possibly, probably, necessarily*
Main verbs	*require, know, hope*
Modal verbs	*could, can, must, may, should, might*

The last class, the modal verbs, are traditionally the focus of studies on modality. In English, this group of words is easy to identify through grammatical analysis: they can fit into the slot after the subject and before *have* marking the perfect: *John ___ have seen Mary*. I'll follow the tradition and base my explanation of modality on this class as well.

Since a sentence with a modal verb in it depends for its meaning on alternate possible worlds, we can classify them in terms of *which* alternate worlds a given modal cares about. Compare (35) and (36):

(35)   Rich people should give money to the poor.

(36)   The book must be in Professor Wong's office.

Sentence (35) is true because rich people give money to the poor in certain possible worlds – the morally good possible worlds. Sentence (36) does not have to do with the morally good possible worlds. Instead, it is true because the book is in Professor Wong's office in those possible worlds where certain known facts hold true. This may be easier to see by putting (36) into some context:

(37)   The book is listed in the catalogue, but it's not in the library. It's on the topic of tomato/pig hybridization. Only Professor Wong works on this topic. So, *the book must be in Professor Wong's office.*

(37) says that a bunch of facts together entail that the book is in Professor Wong's office. These facts are that the book is listed in the catalogue, it's

not in the library, it's on tomato/pig hybridization, and only Prof. Wong works on tomato/pig hybridization. Check back to chapter 1 to remember what entailment is. A sentence entails another if, and only if, the set of worlds in which the one is true is a subset of the set of worlds in which the other is true. So what (37) says is that the set of worlds in which the book is listed in the catalogue, it's not in the library, it's on tomato/pig hybridization, and only Prof. Wong works on tomato/pig hybridization is a subset of the set of worlds in which the book is in Professor Wong's office. More briefly, in every world in which the relevant facts are true, the book is in Professor Wong's office. (See diagram 44.)

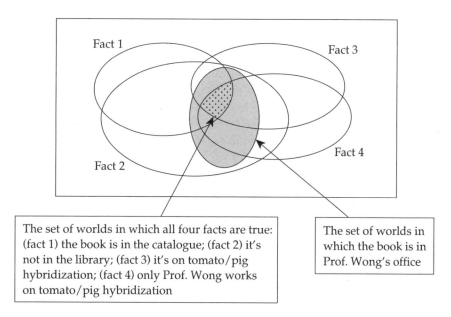

The set of worlds in which all four facts are true: (fact 1) the book is in the catalogue; (fact 2) it's not in the library; (fact 3) it's on tomato/pig hybridization; (fact 4) only Prof. Wong works on tomato/pig hybridization

The set of worlds in which the book is in Prof. Wong's office

Diagram 44

Any sentence with a modal in it depends for its meaning on the identification of which possible worlds are relevant to its truth or falsity. This identification of relevant worlds is partially accomplished by the choice of modal verb, but in general this is not enough. Whereas (35) depends on morally good worlds, (38) – which contains the same modal verb *should* – depends on those worlds in which we take the best route home, even though this has little to do with morality:

(38)   We should turn onto Clarendon Boulevard, not onto Wilson Boulevard.

Since precisely which worlds are relevant to a modal sentence cannot be recovered from its grammatical form, for a hearer to understand the meaning of a modal sentence, he or she must know, or be able to figure out, just which worlds are intended. This is a pragmatic matter, essentially a presupposition. Just as understanding a sentence containing a pronoun or definite noun phrase depends for its meaning on knowing what that pronoun or definite refers to, understanding a modal sentence depends on knowing which worlds are relevant.[17]

With this point in mind, let's think about what it takes to specify the meaning of *should* in (35) in a more precise way. Someone who utters (35) counts on the addressee knowing that he or she counts "morally good" worlds as relevant. Now of course what's morally good is not set once and for all by logic alone. It happens to be true that charity is a moral good in our world, but it didn't have to be that way. If what is moral is determined by God and not by human convention, it could have been that God decided that letting the rich get richer is morally good. If what's morally good is determined by human conventions, then we could have selected alternative conventions. So, if we're wondering whether (35) is true in our world, we have to look to worlds which are good according to the standards of our world, but if we want to know if it's true in another sort of world, we have to look at worlds which are good according to the standards of that world.[18] That is, what we need is a specification, for each world, of what possible worlds are relevant to the sentence's truth in that world – something like (39):

(39)　a.　Worlds in which people behave charitably:　　worlds 1, 2, 3
　　　　　　Worlds in which people behave greedily:　　worlds 4, 5, 6
　　　　　　Worlds without money:　　world 7
　　　　b.　Worlds in which morality dictates charity:　　worlds 1, 5
　　　　　　Worlds in which morality dictates greed:　　worlds 2, 4
　　　　　　Worlds in which morality dictates the
　　　　　　absence of money:　　worlds 3, 6, 7

See diagram 45.

A specification of world-to-world relations like this is known as an *accessibility relation*. Notice that world 1 has three arrows coming out of it, and they point at world 2, world 3, and world 1 itself. We say that worlds 1, 2, and 3 are *accessible* to world 1 under this accessibility relation. This encodes the fact that worlds 1, 2, and 3 (the charity worlds, cf. (39a)) are the ones relevant to determining whether (35) is true or false in world 1 (a world in which charity is good, cf. (39b)).

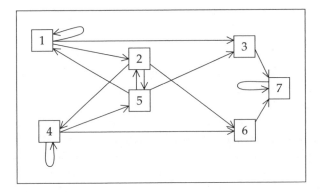

Diagram 45

We can use the accessibility relation to explain the meaning of (35) in more detail. Sentence (35) is true in a given world in diagram 45 if all of the worlds accessible to it are ones in which rich people give money to the poor. Worlds 1 and 5 are the only worlds in which (35) is true. Notice that in world 1, people should give money to the poor (the charity worlds 1, 2, and 3 are accessible), and moreover people *do* give money to the poor. It's a world which is good by its own charitable standards (and this is indicated in the diagram by the fact that an arrow leading out of world 1 turns back and points at world 1 itself). World 5 is one in which people should give money to the poor, but not one in which they do give money to the poor. It's more like our world.

Accessibility relations can be classified into groups. One important group is the *deontic* accessibility relations. Deontic accessibility relations pick out worlds which are "good" according to some measure. A modal which makes use of a deontic accessibility relation is a deontic modal, like *should* in (35). Deontic accessibility relations are diverse, however, in that what is good can be determined from various perspectives. We have good according to the law, according to the teachings of a particular religion, according to utilitarian calculation, and so forth. There are many different shades of deontic meaning. Another important group of accessibility relations is the *epistemic* relations. These concern what is known, for example (36)–(37).

Modals may differ not only in *which* worlds are relevant to their meanings, but also – roughly speaking – in *how many* worlds are relevant. Consider the difference between (40a) and (40b):

(40) a. The book may be in Professor Wong's office.
      b. The book must be in Professor Wong's office.

Both of these modals are epistemic, but they certainly differ in meaning. According to (40a), in *some* world compatible with the known facts (the book is listed in the catalogue, it is not in the library, etc.), the book is in Prof. Wong's office; however, according to (40a), we can also imagine worlds in which all the known facts hold but it's not in his office. All we're saying is that it *may be* there. On the other hand, with (40b) we don't admit the possibility that the book is anywhere else. In other words, (40b) requires that the book be there in *all* worlds compatible with the known facts. We call *may* a *possibility* modal: it just says that the book's being in Prof. Wong's office is a possibility, and the possibility that it's not there may exist as well. We call *must* a *necessity* modal: it says that the book's being in Prof. Wong's office is a necessary conclusion from the known facts.

Deontic modals also can be labeled as possibility or necessity modals. In fact, when *may* functions as a deontic modal, it indicates possibility, just like when it functions as an epistemic modal. (41) says that departing at 5:00 is compatible with the rules, but leaves open the possibility that leaving at another time is OK too. When *must* functions as a deontic modal, it indicates necessity, just like when it functions as an epistemic modal: (42) says that the only option compatible with the rules is to depart at 5:00; any other time will violate the rules.

(41) You may depart at 5:00 p.m.

(42) You must depart at 5:00 p.m.

> Work through a number of other English modals, and categorize them as possibility modals, necessity modals, or something else. Then categorize the same modals as deontic, epistemic, or something else. You should find some cases in which more than one modal is classified the same way (more than one deontic necessity modal, for example); in such cases, how would you explain any difference in meaning which you perceive? Spend some time trying to characterize any models which you label as "something else." If you can, perform the same exercise for the modals of some other language.

There is an enormous literature on modality, and much of it has to do with refining the theory of accessibility relations. This gives rise to more sophisticated classifications of modals.[19]

NOTES

1   This diagram is for one world only. If we wanted to indicate the way a predicate is sensitive to worlds and to times simultaneously, we'd have a diagram like 41 for each world. As an artistic exercise, you may want to combine diagrams 18–19 and 41 in the relevant way.

2   See Partee (1973).

3   Reichenbach (1947).

4   W. Klein (1994).

5   The distinction between events and states can be traced back to Aristotle, and has an intense history within philosophy and semantics. For discussion and references, see Dowty (1979).

6   The literature abounds with variations on the classification of events, but this one is pretty standard and captures the most popular distinctions.

7   This discussion is based on Portner (2003).

8   See Portner (2003) for a recent analysis of these matters.

9   From McCoard (1978), based on Dietrich (1955).This example is less odd if we imagine it being uttered by a god who manipulates human affairs: "Now that Gutenberg has discovered the art of printing, I can move on to my next project." Inoue (1979) and Portner (2003) discuss why this might be so.

10   From Chomsky (1970). This sentence also becomes much better in the right conversational setting, as discussed by Inoue (1979). (Can you come up with such a context?)

11   See Parsons (1990).

12   See Smith (1999).

13   See Dowty (1977). The heavy reliance on events in the explanations which follow doesn't come from Dowty's discussion, but the central idea of using modality in the analysis is his.

14   See also Landman (1992); Portner (1998).

15   I have taken the tense out of the example, so we have the tenseless verbs *be* and *cross*. This is both to simplify things and because it's probable that tense and aspect modify sentences in the strict order aspect-before-tense.

16   If we had something like the progressive for nouns, we might have been able to say (in 2002) that Al Gore was the president-ing, where a "president-ing" is someone who is president in all worlds in which the normal course of events is not interrupted. (Years down the road, this example might not be so comprehensible. The essential facts to know are that the 2000 United States presidential election was very close, and many people thought that if the count in the state of Florida had been conducted properly, Al Gore would have become president rather than George W. Bush.)

17   This does not imply that the hearer must know the facts in question; or in the case of *should*, that the hearer must know the relevant moral code in detail. In many cases, the hearer just knows a description of the set of possible worlds ("the good worlds according to a particular moral code," "the facts that the

speaker has in mind"), and then can infer backwards from the modal sentence to a better understanding of that set of worlds. For example, if I don't know anything about your religion, and then you tell me *According to my religion, we should give money to the poor*, I thereby learn something about the set of worlds which your religion specifies as morally good.

18 You may think that what's morally good can vary by place and time as well as by possible world. If so, what is said below can be made more sophisticated to accommodate this variability. The way we allow which worlds are relevant to vary by world below can be a model for how we let them vary by place and/or time.

19 See the following papers by Kratzer, for example: (1977; 1981; 1991).

9 Propositional Attitudes

In chapter 7, we saw that verbs like *think, believe, want,* or *doubt* create intensional constructions. An example from that chapter was (1):

(1)   a.   Mary thinks that her house is the tallest building in New York.
      b.   Mary thinks that her house is the Empire State Building.

We know that this is an intensional construction because (1a) and (1b) are not equivalent, even though *the tallest building in New York* and *the Empire State Building* refer to the same thing. *Think* can be labeled a sentence-embedding verb because a sentence like *that her house is the tallest building in New York* plays a grammatical role similar to that of a direct object; we say that this sentence is "embedded in" the larger sentence (1a), and it is the verb *think* which allows this embedding. Verbs like *think* are also frequently called *propositional attitude verbs,* because they seem to indicate that the person referred to by their subject has a certain relation with (or "attitude toward") the proposition expressed by the embedded sentence. In the case of (1a), it seems that the sentence tells us something about the relationship between Mary and the proposition that her house is the tallest building in New York: she thinks that this proposition is true. If instead of *think,* the verb were *hope,* the sentence would tell us that she hopes that this proposition is true.

In this chapter, we develop these ideas about the meaning of sentences like (1) in more detail. This project leads to some interesting insights about the propositional attitude verbs and reveals some disturbing problems for the idea that we can understand propositions simply as sets of possible worlds. This chapter therefore has a dual role: it both continues the project of applying the ideas of formal semantics to more and more constructions, and confronts some of the deepest foundational issues which face semantic theory.

9.1   A Possible Worlds Semantics for Belief and Desire

The most popular way of thinking about the semantics of words like *believe* and *hope* within the formal semantics tradition treats them as very similar to other intensional words, particularly modals. An epistemic modal like *must* describes a proposition as true in all worlds of a certain sort (those in which certain known facts hold true). Similarly, we can think of *believe* as describing a proposition as true in all worlds which match the subject's beliefs. For example, in the case of (2), we focus on certain worlds: those which match Noah's beliefs.

(2)   Baby Noah believes that there is applesauce in the bowl.

In all of "Noah's belief worlds," there is applesauce in the bowl. (There may also be other worlds – not belief worlds for Noah – in which there is applesauce in the bowl. For example, there are possible worlds in which there is applesauce in the bowl, and in which grandmothers are mean. But these are not among Noah's belief worlds.)

Diagram 46 illustrates this in a way that makes clear the role of an accessibility relation. Accessible from w1 is a set of worlds (the light gray ones),

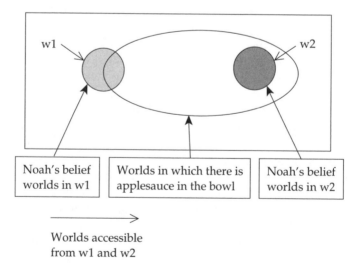

Diagram 46

and accessible from w2 is a different set (the dark gray ones). The light gray worlds are the ones Noah believes in in w1, and the dark gray ones are the ones he believes in in w2. The latter, but not the former, is a subset of the worlds in which there is applesauce in the bowl. Therefore, (2) is true in w2, but not true in w1. Notice that in neither w1 nor w2 is there actually applesauce in the bowl – poor Noah!

> Fill in diagram 46 to indicate a world w3 in which Noah correctly believes that there is applesauce in the bowl, and another world w4 in which he incorrectly believes that there isn't. Remember that what Noah believes in a given world is indicated by linking him (with an arrow) to a set of belief worlds.

A first draft of a semantic analysis for all sentence embedding verbs can be made along these lines. To think about (3), with the verb *hope*, we have diagram 47:

(3) Noah hopes that there is applesauce in the bowl.

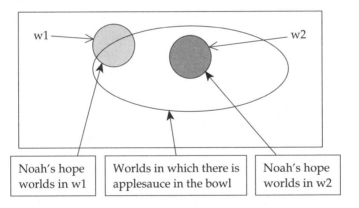

Diagram 47

In diagram 46 the accessibility relation links worlds w1 and w2 with the set of worlds matching Noah's beliefs in that world. Similarly, in diagram 47, an accessibility relation links worlds w1 and w2 with the set of worlds matching Noah's hopes in that world. According to diagram 47, (3) is false in w1 and true in w2.

9.2   Logical Consequences of the Modal Analysis of Propositional Attitude Verbs

Take a moment to recall the definitions of synonymy, contraction, and entailment within possible worlds semantics from chapter 1. Two sentences are synonymous if they describe the same sets of possible worlds; they contradict one another if they describe non-overlapping sets; and one entails the other if the first is a subset of the second. These definitions have some important consequences when combined with the modal analysis of propositional attitude verbs we have been discussing.

Consequence 1: If X *believes/wants* S is true, and S is synonymous with T, X *believes/wants* T must also be true.

Consider this in terms of diagram 46. In w2, (2) is true. Noah believes that there is applesauce in the bowl. This is because the dark gray set is a subset of the worlds in which there is applesauce in the bowl. If another sentence (*The bowl contains applesauce*) is synonymous with *There is applesauce in the bowl*, it will describe the same worlds. So, the dark gray set will inevitably be a subset of that set as well.

Consequence 2: If X *believes/wants* S is true, and S contradicts T, X *believes/wants* T must be false.

Consequence 3: If X *believes/wants* S is true, and S entails T, X *believes/ wants* T must also be true.

Prove consequences 2 and 3.

This exercise has an answer, no. 8, in the appendix.

These consequences are to some extent desirable. If Noah believes that there's applesauce in the bowl, it seems correct to conclude that he also believes that the bowl contains applesauce (consequence 1). If Noah believes that there's applesauce in the bowl, it seems correct to conclude that he doesn't believe that the bowl is empty (consequence 2). If Noah believes that there's applesauce in the bowl, in seems correct to conclude that he believes that the bowl contains food (consequence 3).

However, the consequences aren't always desirable. They are much more clearly undesirable when it comes to desire verbs than belief verbs. With respect to desire verbs, consequence 2 means that we cannot have incompatible desires. If Robert wants to marry Jane, it implies he can't also want to marry Sue (assuming bigamy to be impossible). But our experience tells us that we can want incompatible things. Likewise, consequence 3 means that we must desire all consequences of our desires; so, if Robert wants to marry Jane and be loyal to her, then he must want to break up with Sue. But it is possible for us to be so conflicted as to have desires while wishing to avoid the consequences of our desires, even though we might be happier if it weren't.

It is possible to solve some of these problems by employing a deeper understanding of what it is to desire something. As pointed out by Irene Heim,[1] Stalnaker's discussion of the relation between belief and desire in a theory of rational action (see chapter 1) can give us some insights into the semantics of desire predicates, words like *hope, want,* and *wish.* According to the belief–desire theory of rational action, the role of belief in our lives is to set up the space of possibilities in which we try to realize our desires. If we believe that it will rain, and we want to stay dry, we will carry an umbrella; but if we believe it won't rain, we won't carry an umbrella (assuming that we also want to carry as few things as possible). So what desires are is a specification, given a range of possibilities which we believe to be open to us, of which of these possibilities we should strive to make real.

Here's another example: Noah most wants to attend Princeton; if he can't attend Princeton, he prefers to attend Stanford; if he can't attend Stanford, he prefers Georgetown; and if he can't attend Georgetown, he prefers the University of Virginia. His desires amount to an ordering of possible worlds, so that (other things being equal), worlds in which he attends Princeton are best, those in which he attends Stanford are second best; Georgetown third best; and Virginia fourth best. (See diagram 48.)

At first he believes that he can get into any of the schools (belief worlds 1), so he will act so as to achieve the best worlds according to his desires – the Princeton worlds. But suppose he learns that he will not get into Princeton (his belief worlds shift to no. 2); then his desires will lead him to act so as to achieve his new best (formerly second best) worlds – the Stanford worlds.

All of this suggests that the meanings of words like *hope* and *want* should have a comparative character; they are about what worlds are better than others, given certain assumptions about what's possible. When Noah's beliefs are as in belief worlds 1, (4) is true and (5) is false; but when he switches to belief worlds 2, (5) becomes true and (4) becomes inappropriate (to me, it's unclear whether to say it's false, but it's certainly not the right way to describe Noah's desires).

(4)   Noah hopes to attend Princeton.

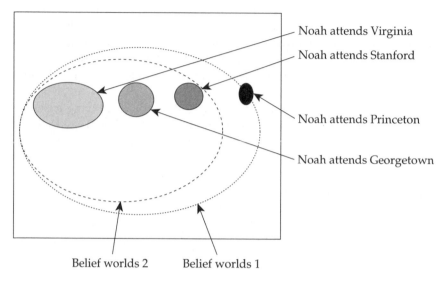

Noah attends Virginia

Noah attends Stanford

Noah attends Princeton

Noah attends Georgetown

Belief worlds 2   Belief worlds 1

Diagram 48

(5)   Noah hopes to attend Stanford.

(Diagram 48 is a bit clumsy. It doesn't indicate Noah's preferences for certain worlds over others in a very clear way. Roughly, he prefers worlds to the right over worlds to the left. But if we took this diagram to be an exact description of his beliefs, it would mean he prefers any world in which he attends Princeton over any world in which he attends Stanford. But of course his preferences wouldn't work this way; he would not prefer a world in which he attends Princeton but is poor his whole life over worlds in which he attends Virginia and is wealthy. Roughly, (4) means that a world in which he attends Princeton is preferable to the worlds in which he attends other schools, everything else being pretty much equal in the two worlds.)

9.3   Two Foundational Problems: Coreferential Terms and Logical Truths

While the difficulties with our original modal analysis of desire predicates (diagram 47) could be diagnosed and cured with a more sophisticated way of thinking of their meaning, there are problems with belief predicates (as well as desire predicates and other words which create intensional constructions) which are of a more fundamental nature. These problems have to do with the fact that we often intuit differences of meaning where the basic ideas of our semantic theory say there should not be differences. If you recall from chapter 1, we built our semantic theory on two basic associations of language with non-language:

(6)   The meaning of a name is a thing (its referent).

(7)   The meaning of a sentence is its truth-conditions.

Principle (6) implies that if you have two names with the same referent, they have the same meaning; principle (7) implies that if you have two sentences with the same truth-conditions, they have the same meaning. For the most part, these implications seem just right. However, when it comes to belief sentences (and other intensional constructions), they lead to some grief.

The problem with (6) looks like this: the baby has an English name, *Noah*, and a Chinese name, *Weihan*. According to (6), *Noah* and *Weihan* are synonymous. In most cases (like (8)), this seems correct. But in a belief sentence, sometimes it doesn't ((9)):

(8)   a.   Noah is crying.
      b.   Weihan is crying.

(9)   a.   Susan believes that Noah cries a lot.
      b.   Susan believes that Weihan cries a lot.

(8a) and (8b) are synonymous at least to the extent of having the same truth-conditions. (9a) and (9b), however, can differ in the case where Susan has heard of both Noah and Weihan, but doesn't know that they name the same baby. Noah's mother Sylvia told Susan "Our baby Noah is a crabby baby who is always crying." Noah's grandmother Linna told Susan "Our grandchild Weihan is a perfect baby who never cries." She doesn't know that Noah's grandmother is the mother of Noah's mother, and thinks she has heard about two different children. Therefore, it seems, (9a) is true and (9b) is false. If one can be true and the other false, they can't be synonymous. Since the sentences are just alike except for the fact that one uses the name *Noah* and the other uses the name *Weihan*, it seems that the difference in meaning between (9a) and (9b) must be due to a difference in meaning between the two names.

The problem with (7) looks like this: *two plus two is four* is true in every possible world. *The square root of 60,025 is 245* is also true in every possible world. These two sentences have exactly the same truth-conditions. This means that, according to (7), they are synonymous. This seems alright in some cases (like (10)), but not in many others ((11)):

(10)   a.   It's a truth of mathematics that two plus two is four.
       b.   It's a truth of mathematics that the square root of 60,025 is 245.

(11)   a.   Susan knows that two plus two is four.
       b.   Susan knows that the square root of 60,025 is 245.

It could easily be that (11a) is true while (11b) is false. Since the sentences are alike except for the fact that one includes the sentences *Two plus two is four* while the other includes the sentence *The square root of 60,025 is 245*, it seems that the difference in meaning between (11a) and (11b) must be due to a difference in meaning between the two sentences included.

Frege came up with a way out of these problems. His solution was essentially to say that a word, phrase, or sentence can have different meanings in extensional vs. intensional contexts. Recall from chapter 5 Frege's distinction between *sense* and *reference*. There I reported that reference is the compositionally relevant aspect of meaning, while sense is a way of identifying the reference in particular situations, but this was not quite accurate. According to Frege, reference is the compositionally relevant aspect of meaning for ordinary, extensional constructions, but sense is the compositionally relevant aspect of meaning for intensional constructions. So, let's assume the ordinary sense and reference for *the dog which lives at Paul's house* as follows:

(12)   a.   The **sense** of *the dog which lives at Paul's house* tells us that, given the facts as they are, it refers to Shelby; given a possible world in which Hannibal lives at Paul's house, it would refer to Hannibal; given a possible world in which Hobo lives at Paul's house, it would refer to Hobo, etc.
       b.   The **reference** of *the dog which lives at Paul's house*: Shelby.

According to Frege, in (13) *the dog which lives at Paul's house* refers to Shelby, but in (14) – and intensional construction – it refers to the sense specified in (12a):

(13)   The dog which lives at Paul's house is cute.

(14)   Bob thinks that the dog which lives at Paul's house is cute.

There is something odd about Frege's idea. He says that, in (14), the phrase *the dog which lives at Paul's house* refers to the procedure "given the facts as they are, it refers to Shelby; given a possible world in which Hannibal lives at Paul's house, it would refer to Hannibal; given a possible world in which Hobo lives at Paul's house, it would refer to Hobo, etc." If *the dog which lives at Paul's house* refers to the procedure, it seems at first glance that (14) says that Bob believes that this procedure is cute. Now, Bob may indeed find procedures cute, but that is not what (14) is saying. This implies, if Frege is right, that semantic procedures work quite differently in intensional constructions and extensional ones. But this makes it a mystery why exactly the same grammatical structures should be employed.

If Frege is right in his idea that senses are important in intensional constructions in a way that they are not in extensional ones, the notions of sense and reference may be helpful in solving the problems posed by (9) and (11). These notions will be helpful if there is a difference in sense between *Noah* and *Weihan*, or between *two plus two is four* and *the square root of 60,025 is 245*. Frege certainly thought that two names with the same reference could differ in sense, and this is why he thought he had solved the problem of (9). But actually it is quite a challenge to come up with a precise explanation of what senses are which both fits into linguistic theory and gives us a difference in sense between *Noah* and *Weihan*. How could we explain the sense of *Noah* and the sense of *Weihan* in a way that tells us in a clear way what the difference between them is? One intuitive idea is that the senses are descriptions: for Susan, the sense of *Noah* is "the son of Sylvia" and the sense of *Weihan* is "the grandson of Linna." That sounds plausible. However, we already have seen in chapter 5 that there are serious problems with the description theory of names. Moreover, the philosophical literature is filled with many related problems, and most semanticists agree that sense and reference are not enough to solve them.

The difficulties for semantic theory posed by (9) and (11) are clearly not trivial. Dealing with them is a serious challenge. There are really three approaches one can take. The first is to say that the fundamental assumptions of our semantic theory are wrong; perhaps we should have gone with the idea theory of meaning (despite its real problems), rather than move to a theory which says that meanings are out in the world. The second is to challenge some of the assumptions which we made in thinking about (9) and (11); we'll look at this possibility in the next section. The third is to deny that there's a problem for semantics at all; in the section after the next one we'll consider the possibility that these examples show something about meaning, but not the kind of meaning which formal semantic theory is accountable for.

9.4   Structure and Meaning

A hidden assumption in our discussion of (9) and (11) was that the sentences have the same structure in relevant respects. For example, in the case of (11), we reasoned like this:

> It could easily be that (11a) is true while (11b) is false. Since the sentences are alike except for the fact that one includes the sentences *Two plus two is four* while the other includes the sentence *The square root of 60,025 is 245*, it seems that the difference in meaning between (11a) and (11b) must be due to a difference in meaning between the two sentences included.

Recall that compositionality says that the meaning of a phrase is determined by the meanings of its parts and the way in which they are combined. (11a) and (11b) differ in meaning, and this difference could be due to a difference in meanings of their parts, or a difference in the way in which they are combined (or both). The argument we gave, quoted above, says that "the sentences are alike except for the fact that . . .": it assumes that their structures are the same. The structure which most linguists would assume is indicated by the bracketing below:

(15)   [Susan [knows [that [two plus two is four]]]]
        [Susan [knows [that [the square root of 60,025 is 245]]]]

One crucial implication of this structure is that everything within the subordinate clause (*two plus two is four, the square root of 60,025 is 245*) is combined together before any of it is combined with *know*. This means that *know* is no more related to any part of the subordinate clause than any other part. Perhaps this implication is not correct.[2] Let's think about (11a). Suppose that Susan took a math test with the question on it "What is two plus two?" Then if we say (11a), we'd say it tells us what Susan knows about $2 + 2$. But if the question had been "What plus two is four?," we'd say it tells us what Susan knows about adding something to two to get four (what we might write as "$x + 2 = 4$"), namely that two is that kind of thing. We might even pronounce (11a) differently in the two cases:

(16)   a.   [The test asked: What is two plus two?]
              Susan knows that two plus two is FOUR.
        b.   [The test asked: What plus two is four?]
              Susan knows that TWO plus two is four.

In what situations would you pronounce the sentence these ways?

- Two PLUS two is four.
- TWO plus TWO is four.
- Two plus two IS four.

These differences in pronunciation seem to reflect real differences in meaning. If Susan is just in first grade, it seems possible that *Susan knows that two plus two is FOUR* is true, while *Susan knows that TWO plus two is four* is false. She is able to solve the simple addition problem by counting on her fingers, but gets lost with "what plus two is four?"

Since we have the intuition that (11a) tells us different things when in the situations (16a) and (16b) – it tells us what Susan knows about two plus two in one case, and what she knows about $x + 2 = 4$ in the other – we might think that this difference should be recognized within linguistic theory somehow. We need to understand what it is for somebody to know something *about* something, not just for somebody to know something. In other words, sentences with *know* really involve three things: the knower, the thing about which something is known, and the knowledge (what the knower knows about that thing). The structure in (15) only has the knower and knowledge. The thing about which something is known is missing.

Following Max Cresswell and Arnim von Stechow, we can remedy this situation by dividing the meaning of subordinate clause into two parts, the thing which is known about, and the knowledge about that thing:

(17)   a.   Susan knows that <two plus two is, four>
         b.   Susan knows that <plus two is four, two>

The material in angled brackets is a rough indication of what is called a *structured meaning*. The complement clause *two plus two is four* does not simply express a proposition – that is, its meaning is not just truth-conditions – but rather it gives us a collection of smaller meaning-pieces. In the case of (17a), the meaning pieces are the property "two plus two is" (the unsaturated proposition which when saturated by four says "true," and when saturated by anything else says "false"), and four. In (17b), the pieces are the property "plus two is four" (the unsaturated proposition which when saturated by two says "true," and when saturated by anything else says "false"). Both structured meanings have the general form

<piece1, piece2>, but the pieces are different. This amounts to a difference in structure between (11a) when it's used as in (16a), and (11a) when its used as in (16b). We are then free to say that the difference in meaning between (11a) as in (16a) and (11a) as in (16b) is due to this difference in structure.

Provide structured meanings along the lines of (17) for the sentences in the previous exercise.

This exercise has an answer, no. 9, in the appendix.

The same trick can then let us explain how (11a) and (11b) differ in meaning. The true semantic structure of (11a) might be (17a). The true structure of (11b) might be (18):

(18)   Susan knows that <the square root of 60,025 is, 245>

Though (17a) and (18) are similar (they both have the form *Susan knows that <PROPERTY, NUMBER>*), they are different enough. In the case of (17a), we report Susan's knowledge about what two plus two is, while in (18) we report her knowledge about what the square root of 60,025 is. Since she might have knowledge about one thing but not the other, it's perfectly possible for (11a) to be true and (11b) to be false.

We have seen how structured meanings can solve the problem of (11). That's great for proponents of formal semantics. However, as it stands structured meanings don't do much for the problem of (9). It seems that (9a) tells us what Susan believes about Noah, and that (9b) tells us what she believes about Weihan. So, the structured meanings would be as in (19):

(19)   a.   Susan thinks that <Noah, cries a lot>
        b.   Susan thinks that <Weihan, cries a lot>

However, since Noah and Weihan are the same baby, if the meaning of a name is just its reference, then these structured meanings are identical. It makes no difference that Noah/Weihan was referred to with the name *Noah* in one case and with the name *Weihan* in the other. "Noah" in (19a) and "Weihan" in (19b) are not names, but the actual baby, so we could have written this as:

(19) c. Susan thinks that <☺, cries a lot>

Structured meanings are just ways of dividing up the meaning-pieces of a sentence, and the two names provide us with exactly the same meaning-piece, so structured meanings don't make a difference.

To solve the problem posed by (9), it would be sufficient to let the meaning of (9a) and (9b) depend not just on the meanings of their parts (and the way they are put together), but also on the words which are used to present those meanings.[3] Going into how this would work is a pretty advanced topic, and I won't do much with it here. But the general idea could be reflected in a paraphrase for (9a) and (9b) like (20a) and (20b):

(20) a. Susan's beliefs are like what I present to you with the sentence "Noah cries a lot."
      b. Susan's beliefs are like what I present to you with the sentence "Weihan cries a lot."

To some extent, what I present to you with the sentence *Noah cries a lot* and what I present to you with the sentence *Weihan cries a lot* are the same. They both present the proposition that this particular baby cries a lot. However, in some situations it may be that I present more than this to you. For example, even though both I the speaker and you the hearer know that Noah and Weihan are the same baby, by saying *Noah cries a lot* I may be indicating that Susan would call this baby "Noah" – and not "Weihan" – when she is saying things based on the complaint that she heard: "Our baby Noah is a crabby baby who is always crying." Now, it is a radical and controversial move to allow the semantic meaning of a sentence to depend on the form of the sentence which expresses it in any other way than through the ordinary compositional rules. (It would not be controversial to allow the *speaker's* meaning of a sentence to depend on the form of the sentence which expresses it – more on this below – but the proponents of the theory I'm talking about want to say that the sentence's form is relevant to both the semantic meaning and the speaker's meaning.) It's controversial because it goes against the usual way of understanding the principle of compositionality as allowing form to be relevant to meaning only insofar as it guides the way in which pieces of meaning are put together thorough saturation, modification, or whatever. Nevertheless, the problem posed by cases like (9) is a serious one, and solving it may require radical, controversial steps.

9.5   Or, Have We Reached the Limits of Semantics?

It's obviously not an easy thing to respond in terms of the basic ideas of formal semantics to the problems we've been discussing. Though it may be possible – as we see, many people think it is – philosophers and linguists have been discussing these issues for a long time, and yet they haven't reached a clear resolution. Perhaps the reason for this is not that we're not smart enough to figure out the solution, but rather that we don't properly understand the problem. We have assumed that the difference in meaning between (9a) and (9b), and between (11a) and (11b), should be explained by semantic theory; after all, semantics is the study of meaning, and these differences have to do with meaning. However, remember that there are various sorts of meaning, most famously speaker's meaning and semantic meaning. Formal semantics is about semantic meaning, which we take to be truth-conditional meaning unless it's proven otherwise. These problems may prove otherwise. But alternatively, could (9) and (11) have to do with speaker's meaning (or some other kind of meaning besides semantic meaning) instead?[4]

The way in which a thought is expressed can certainly have a major impact on speaker's meaning. For example, by saying (21a), I can communicate that Elizabeth is English, even though the sentence is synonymous with (21b) in terms of semantic meaning:

(21) a. Elizabeth said that we should take the lift.
      b. Elizabeth said that we should take the elevator.

(It is most likely to communicate this if you know that I am not English, and speak American English, since otherwise you would think that my using the word "lift" is due to my dialect, rather than my desire to imitate hers.) Is the difference between *lift* and *elevator* in (21) like that between *Noah* and *Weihan* in (9)? In both cases, the meaning is affected by the particular word chosen, and not the semantic meaning of that word. In both cases, this meaning can only be understood by a hearer who figures out that a particular word is chosen because that is the word that the person being talked about would use: Susan would say "Noah" in describing him as a baby who cries a lot; Elizabeth would say "lift" in expressing the opinion that we should take the elevator. These are some interesting similarities. On the other hand, there is at least one difference. The special piece of meaning in (21a), "Elizabeth is English," is independent of the semantic meaning of the sentence; whether or not she is English, or would use the word "lift," has nothing to do with whether she said we should go by elevator or not. In contrast, the special piece of meaning in (9a), "Susan associates the crying Noah with the name 'Noah,'" is not independent of the sentence's semantic meaning; both the non-controversial meaning, "Susan believes that a certain baby cries a lot," and the special meaning have to do with what Susan believes, and this makes it difficult to separate the two. Still, if they can be disentangled, perhaps the correct conclusion is that some of the examples we've been worrying about have to do not with semantic meaning, but with speaker's meaning alone, and so are not relevant to semantics.

NOTES

1 Heim (1992).
2 Cresswell and von Stechow (1982).
3 See Larson and Ludlow (1993); Richard (1990). For a critique, see Soames (2002); for a paper that addresses some issues in the critique, see Ludlow (2000). Thanks to Richard Larson and Peter Ludlow for feedback on these paragraphs.
4 Some works which have advocated thinking about these problems in pragmatic terms include the books by Salmon (1986) and Soames (2002) cited earlier, as well as Barwise and Perry (1983).

10 The Pragmatics of What's Given

Though this is a book about semantics, this chapter and the next are about pragmatics. It is essential to know something about pragmatics if one is to understand semantics, for two reasons. First, it is not always clear whether a particular aspect of meaning has to do with speaker's meaning (pragmatics) or semantic meaning. Knowing a bit about pragmatics will help. Second, and more fundamentally, it turns out that semantics and pragmatics are interwoven in a way that makes it impossible to really study semantics without simultaneously doing some pragmatics, and vice versa. We've already seen this to some extent; for example, sentences with definite noun phrases (*the dog*), vague adjectives (*tall*), and modals (*must*) can't be assigned a semantic meaning without the input of contextual information. Turning things around, it is obviously impossible to figure out speakers' meanings without first understanding the literal semantic meaning of what they say. (We'll see this in more detail in chapter 11.)

These theoretical points can be seen "on the ground" in the lives of linguists today. Formal semanticists are in a way a misnamed breed, since they are all constantly and deeply involved in various aspects of pragmatics. The scholarly papers written by formal semanticists are full of such things as "discourse representations" and "context change potentials," notions having to do with the integration of semantic and pragmatic components of meaning. So, if you want to understand what formal semanticists *do*, you will need to know something about pragmatics.

This book is not going to provide much of an introduction to pragmatic meaning, but I hope that it will help you begin thinking about some of the relevant concepts. It can also serve as a guide to some of the major topics which you can study in more detail through other readings.[1]

Pragmatics is a very diverse field, incorporating all of those topics having to do with the notions of speaker's meaning and the contribution of information from outside of the linguistic code (lexicon and grammar) to meaning. One convenient way to divide up the diversity of pragmatics is roughly into the parts having to do with what you know before you hear something, and with what you know after you hear it. If I say to you *The guy I mentioned before is dangerous*, you need to know something already: which guy I mentioned before. Only if you know that can you understand what I'm trying to say. Then, given that you know who I'm talking about, after you understand the semantic meaning of what I say, you may figure that my speaker's meaning involves still more than this; perhaps you can tell that I'm warning you to stay away from that guy.[2]

"beforehand" pragmatics	→	semantics	→	"afterwards" pragmatics
Knowledge of who the guy is		The literal meaning		This is a warning!

In this chapter, I'll focus on the kind of pragmatic meaning which comes "before" semantics, and in the next chapter I'll introduce that kind of pragmatics which has to do with what comes "after."

10.1 Indexicality and Deixis

The meaning of certain words depends on the situation in which they are used. For example, the word *I* refers to me if I use it, and it refers to you if you use it. The word *you* refers to Sylvia if I'm talking to her, and to Mary if I'm talking to her. Such words are known as *indexicals*. We've already seen a number of other pieces of language which may depend for their meaning on the situation in which they are used; for example, vague adjectives like *tall*, pronouns like *she* or *he*, and definite noun phrases. Another important kind of phrase which depends on the situation of use for its meaning is the *demonstratives*, things like *that pig* or *this baby*.

We can classify all of these according to the way in which they depend on the situation for their meaning. Words like *I, you, now,* and *here*, what you might call the classic indexicals, depend on an objective non-linguistic property of the speech situation. The vague adjectives, pronouns, and definites depend on an aspect of the situation which cannot be directly observed. In some cases, it is previous linguistic context which makes clear what meaning is intended (that is, they can be anaphoric); in others, someone trying to understand what is said must infer what the speaker has in mind. The phrases like *this pig* or *that baby* often involve some sort of pointing gesture or demonstration to indicate what precisely is meant; it is for this reason they are known as "demonstratives." (Note that pronouns and definites can have demonstrative-like uses: I can point to someone and say *He is odd*, just as I can point and say *That guy is odd*.)

> - List as many classic indexicals as you can, and specify what feature of the speech situation they depend on for their meanings.
> - List as many items which, like pronouns, can be either anaphoric or depend on a hearer's ability to infer what the speaker intends.
> - List as many types of demonstratives as you can.
> - Take a letter to the editor from your favorite newspaper, and locate some examples of each of these types of context-dependent elements.

10.2   Presupposition[3]

If someone utters (1), they take for granted that John has left work early before:

(1)   John left work early again.

But of course speakers take things for granted all the time. Linguistic presupposition occurs when the utterance of a sentence tells the hearer that the speaker is taking something for granted. It seems that the presence of *again* in (1) signals what the speaker is taking for granted.

Let's have a typographical conventions for this chapter:

For any sentence S, S^P will refer to the presuppositions of S.

(2)   It stopped raining.

$(2)^P$ = the proposition that it was raining before (which is presupposed by (2)).

The presuppositions of a sentence are different from its ordinary entailments. Ordinary entailments are a function of the literal, semantic meaning of a sentence. So (2) entails (3):

(3)   There was a time (after the reference time of (2)) during which no drops of water were falling from the sky.

Though we want to say that presuppositions contrast with entailments, notice that, technically speaking, presuppositions are entailments: if (2) is true, $(2)^P$ must be true too. This shows that presuppositions are really a special species of entailment. They are entailments which are "taken for granted." This concept of being "taken for granted" is rather fuzzy, and we would do well to come up with some clearer criteria for identifying presuppositions.

Over the years, linguists have noticed that those pieces of meaning which give the feeling of being taken for granted have some special properties. They "survive" embedding in certain linguistic contexts where entailments don't "survive." For example:

Negation
(4) It didn't stop raining.

(4) is the negative version of (2). Notice that, if (4) is true, we still know that (2)^P must be true. We can say that the presupposition survives negation. But, if (4) is true, we do not know that (3) is true. The entailment does not survive negation.

(5)

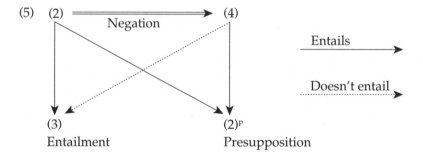

The reason for this difference between presupposition and entailment is that negation denies the semantic meaning of a sentence. For this reason, entailments (which are due to semantic meaning) don't survive negation. Negation leaves the presuppositions of a sentence intact, since they are part of pragmatic meaning, not semantic meaning.

Sometimes we talk about presupposition in terms of "inheritance" rather than "survival." We say that the presuppositions of a sentence are *inherited* by the negation of the sentence, while entailments are not. The reason for this terminology is apparent if we think about the structure of the sentence:

(6)

Think of this as an upside-down family tree. The topmost node is the child of *not* and *it stopped raining*. Likewise, *it stopped raining* is the child of *it* and *stopped raining*. By itself, *it stopped raining* presupposes that it was raining before. The child of this sentence, *it didn't stop raining* (*not* + *it stopped raining*), "inherits" the presupposition from its parent. But it doesn't inherit the entailment (3).

Other constructions allow inheritance of presuppositions too, for example:

If clauses
(7)   John left work early again, he will be fired.

Modals
(8)   Maybe John left work early again.

We can use the fact that negation, *if* clauses, and modals allow inheritance of presuppositions as a presupposition detector. Suppose we wonder whether *Noah stopped crying* presupposes anything. We can just negate it (*Noah didn't stop crying*), put it in an *if* clause (*If Noah stopped crying, we could sleep*), and modify it with a modal (*Maybe Noah stopped crying*). Notice that each of these shares with the original sentence the implication that Noah was crying before. This indicates that Noah's crying before is a presupposition.

• Use the inheritance tests to show that (1) really does presuppose that John left work early before.

This exercise has an answer, no. 10, in the appendix.

• What do the following sentences presuppose? Provide arguments using the inheritance tests.
   (a)   Mary regrets that she ate an apple.
   (b)   It was John who brought an apple to the party.
   (c)   Frank$_F$ ate an apple too.
          (α_F indicates that α is pronounced with intonational focus.)
   (d)   Frank ate$_F$ an apple too.
   (e)   Frank ate an apple$_F$ too.
   (f)   Each student from Mexico did well on the exam.
   (g)   The King of France is bald.
   (h)   Even Jill likes Frank.
• Name at least one entailment of each sentence in (a)–(h).

How do presuppositions fit into a more general view of meaning? There are two major views on this question within the modern linguistics literature:

i   *The two-component model.* Presuppositions have a special status. Sentences have two kinds of content, their ordinary semantic content and their presuppositional (pragmatic) content. (Gazdar; Karttunen and Peters)

ii *Pragmatic presupposition.* Presuppositions are admittance conditions for sentences into a context. (Stalnaker; Heim; van der Sandt)

10.2.1 The projection problem

In order to understand the differences between "the two-component model" and "pragmatic presupposition," we need to consider the primary empirical problem which has exercised presuppositionologists. We noticed already that certain constructions (negation, *if* clauses, modals) inherit the presuppositions of their parts. Do all constructions behave this way? Consider these data:

(9)   It stopped raining and then it started raining.

(10) It started raining and then it stopped raining.

(11) If it was raining, then it stopped raining by noon.

(12) If John came to the party, then it stopped raining by noon.

(13) Either it stopped raining or Mary had an umbrella.

(14) Either it stopped raining or it never was raining in the first place.

Even though all of these sentences contain *it stopped raining* as a part, it seems that only (9), (12), and (13) presuppose what *it stopped raining* presupposes: that it was raining before. Thus we cannot say that presuppositions are always inherited. The issue of which constructions inherit the presuppositions of their parts and which do not is called the *projection problem for presuppositions.*

10.2.2 The inheritance rule approach

Karttunen and Peters[4] follow the two-component model of meaning; they claim that every phrase or sentence is associated with both an ordinary semantic meaning and a secondary pragmatic meaning (what they call *conventional implicature*, which for our purposes we can identify with presupposition). When syntactic rules combine phrases or sentences to create larger phrases or sentences, there are correlated rules which determine what the ordinary meaning and presuppositions of the new phrase or sentence are. For example:

(15)   a.   <u>Semantic rule for negation</u>
$\| \text{it is not the case that } \varphi \| = $ the set of worlds not in the set $\| \varphi \|$
       b.   <u>Presupposition rule for negation</u>
$(\text{it is not the case that } \varphi)^P = \varphi^P$

The double lines in (15a) are used to indicate "the proposition expressed by" what's inside, so this says that, semantically, a negative sentence is true in all those worlds in which the non-negative sentence is not true. (15b) says that the presupposition of a negative sentence is the same as the presupposition of the corresponding positive sentence.

Conjunction is more complicated. First we take three simple sentences, (16)–(18), and note whether they have any (relevant) presuppositions.[5]

(16)   John arrived on time too.

(16)^P Someone else arrived on time.

(17)   Mary arrived on time.

(17)^P (none relevant)

(18)   Mary is happy.

(18)^P (none relevant)

Next, let's think about some complex sentences built out of these simple ones using *and*.

(19)   Mary is happy, and John arrived on time too.
       "(18) and (16)"

(19)^P = (16)^P.

(20)   Mary arrived on time, and John arrived on time too.
        "(17) and (16)"

(20)^P (none)

Sentence (19) inherits the presupposition (16)^P that somebody other than John arrived on time. (*Too* can have other meanings here; for example, we may feel that arriving on time implies being happy, and so *too* informs us that John is happy in addition to Mary. But we want to focus on the presupposition "someone else arrived on time." That (19) presupposes this can be made more apparent by putting it into context. Earlier I told you that Bill arrived on time. Now I tell you "Mary is happy, and John arrived on time too.") Why doesn't (20) inherit this presupposition as well? Intuitively, (20) doesn't presuppose that someone arrived on time because the first clause, *Mary arrived on time*, already informs us of this fact. That is, the first part of (20) entails the presupposition of the second part, and so it is not presupposed. So we can formulate the inheritance rule this way:

(21) $(\varphi \ \& \ \psi)^P = \varphi^P$ plus as much of ψ^P presupposes as can't be deduced
        from the semantic meaning of φ.

This projection rule approach to presupposition has some problems (examples from Soames, with minor variations).

(22)   a.   There is no king of France.
        b.   Therefore, the king of France isn't in hiding.

(23)   I regret/realize that I haven't told the truth.

(23)^P I haven't told the truth.

(24)   If I regret that I haven't told the truth, I will confess it to everyone.

(25)   If I realize that I haven't told the truth, I will confess it to everyone.

A definite noun phrase like *the king of France* presupposes that there is a unique salient reference – in this case that there is a king of France. Therefore, according to Karttunen and Peters's theory, (22b) should presuppose that there is a king of France, but it doesn't. Both (24) and

(25) should presuppose that I haven't told the truth (because they put (23), which by itself presupposes that I haven't told the truth, into an *if . . . then* sentence, which follows inheritance rule (21), but only the former really does. We need to look for some new ideas to help us understand presupposition better.

10.2.3 The cancellation approach

Gazdar[6] and Soames suggest that we need to distinguish between *potential presuppositions* of a sentence and *actual presuppositions*. A sentence inherits all of the potential presuppositions of its parts, but some of these may be canceled by other information present in the conversation. A presupposition will only become actual if nothing else undoes it. For example, if (22a) is uttered before (22b), the potential presupposition of (22b) that there is a king of France is canceled. Similarly, (25) suggests that I am unsure whether I have told the truth. (Question: how does it suggest this?) This cancels the potential presupposition (23)[P] of the sentence, since I can't be taking for granted that which I am unsure of.

The cancellation approach has problems with some data too. For example (from Soames):

(26)   If all the Smith brothers have children, then John Smith's children will probably inherit the family fortune.

Example (26) has a potential presupposition that John Smith has children. There is no apparent reason to cancel this presupposition. Even though saying *If all of the Smith brothers have children* indicates that the speaker doesn't know whether all the Smith brother has children, this doesn't conflict with the idea that John Smith has children. And yet the sentence as a whole does not presuppose that John Smith has children.

This example works out fine on the Karttunen and Peters approach, by the way. Since *all the Smith brothers have children* entails that John Smith has children, inheritance rule (21) implies that the presupposition in not inherited.

Another difficulty is that not all presuppositions seem cancelable:

(27)   ??John came to the party too, though nobody else did.

Both the inheritance rule approach and the cancellation approach work well for many examples, but seem unable to account for all of the data.

This is why the two-component model of presupposition is no longer in much favor among linguists who study presupposition. (However, the research done in terms of these theories uncovered most of the important data on presupposition which we know about today. This shows that a lot of good can come out of working on a theory which is ultimately proven wrong.)

10.2.4 Pragmatic presupposition

Pragmatic presupposition takes presuppositions to be conditions on whether a sentence can be admitted into a conversational context. That is, if we think of language use as a kind of game, presuppositions tell us whether a particular move in the game is currently allowed.[7]

Some concepts invented by Stalnaker:[8]

(28) <u>Common Ground (CG)</u>
      The set of propositions which the participants in a conversation agree to be uncontroversial for the purposes of this conversation.

(29) <u>Context Set (C)</u>
      The set of possible worlds in which every proposition in the Common Ground is true.

For example, in a particular conversation the participants have agreed on three facts: it's raining, Mary is in the room, and Shelby is a nice dog. They know these things because they can see that they are true. (This is a phony example, since the participants in any real conversation will always agree on much more than this, at least implicitly. But we need to keep the example simple so I can draw pictures.)

(30) CG = {The proposition that it is raining, the proposition that Mary is in the room, the proposition that Shelby is a nice dog}

In these terms, the Context Set C is the set of possible worlds – that is, the proposition – in which it is raining AND Mary is in the room AND Shelby is a nice dog.

(31) C = the set of worlds in which it is raining and Mary is in the room and Shelby is a nice dog.

See diagram 49.

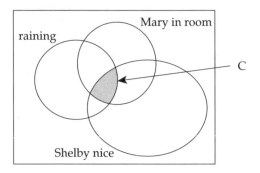

Diagram 49

The notions of Common Ground and Context Set provide us with some ability to talk about the state of a conversation at a given point in time. The Common Ground and Context Set in diagram 49 indicate the state of our hypothetical conversation. And in terms of these notions, we can explain the idea that presuppositions are conditions on whether a sentence is admissible into a conversation. In general, the theory of pragmatic presuppositions says that a presupposition is a statement of the form: "Sentence S can only be used in C if..." For example, the sentence *HANNIBAL is a nice dog too* presupposes that some other dog is nice:[9]

(32)   For any Context Set C, *HANNIBAL is a nice dog too* can only be used in C if C entails that some other dog is nice.

Given the Common Ground in (30), the sentence *HANNIBAL is a nice dog too* can be used, since the Context Set illustrated in (31) entails that some other dog (namely Shelby) is nice.

10.2.5   Accommodation

What happens if a sentence is uttered in a context which does not satisfy its presupposition? For example, you've been working inside all day and have no idea that it had been raining. I come in and the first thing I say is (33):

(33)   It stopped raining.

The legalistic line to take would be to object: "But you haven't said that it was raining!" But nobody behaves this way. Unless you wish to dispute the idea that it was raining, the cooperative thing to do in such a situation is to act as if the proposition that it was raining had been in the Common Ground, discreetly adding it and moving on. This process, discussed carefully by Lewis, has been labeled *presupposition accommodation*.

Accommodation serves the end of allowing conversations to proceed more smoothly, allowing the conversation not to get hung up on having to establish explicitly every uncontroversial background assumption. But it also sometimes allows a speaker to subtly insinuate a controversial proposition into the Common Ground (*My opponent is not telling the truth again!* or *When did you stop embezzling money?*).

An important issue for accommodation theory is the fact that not all presuppositions seem to be equally accommodatable. For example, the following are very odd out of the blue, with no information on who else arrived late or who the woman is:

(34) Mary arrived late too.

(35) The woman likes beans.

10.2.6 Context change potential and presupposition projection

Irene Heim[10] and others have tried to derive the presupposition inheritance properties of various constructions within the general framework of the theory of pragmatic presupposition. A fundamental idea which comes out of this project is that the meaning of a sentence is the instructions it provides as to how to update the Common Ground. On this perspective, the meaning of a sentence is its *context change potential*. A semantic theory which incorporates this notion of meaning as context change potential is often called a theory of *dynamic semantics*.[11] Dynamic semantics can be opposed to *static semantics*, which is what we've been doing so far in this book. Because it lets us integrate meaning below the sentence level with meaning above the sentence level, many semanticists would argue that the advent of dynamic semantics represents one of the most important advances in semantic theory since formal semantics originated in the 1960s and 1970s. As we'll see, dynamic semantics lets us understand presupposition much better.

Within a dynamic approach to meaning, we need a way of adding a sentence to the evolving conversation. Framing her principle in terms of the Context Set, Heim uses what we can call the basic rule. The basic rule tells us that the context change potential of a sentence S is: when you update a Context Set C with S, discard from C all of those worlds in which S is not true.

(36)   For any Context Set C and simple sentence S, C + S = C ∩ ∥S∥.

"C ∩ ∥S∥" is the intersection of C with the proposition expressed by S. Since the Context Set C is defined as the intersection of the propositions in the Common Ground, this is equivalent to saying that the proposition expressed by S is added to the Common Ground. That is, it becomes a proposition which the participants in the conversation take as uncontroversial. Notice that the context change potential for a sentence S is based on the proposition it expresses, ∥S∥. This proposition is the sentence's static meaning, so all the work we've done in understanding static meaning in terms of propositions is not wasted.

Diagram 50 shows how the interpretation of *Shelby likes bones* would work, given a Common Ground in which it is presupposed that it's raining, that Mary is in the room, and that Shelby is nice.

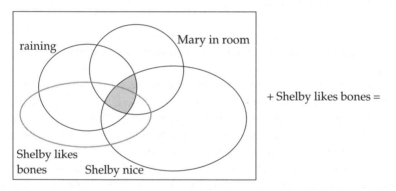

+ Shelby likes bones =

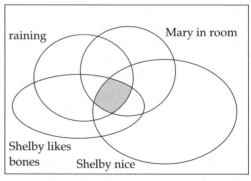

Diagram 50

The basic rule says that when you add a simple sentence to a conversation, you take the current Context Set and toss out all of those worlds in which the sentence is not true. So, in the example illustrated, we start off with the Context Set "It's raining AND Mary is in the room AND Shelby is nice." In this Context Set, there are worlds in which Shelby likes bones, and worlds in which he doesn't. When somebody says *Shelby likes bones*, the old Context Set has to lose those worlds in which he doesn't like bones, giving us the new Context Set. We're now ready for this extremely dull conversation to continue. The next sentences which enters is a conjunction, (37).

The conjunction rule
(37)   Shelby ate a bone and Hannibal ate a bone too.

(38)   For any Context Set C and conjoined sentence φ *and* ψ, C + (φ and ψ) = ((C + φ) + ψ).

(39)   C + *Shelby ate a bone and Hannibal ate a bone too* = ((C + *Shelby ate a bone*) + *Hannibal ate a bone too*).

We want to add the sentence (37) to some Context Set C. Since (37) contains *and*, rule (38) tells us that the way to do this is to first add *Shelby ate a bone* and then add *Hannibal ate a bone too*. So we start out with some Context Set C. Then we follow rule (36) and add *Shelby ate a bone*. We toss out all of those worlds in which Shelby did not eat a bone, giving us a new Context Set (let's call it C*). Now we're ready to add *Hannibal ate a bone too*. This sentence has a presupposition: it can only be added to C* if C* entails that some other dog besides Hannibal ate a bone. Fortunately, C* does entail this – we know that it does, because we just made C* by adding *Shelby ate a bone* to C.

Notice that we have just explained Karttunen and Peters's presupposition projection rule for conjunction. According to Karttunen and Peters, sentence (37) does not presuppose that some other dog besides Hannibal is nice because the first conjunct, *Shelby ate a bone*, entails this presupposition. This projection rule works right, but it is just stipulated; we have no idea why it works. On the other hand, in terms of the pragmatic presupposition theory, we can see why sentence (37) presupposes what it does. There is no need for the participants in the conversation to take it for granted in the original context C that some other dog besides Shelby ate a bone. This is so because the first part of (38), *Shelby ate a bone*, gets into the Context Set before we have to worry about the presupposition and takes care of it for us. You could say that the presupposition is handled through the internal workings of rule (38).

Notice that if the first conjunct did not entail the presupposition of the second (as in (40)), or if the presupposition came from the first conjunct (as in (41)), this reasoning would not apply. In these cases, the presupposition would not be handled internally. The only way that the sentence with the presupposition could be admitted into the context would be if the participants in the conversation already took the presupposition for granted from the start. Thus, (40) and (41) both presuppose that some other dog besides Hannibal ate a bone:

(40)   It is raining, and Hannibal ate a bone too.

(41)   Hannibal ate a bone too, and Shelby also ate a bone.

Explain how these sentences are added to the Context Set in step-by-step fashion.

This exercise has an answer, no. 11, in the appendix.

I hope that this discussion has given you a taste for how presupposition can be studied from the perspective of dynamic semantics and the theory of pragmatic presupposition.

10.3   Speech Acts

The theory of speech acts develops from Austin's[12] observation that the meaning of many sentences does not seem particularly tied up with their judging the world to be a certain way; rather, what's crucial about them seems to be that they have a certain kind of effect on the world (on the speaker, hearer, or social environment):

(42)   I now declare you man and wife.

(43)   I hereby warn you not to come onto my property again!

(44)   I promise.

Austin sets up a distinction between sentences of this type, *performatives*, and sentences whose meaning involves describing the world as being a certain way, *constatives*.

There's nothing magical about the words in (42)–(44), and so in order for them to have an effect on the world, performatives must be embedded into a social context that gives them the power to affect the world. Only when performatives are rightly used, in terms of this context, can they have a performative effect. These extralinguistic conditions which must be satisfied, if a sentence is to function as a performative, are its *felicity conditions*. For example, for (42) to work:[13]

i a. There must be a conventional procedure (the "ceremony") for getting people to be married. (This is partially specified by relevant laws, but otherwise it's pretty complex. We have concepts like being married "in the Catholic church," which adds its own requirements.)

b. The circumstances and people involved in the ceremony must be appropriate (i.e., the people must be free to marry, the official performing the ceremony must have the right to do so, etc.).

ii The ceremony must be correctly and completely executed.

iii The people involved must have appropriate thoughts (e.g. one must understand what one is promising in the wedding ceremony).

Felicity conditions are essentially presuppositions within the realm of performatives. In fact, ordinary presuppositions for constatives are sometimes called felicity conditions too.

Most people find the concept of a performative pretty intuitive. To accept the concept is to step on a slippery slope, however, as Austin knew well. Once we get into the habit of thinking about the fact that in using language we perform actions of various kinds, the conceptual distinction between performative and constative seems to break down. Consider (45), an example one would probably consider a clear constative:

(45) That dog is cute.

Still, don't I, in fact, do a variety of things by uttering this sentence? I *utter* some sounds. I *express* the proposition that Shelby is cute (assuming that, in the context, *that dog* refers to Shelby). I *assert* that Shelby is cute. The assertion in particular is quite parallel to the kind of actions we saw in (42)–(44) above. This point is made clear by the idea of dynamic semantics that meaning is context change potential. To assert something is to add it to the Common Ground, and that certainly sounds like an action.

> What about questions and imperatives? Can we think of them in a way similar to (45)?
>
> • Who did you see at the party?
> • Eat your beans!

Austin's more general theory of speech acts, elaborated on by Searle[14] and others, distinguishes three kinds of acts which can be associated with any utterance:

i The <u>locutionary act</u>: phonetics, phonology, syntax, semantics. The utterance of certain sounds, in a certain linguistic system (of sound and form), expressing a particular proposition.
ii The <u>illocutionary act</u>: the communicative action which the speaker intends to perform by getting the hearer to understand that this is his (the speaker's) intention.
iii The <u>perlocutionary act</u>: the effects which the speaker brings about *by means of* the locutionary and illocutionary acts.

For example, with (45) the locutionary act is to say those words, in a certain structure, expressing the proposition that Shelby is cute. The illocutionary act might be to assert this proposition. A perlocutionary act performed by this sentence might be to convince the hearer to dog-sit Shelby while his owner goes out of town during Christmas break.

We can speak of a sentence's illocutionary *force*. For example, (45) has the force of assertion. Illocutionary force is often seen as a semantic/pragmatic object which is a component of the sentence's overall meaning. Searle, for example, claims that sentences typically are divided into two parts: a force indicator (which expresses the force) and a propositional part (which has a truth-conditional meaning).

It can be pretty hard to tell the difference between illocutionary and perlocutionary force. According to Austin, a rule of thumb is that the illocutionary force is what the speaker does *in* saying the sentence, and the perlocutionary force is what she does *by* saying it. But this is pretty vague. Perhaps the best way of making precise the difference is to say that the illocutionary act is the one giving rise to the sentence's *Gricean non-natural meaning*.[15]

Grice's theory of meaning is complicated, and this book is not the place to learn all of its details. The basic idea is that non-natural meaning is present whenever a speaker wants to have some communicative effect on a hearer, and tries to achieve this effect by saying something which will let the hearer figure out, using his or her knowledge of the language among other things, that this is what the speaker wants. So for example, I say *Sit down!* with the aim of getting you to know that you need to sit down, on the assumption that you'll use your knowledge of English to figure out what the sentence means and then determine that I probably said this sentence because I want you to sit down. In that case, we could say that the non-natural meaning of the sentence is that you should sit down. If I know that you hate being told what to do, and I said *Sit down!* in order to annoy you, this would probably not be non-natural meaning. My annoying you would be part of the sentence's perlocutionary effect, but it would not be part of the illocutionary meaning. It would not be non-natural meaning because I don't intend that you become annoyed by recognizing that I want you to become annoyed – I intend that you become annoyed because you think that I'm telling you what to do.

By the way, non-natural meaning contrasts with *natural* meaning. Natural meaning comes about when information is present in a way that doesn't involve any communicative intentions on anyone's part. For example, the honeybees' dance – when honeybees move in certain very complex ways and thereby give other bees the ability to locate a food source – has natural meaning, not non-natural meaning, because the bees don't have any intention to communicate with the other bees.

The classification of speech acts into three levels (locutionary, illocutionary, perlocutionary) raises many questions. Many of these pertain to *indirect speech acts*, speech acts where the illocutionary force is not revealed in the sentence's form in any clear way. For example, we tend to think of declaratives as being associated with the illocutionary force of asserting. However, consider this example:

(46)   I'd like for you to sit down now.

This sentence has the form of a declarative. But its illocutionary force, in this context, is that of requesting or perhaps ordering. The usual conclusion is that illocutionary force is largely or purely a pragmatic matter. It must be recoverable somehow from a sentence's context and form, but it need not be encoded in the form. This leaves scholars interested in speech acts with plenty to do.

Though it seems correct that illocutionary force must be ultimately a pragmatic matter, we don't want to go too far in the direction of saying that formal matters are irrelevant. The pattern of *sentence types* – declarative, interrogative, imperative, etc. – within a language does seem linked with the notion of illocutionary force. Interrogatives seem to fundamentally have to do with the force of asking, imperatives with those of ordering or requesting, and declaratives with that of asserting. But they are not exclusively linked with these forces, as examples like (46) make clear. We need to distinguish a sentence's *sentential force* (or *sentence mood*),[16] the force indicated by its form (in particular, its sentence type), from its ultimate illocutionary force. The sentential force of (46) would be that of assertion, even though its illocutionary force is most like requesting or ordering. Notice that there are many more illocutionary forces than sentential forces. The three clause types of *declarative, interrogative,* and *imperative* seem to be universal. There are other, "minor" clause types, like exclamatives and optatives, in some languages. But even all of these do not match the diversity of illocutionary acts, which include promising, threatening, hinting, proposing, denying, . . .

> Do you have any ideas on why every language has a sentence type for questions, namely interrogatives, while very few languages have a sentence type for promises (though some do, e.g. Korean), and (as far as I know) none does for threats? Does it seem likely that there is a pragmatic explanation for this pattern, or is it more plausibly based in syntax and/or semantics?

The recent trend of dynamic semantics discussed in connection with the pragmatic theory of presupposition (that is, the trend toward theories which view meaning as context change potential) offers an interesting way of looking at the notions of sentential and illocutionary force.[17] We've already seen that the context change potential for a declarative provides a model of assertion as the addition of a proposition to the Common Ground. It seems reasonable to pursue parallel analyses for other sentential forces, so that the sentential force of an interrogative is to add a question meaning (a set of answers, cf. chapter 1) to a question list[18] and the sentential force of an imperative is to add an imperative meaning (a proposition or perhaps a property[19]) to a requirement list.[20] This approach suggests that traditional speech act theory is based on an outmoded view of semantics. Static meanings could be relegated to the level of locutionary force, with the illocutionary and perlocutionary levels being of a purely pragmatic nature. In contrast, dynamic meanings exist right on the border line between semantics and pragmatics; they integrate semantic and pragmatic aspects of meaning, and as a consequence they become useful for understanding sentential, and perhaps even illocutionary, force.

10.4   Focus and Topic

Another area of pragmatics which is closely related to semantics concerns the ways in which speakers can indicate how what they are saying fits into the larger conversation. For example, if Nick says (47a), and Julie replies (47b), it is likely that Julie will emphasize the word *Oakland*, indicating that this is where she disagrees with what Nick said:

(47)   a.   Nick: My parents' flight is landing at San Francisco airport.
       b.   Julie: No, they're arriving in OAKLAND.

The type of emphasis indicated here with all caps is known as *intonational focus*, as mentioned earlier.

Another related pragmatic construction is *topic*. Some languages have the ability to indicate in the form of a sentence what the sentence is "about." English has only a marginal ability to do this (see (48)); Japanese provides a better example (as in (49)):[21]

(48)   As for John, he's waiting in the next room.

(49)   Jon   wa   kafe   de   onna-no-hito   ni   aimashita.
       John   TOP   café   at   woman   to   met
       Kanojo wa   pianisuto   deshita.
       She   TOP   pianist   was
       "John met a woman at a café. She was a pianist."

Sentence (49) contains two sentences, and each of them contains a word followed by *wa*. These *wa*s indicate that the preceding word refers to the topic of the sentence, so that the first sentence is felt to be about John, and the second about the woman he met.

Like recent research on presupposition, topic and especially focus lie in the region where semantics and pragmatics overlap. I will illustrate this point with regard to focus (since semanticists still don't understand the semantics and pragmatics of topic all that well). Focus can have a great many apparently different functions. The primary one seems to be pragmatic, marking presuppositions:

(50)   MARY likes Joe. *presupposes* Somebody likes Joe.
Mary likes JOE. *presupposes* Mary likes somebody.

However, in some sentences it contributes to semantic meaning. The pairs of sentences in (51)–(52) differ in their truth-conditions, that is in their semantics:[22]

(51)   a.   In St Petersburg, OFFICERS always danced with ballerinas.
b.   In St Petersburg, officers always danced with BALLERINAS.

(52)   a.   I only eat FISH.
b.   I only EAT fish.

Example (52a) entails that I don't eat beef, chicken, lamb, pork, etc., while (52b) entails that I don't catch fish, train fish, study fish, etc. These are differences in semantic meaning.

Moreover, as we saw already in (47), focus can tell us how a sentence fits into a larger text. With the question in (53), (a) is a natural reply, but (b) is odd. The situation is reversed in (54).

(53)   Who went to the party?
a.   MAX went to the party.
b.   ??Max went to the PARTY.

(54)   Where did Max go?
a.   ??MAX went to the party.
b.   Max went to the PARTY.

The essential meaning of focus is to indicate that what the speaker said is drawn from a set of possibilities he or she might have said. So, by putting the focus on *fish* in (52a), a speaker indicates that a number of things might have been mentioned: beef, chicken, lamb, pork, fish, etc. This implies that she might have said that she eats beef, or that she eats chicken, or that she eats lamb, or that she eats pork, or that she eats fish, etc. We can then easily understand the meaning of *only*. *Only* says that of all these things that she might have said, the only true one is that she eats fish.

(55)

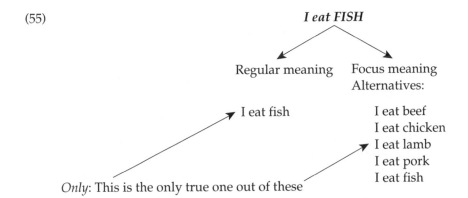

Here we see semantics and pragmatics thoroughly intertwined.

NOTES

1   Here are a few references to begin such a project with: Davis (1991); Green (1996); Kadmon (2001); Levinson (1983).

2   This picture is certainly too simple. For example, perhaps I mentioned several guys earlier, and only after you see what I'm saying (that I'm calling some guy dangerous) can you figure out which of them is the one I intend to refer to with *the guy I mentioned earlier*. However, this simple way of thinking about matters is good enough for getting started.

3   A good source on theories of presupposition up until the 1980s is Soames (1989). A good deal of my discussion is inspired by his presentation.

4   Karttunen and Peters (1979).

5   Presupposition is extremely pervasive in language. If you look hard enough, you can find presuppositions for every sentence. What additional presuppositions can you detect in these simple examples?

6   Gazdar (1979).

7   The idea of understanding presupposition in terms of the metaphor of a game comes from Lewis (1979).

8   Stalnaker (1974; 1978).

9   Printing HANNIBAL in all capital letters is meant to suggest that it is pronounced with what is called "intonational focus." This pronunciation can informally be called "emphasis."

10   Heim (1982; 1990).

11   Hans Kamp (1981) brought the fundamental ideas of dynamic semantics into linguistics at about the same time as Heim. Kamp's theory is called "discourse representation theory," while Heim's is known as "file change semantics." Since the original work of Kamp and Heim, a variety of other approaches to dynamic semantics has been developed.

12   Austin (1962).
13   This discussion is to some extent modeled on that of Levinson (1983).
14   For example, see Searle (1969; 1975a; 1975b).
15   See, for example: Grice (1957); Searle (1965).
16   See Chierchia and McConnell-Ginet (2000) and Reis (1999) for further discussion of these terms.
17   Some works which can help you start studying this topic: Hamblin (1971); Stalnaker (1978); Lewis (1979); Hausser (1980); Gazdar (1981); Ginzburg (1995a; 1995b); Portner (forthcoming).
18   Ginzburg (1995a; 1995b).
19   Hausser (1980).
20   Lewis (1979); Han (1998); Portner (forthcoming).
21   From Portner and Yabushita (1998). See also Reinhart (1982).
22   From Rooth (1985). This discussion of focus is based on Rooth's theory. See also: Rooth (1992); Jacobs (1983); von Stechow (1991).

11 The Pragmatics of Inference

Speaker's meaning is not always the same as semantic meaning. This is so even taking into account all of the ways in which context can contribute to semantic meaning (some of which were outlined in the previous chapter). It is obvious that, in many situations, people don't mean just what they literally say. They may mean what they literally say plus some more besides, or they may mean something which is altogether different from what they literally say. For example, in situations which you can easily imagine, the following utterances have speaker's meanings not identical to their truth-conditions:

(1) I'm not hungry.
    Speaker's meaning: I'm not hungry so let's not eat right now.

(2) I would pay $100 for that vase.
    Speaker's meaning: I would pay $100 for that vase, but I would not pay much more than $100 for that vase.

The theory of *conversational implicature* says that the differences between semantic meaning and speaker's meaning can be calculated on the basis of a well-defined set of principles. The concept of implicature was introduced by Grice,[1] and his ideas about the topic are still the best known. The core of Grice's theory of implicature is the cooperative principle:[2]

Cooperative principle:
Speaker's meanings should be calculable on the basis of the assumption that speakers are behaving rationally and cooperatively.

Our goal in this chapter is to see how the cooperative principle can be useful in helping to understand how speaker's meaning may diverge from semantic meaning.

For the cooperative principle to be useful, we need to know what it is to be rational and cooperative. Grice tries to make this explicit through a series of conversational maxims:

- The maxim of <u>quality</u>: make your contribution one that is true.
- The maxim of <u>quantity</u>:
    a.   make your contribution as informative as is required for current purposes of the exchange;
    b.   do not make your contribution more informative than is required.
- The maxim of <u>relevance</u>: make your contributions relevant.
- The maxim of <u>manner</u>: be perspicuous, and specifically avoid obscurity, avoid ambiguity, be brief, and be orderly.

It is easy to misunderstand what the maxims are all about. They are not *rules* to be followed. Instead, they are commonplace *assumptions* people make about how speakers are behaving. As much as possible, hearers will construe the speaker's meaning of an utterance so that it conforms to the maxims. A speaker can count on this and thereby communicate more than the literal meaning of a sentence. Moreover, since a speaker knows that a hearer will interpret what she or he says as conforming with the maxims, she or he must speak in a way that takes account of this fact, or risk being misunderstood, and so cannot fail to conform with the maxims (putting aside truly pathological cases). So the way to think of the maxims is not as parallel to explicit laws like traffic regulations, which can be violated at the risk of sanctions. Rather they are more like the convention of shaking hands with a person you meet for the first time (or whatever is the appropriate convention in your culture). The "maxim" is something like "shake hands to initiate a friendly interaction." People assume you will follow this maxim, and so if you do not shake hands, they will think you are being unfriendly. Because you know that people will interpret your actions this way, you have to shake hands if you don't want to be seen as unfriendly. Your only alternative is to explicitly opt out of the maxim ("I can't shake your hand because I have been sick"), a possibility which exists with the Gricean maxims as well.

Based on these maxims, implicatures may arise in two ways. A simple assumption that a speaker is following the maxims may lead to a conclusion about what she or he means. For example, (3b) implicates that Jim does not know whether it's raining:

(3)   a.   Bob: Is it raining right now?
      b.   Jim: It might be raining.

This implicature follows mainly from the maxims of quantity and quality. Once Bob has asked whether it's raining, it is clearly relevant in this conversation whether it is raining or not. Quantity says that Jim should therefore tell Bob that it's raining or that it isn't. But Jim did not do so. The reason for this must be that Jim cannot confidently provide the required information, since by the maxim of quality, he should not say that it's raining if he is not confident it is, and he should not say that it isn't raining if he is not confident it isn't. Therefore, Bob can conclude that Jim is not in a position to say whether it's raining or not. In other words, he does not know whether it is raining.

Implicature may also arise from the *flouting* of a maxim. This occurs when it is obvious that the literal meaning of what is said does not conform to a maxim, and the hearer must find some alternative speaker's meaning to maintain the assumption of cooperation. For example:

(4)   a.   Bob: I flunked out of law school.
       b.   Jim: That's life.

Literally speaking, (4b) is obviously true and so uninformative. It therefore seems to violate quantity. Since Bob knows that Jim is aware that what he said literally violates quantity, and assumes that Jim is cooperative and following the maxims, he concludes that Jim must not mean what he literally said. Bob must therefore seek some alternative speaker's meaning to attribute to Jim. In this case, *That's life* is a kind of idiom, and it carries a conventional alternative speaker's meaning, something like "Since life is full of bad things, accept this and other similar bad things without getting upset."

Note that people who study implicature get *very precise* about how the maxims (or some updated version thereof), in combination with semantic meaning, generate implicatures about speaker's meanings. It's not just a matter of saying maxim X leads to implicature Y. Though the exact format varies depending on the form of the maxims, it goes something like this:[3]

(5)   It's possible that there's life on Mars.
       Speaker's meaning: It's not certain that there's life on Mars.

    i   S uttered *It's possible that there's life on Mars* to H.
    ii   S is not acting in a play, under the influence of drugs, or the like;
          S knows that H speaks English, is attending to what he says, etc.;

S knows that H knows all of this. And so S is apparently speaking with the intention to mean something by the utterance.

iii   By the cooperative principle, H can assume that S is behaving rationally and cooperatively.

iv   One aspect of behaving rationally and cooperatively is conformity with the maxim of quality.

v   The semantic meaning of S's utterance is that it is possible (perhaps certain) that there's life on Mars.

vi   There is no reason to believe that S is flouting quality by speaking ironically or the like.

vii   Therefore, H can conclude that S intends to communicate that it is possible (perhaps certain) that there's life on Mars.

viii   Another aspect of behaving rationally and cooperatively is conformity with quantity maxim (a).

ix   So H can assume that S intends to provide as much information as is required for purposes of the exchange.

x   S and H are discussing whether there is life on Mars. For these purposes, it is cooperative (by quantity (a)) for S to give all information pertaining to how likely it is that there is life on Mars.

xi   If S believes that it is certain that there is life on Mars, this is relevant.

xii   Therefore if S believed that it was certain that there is life on Mars, he would have said *It is certain that there is life on Mars*, or the equivalent.

xiii   S did not say *It is certain that there is life on Mars*, or the equivalent.

xiv   Therefore, H can conclude that S does not believe that it is certain that there is life on Mars.

xv   All of this reasoning is pretty easy, and so H can assume that S expects for H to go through this reasoning.

xvi   Therefore H can conclude that S intends to communicate that it is not certain that there is life on Mars.

xvii   Steps vii and xvi together allow H to conclude finally that S intends to communicate that it's possible, and not certain, that there's life on Mars.

How does the speaker's meaning of (1) and (2) arise from the cooperative principle and maxims?

11.1   Properties of Implicature

Because implicatures arise, in a specific, calculable way, from the assumption of cooperativeness, they have certain important properties that distinguish them from entailments (which are due to the semantic meaning of a sentence) and presuppositions.

11.1.1   Calculability and non-conventionality

The central idea of Grice's theory is that conversational implicatures can be derived, or calculated, from the semantics of what is said, plus the cooperative principle and maxims. Because of this, they do not have to be learned independently. They are not *conventional* in the sense of being arbitrary, learned associations between form and meaning. In contrast, the semantic meaning of *dog* is conventional. The connection between the form *dog* and the property of being a dog is arbitrary, and you just have to learn it. In general, if you can provide an explanation in terms of the cooperative principle for how some piece of meaning arises, it's a good guess that it's an implicature and not semantics or presupposition.

> Is presupposition more like semantic meaning or more like implicature with regard to calculability and non-conventionality? Think about the presupposition of *the dog*. Does the fact that it presupposes that a unique most salient dog exists seem like an arbitrary fact about its meaning, or one that can be derived from the phrase's semantics? This is a hard question.

11.1.2   Cancellability (or defeasibility)

Implicatures can be cancelled, unlike entailments and (at least some) presuppositions:

(6)   I ate two apples.
      Entailment: I ate at least one apple.
      Implicature: I didn't eat three apples.

      ??I ate two apples, but I didn't eat one. (Failed cancellation of entailment)
      I ate two apples, and in fact I ate three. (Cancellation of implicature)

Implicatures can be canceled because the reasoning which leads to them can be undermined by additional information. Take (6) as an example: The implicature that I didn't eat three apples arises as follows: the hearer reasons that, if the speaker ate three apples, this would be just as relevant as the fact that she ate two. So, by quantity, she would have said that she ate three apples. But she did not say this. The hearer concludes that if the speaker ate three apples, she is not in conformity with the maxims in any simple way. The hearer also knows that the speaker knows that the hearer would reason this way, and so can conclude that the speaker must intend to communicate that she did not eat three apples. (Take a deep breath.) Notice that part of this reasoning is the premise that the speaker did not say that she ate three apples. But in the utterance where the implicature is canceled, *I ate two apples, and in fact I ate three*, she did say that she ate three apples! Therefore, the reasoning which leads to the implicature is undermined.

11.1.3   Non-detachability

Implicatures don't arise from the specific form of an utterance, but rather from its semantic meaning as a whole, plus the context and cooperativeness assumptions. This implies that if you say the same thing in a different way, it will have the same implicatures.

(7)   It's dark in this room.
      There's no light in here.
      I can't see anything.

All of these will implicate, in the right situation, that you should turn the light on. In contrast, the presupposition in (8) arises because of the presence of *again*. You can get rid of the presupposition simply by removing *again*.

(8)   Mary left again.

Although there is an intuitive difference between the implicature of (7) and the presupposition of (8), non-detachability can be a hard property to work with. Suppose you wanted to use the principle of non-detachability to check whether the idea that Mary has left before in (8) is a presupposition or an implicature. You would need to find some other sentences with the same semantic content as (8), and see whether they also indicate that Mary has left before. But what would be such a sentence? Would (9) do?

(9)   Mary left.

We can't know whether (8) and (9) are synonymous unless we've already determined that the contribution of *again* is pragmatic or semantic. But how could we know this without determining whether the piece of meaning "Mary left before" is a presupposition? Thus, calculability and cancellability provide a better basis for identifying implicatures.[4]

NOTES

1   Grice (1975).
2   This summary is modified from Levinson (1983).
3   Example from Levinson (1983).
4   For a critical discussion of tests for implicature, see Sadock (1978).

12 Formal Semantics Today

I think of this book as doing something like offering you a walk along the beach with a marine biologist. I tell you what I think about the shells, plants, and little sea creatures we find along the way – ugly, pretty, and strange ones. With such a walk, you may learn something about sea life. But once night falls, there are no more seashells to look at, so we relax at a beach-side bar, and I turn to telling you what the world of marine biologists is like.

What is the world of formal semanticists like? We study all of the topics discussed in this book and many more. I've tried to convey the main assumptions about meaning which we all consider fundamental. Certainly, not every formal semanticist agrees with everything presented in this book. There is even disagreement on some of the basic points (though in general a semanticist who disagrees with the basic points would have to work under the assumption that most other semanticists agree with them). In this chapter I'd like to outline some of the diversity within formal semantics on the basic question of how the meaning of sentences is to be understood.

Formal semanticists exist in an intellectual world full of relationships with other fields of scholarship, both connections to and conflicts with. In this chapter, I'd also like to explain some of these relationships.

12.1 Diversity within Formal Semantics

Theories of formal semantics are non-psychologistic: meanings are not concepts, but rather things outside of us, "in the world" in some sense. (As I mentioned in chapter 1, this does not imply that the nature of our concepts is irrelevant to formal semantics, or that the things in the world are independent of our conceptualization of them. The basic doctrine of formal semantics is neutral on these things.) But one can think of the nature of these things in the world, and the link between language and them, in various ways. In this book, I've from time to time used one of the most popular tools for representing sentence-level meanings: possible worlds. Here I'd like to mention some of the tools that some formal semanticists use in addition to, or in place of, possible worlds.

12.1.1   Model–theoretic semantics

Recall a few of the semantic claims outlined in this book: Sentences denote propositions, which are sets of possible worlds. Names refer to individuals. Predicates denote properties, which are functions which associate a set of things with each possible world. Quantifiers denote properties of properties. When someone works within semantics, one possibility is that they just accept these claims whole-heartedly, and then ask questions like "Just which individuals are referred to by names in my language?" and "Just which properties of properties are, in fact, used by my language as the meaning of a quantifier?"

Another approach is to consider this talk about possible worlds and individuals and properties/functions as providing a *model* of what reality is like which is useful for semantic purposes.[1] Perhaps we don't believe that the true nature of reality is relevant to doing semantics. For example, astronomy and physics tell us that sunsets are not "real" in the sense of being a fundamental component of our best scientific understanding of the world.[2] Nevertheless, we may want to say that the noun *sunset* denotes a set of things (more accurately, it expresses a function from possible worlds to sets of things) just like other nouns, and those things would presumably be sunsets. The apparent contradiction between saying that sunsets aren't real and saying that *sunset* denotes a set of them can be resolved if we say that the truth-conditions of sentences are defined in terms of a model of reality appropriate to how language works, with it being a further issue how that model relates to reality itself. Sunsets are part of our model though not fundamental pieces of reality (let's assume for the sake of argument), and we can explain how the model relates to reality: a sunset is a change, at a particular location, as a consequence of the rotation of the earth, from having a direct line of sight to the sun to not having a direct line of sight to the sun (close enough – you get the point). A similar argument can be made about the status of the objects we tend to employ as we do formal semantics, such as sets of possible worlds. We might think of sets of possible worlds within a model-theoretic approach as representing propositions while remaining agnostic about whether propositions are actually sets of possible worlds, or just things which are well modeled by sets of possible worlds.

Here's a sample definition of a model:

A model has the following things:

- A set of possible worlds. Call it W.
- A set of individuals. Call it I.
- A set of times. Call it T.
- A description L of which individuals inhabit which worlds. (Technically, this will be a function.)
- A description < of which times are before which other times. (Technically, this will also be a function.)

An interpretation describes the meaning of each word, phrase, or sentence in terms of a particular model. For example:

- Given a model, the meaning of a name must be one of the individuals in that model's I. The meaning of *Shelby*, given a particular model M, would be a particular individual in M's I (let's call it individual no. 1). Individual no. 1 is the part of the model which corresponds to Shelby in reality.
- Given a model, the meaning of an intransitive verb must be a function from worlds in that model's W to sets of individuals in that model's I. The meaning of *barks*, given a particular model M, could be this function:

    W1 → {individual no. 1, individual no. 2, individual no. 3}
    W2 → {individual no. 2, individual no. 4}
    W3 → {individual no. 1, individual no. 9}
    . . .

    This function is how we represent the property "barks" in model M.
- Given a model, the meaning of a sentence must be a set of possible worlds in that model's W. For example, in terms of the model M we've been describing, the meaning of the sentence *Shelby barks* would be a proposition like {W1, W3, . . . }, since as you notice individual no. 1 is in the set linked to W1 and the set linked to W3 by the *barks* function. (This proposition would of course be built up compositionally, through the saturation process.)

The point of this is to see that the semantic description can proceed without saying anything direct about what reality is like. We say what the model is like, and then have to contemplate how the model connects to reality. It's as if you are given a crude drawing of an elephant, never having seen the real thing, and being told "That's the trunk; that's the tusk; etc." You know that the thing pointed out when you're told "That's the trunk" is not really a trunk (it's a line drawn by a pencil), but you count on the picture being good enough to tell you something useful about real elephants and their trunks, tusks, etc. Semanticists sometimes talk about the "intended model" and the "intended interpretation," the model which is an accurate portrayal of reality and the interpretation which links pieces of language to the intended model in the way that English (or whatever language is being studied) is actually linked to reality.

You can see how model-theoretic semantics can be quite neutral as to the role played by mental concepts, social conventions, and the like in meaning. Mental concepts might play a role in determining the structure of the model, because how we come to a model of reality depends on psychological factors. Returning to the analogy of a picture, think about drawing a picture to represent a particular fish which has patterns of color on its body imperceptible to us because they come from wavelengths of light which our eyes aren't sensitive to. We'll draw the fish leaving out an aspect of it (the patterns) which actually might be quite important to the fish. The picture is a model of the fish with similarities and divergences from reality which are determined by the nature of the people trying to represent them. Who knows? Maybe the very idea of an individual or of time, in our semantic models, has the same status – a thing we see because of who we are, and which isn't there from another perspective. Within model-theoretic semantics, it's very clear that this could be so, and not matter to the more nitty-gritty, linguistic aspects of semantic theory at all.

The perspective of model-theoretic semantics is also conducive to asking general questions about what kind of world we need to assume we live in for language to function. For example, we could ask "Can we explain the meanings of all worlds, phrases, and sentences of English without the assumption that the model contains a set of times?" The answer to this question may prove useful from a semantic perspective as we study the diversity of tense systems across languages, and from a philosophical perspective as we think about the nature of time itself. Of course one can still ask this kind of question without the concept of a model, but, as I've mentioned, thinking in terms of a model lends itself to such concerns.

12.1.2 Davidsonian semantics

Though most formal semanticists build their theory of meaning on the idea that the meaning of a sentence is (or should be modeled as) a set of possible worlds, not all do. A group of semanticists who trace their intellectual lineage back to the philosopher Donald Davidson believe that we can do without possible worlds. These Davidsonian semanticists agree with other formal semanticists that the meaning of a sentence consists in its truth-conditions, but think that possible worlds and the like are not the right way to think about truth-conditions. Rather, they say that it's better to simply and directly express truth-conditions with statements like the following:[3]

(1) *Snow is white* is true if, and only if, snow is white.

According to this perspective, sentence meaning is not a *thing*, like a set of possible worlds. Rather, a sentence has truth-conditions, expressed as in (1), and that's it.

Davidsonian theories tend to be parsimonious, compared to the more common approach of using possible worlds, in several respects. First and foremost, of course, Davidsonians don't use possible worlds. To some extent they make up for this by typically making extensive use of events, another innovation of Davidson's, in their semantic analyses, but since many people intuitively consider events to be much more plausible and comprehensible than possible worlds, this may be a good trade-off. I should note, though, that in principle whether a theory uses possible worlds and whether it uses events are independent points – we can have truth-conditions stated as in (1) in a theory without events, and we can have events in a theory which expresses the meaning of a sentence as a set of possible worlds. But this is just part of a bigger picture. Davidsonian theories tend to forgo describing meanings as independently existing, abstract things in general. Recall that we have said that the meaning of a predicate is a property, where a property is an unsaturated proposition (which can be viewed as a certain type of function, from possible worlds to sets of individuals). Therefore, we're committed to the idea that the meaning of a predicate is a "thing": properties or functions are fancy, abstract things to be sure, but things nonetheless. A Davidsonian might say something like the following instead:

(2) For any sentence of the form *x barks*, this sentence is true if, and only if, the thing referred to by *x* barks.

(Really, of course, this rule should not be specific to the predicate *barks*, but should be generalized to cover all subject–predicate sentences. I just want to convey the basic idea.) Notice that *barks* by itself is not given a meaning. We just have a general statement in (2) about what a whole bunch of sentences containing it means. This statement can be combined with the principle in (3) to yield a truth definition through the reasoning in (4).

(3)   *Shelby* refers to Shelby.

(4)   *Shelby barks* is of the form *x barks*.
      So, it's true if, and only if, the thing referred to by *x* barks.
      In this case, *x* refers to Shelby.
      Therefore, the sentence is true if, and only if, Shelby barks.

Davidsonian semantics can to some extent be characterized as holistic, because the meanings of words and phrases smaller than a whole sentence are characterized in terms of the truth-conditions of sentences containing them. This is not an "atomic" theory which builds the meanings of whole sentences out of independently existing little parts, but rather an "abstracting" one which informs us about the little parts on the basis of what they contribute to the whole.

As you can see, Davidsonian semantics is different from possible worlds semantics in some fundamental ways. Despite this fact, since they both take a truth-conditional perspective on sentence meaning, they are very close relatives. Moreover, most of the ideas about language presented in this book (those which don't make use of possible worlds in a really fundamental way) can be carried over into a Davidsonian theory without a problem, and indeed there is a lively interchange of ideas between Davidsonian semanticists and possible worlds semanticists.

Davidsonian semantics tends to be practiced with a very particular orientation toward the rest of linguistics. Though they could have had the opposite bias while still doing Davidsonian semantics just fine, in fact the Davidsonians by and large understand their project in light of the conception of language and the theories of syntax put forward by Noam Chomsky, the twentieth century's most important syntactician. While this is no place to try to explain Chomsky's linguistic ideas, what this means is that, if you decide to learn more about Davidsonian semantics, you can expect to learn something about formal theories of syntax as well. (Possible worlds semantics is compatible with Chomskian syntax, and many researchers integrate the two closely, but there are plenty of formal semanticists who are neutral about or even hostile toward Chomskian syntax.)

12.1.3   Situation Semantics

Another important approach to semantics which falls within the formal semantics tradition is Situation Semantics.[4] Many formal semanticists use the concept of a "situation" in their work, the unifying idea being that we want to have something less than a complete possible world to base our notion of meaning on.[5] Recall that possible worlds are thought of as complete realities, and as such they settle every possible question with a "yes" or "no." A semanticist talking about situations has in mind a partial reality (or partial model of reality). Situations can be understood as a not-too-radical departure from the ordinary possible worlds framework, with situations seen as just parts of possible worlds. But within this general trend of using situations, the theory of Situation Semantics – capital S, capital S – has some quite distinct characteristics. The most obvious difference is that situations are not viewed as alternative ways reality could be, but as parts of the one reality which we all know and love. The role of a sentence is to classify situations according to some more general features of reality. Let's think about sentence (5):

(5)   Shelby was barking.

This sentence invokes various aspects of reality: Shelby, the property of barking, some past time t (let's say yesterday evening at 11:00 p.m.), and "truth." These it clusters into a classificatory scheme called a *state of affairs* (*soa*):[6]

(6)   soa no. 1: Shelby + barking + yesterday 11:00 p.m. + True

A given piece of the world, or situation, may or may not be properly classified by this state of affairs; that is, it might or might not be a part of reality which has Shelby barking yesterday at 11:00 p.m. If it is, we say that "the situation *supports* soa no. 1."

Another important feature of Situation Semantics is the way it views linguistic meaning as fitting into a broader view of the regularities which let us navigate our world. In lots of ways, people are attuned to various regularities among situations. There are *constraints* which relate situations of one kind to situations of another kind. For example, you know about this constraint: if a situation exists of smoke coming out of a house, it is likely that there is a situation of something burning inside the house. And this one: if a situation exists in which Shelby is barking, there is not a simultaneous situation in which Shelby is quiet. We can use these constraints to reason about and make good decisions as we live in our world.

Languages provide constraints which are also very useful to us. So, there's a constraint like this: if there's a situation in which someone says *Shelby was barking*, and that situation provides enough clues to let the hearer figure out that a particular dog and time were being talked about (my dog Shelby and yesterday evening at 11:00 p.m.), then what they said was true if (and only if) soa no. 1 correctly classifies some actual situation in the world. (This constraint is built up from other constraints which relate to the structure of the sentence, so the theory is compositional.) Importantly, the bottom line of all this talk about situations and states of affairs is a statement of truth-conditions: the speaker's utterance was true if, and only if, Shelby was barking yesterday at 11:00 p.m. Therefore, this is a truth-conditional theory like possible worlds semantics and Davidsonian semantics.

Situation Semantics is a theory which sits resolutely at the point where linguistics, philosophy, and logic meet. Much work in Situation Semantics is more focused on the kinds of logic and mathematics which are necessary to make Situation Semantics coherent, or the philosophical consequences of viewing meaning in this way.[7] (There is plenty of work in possible worlds semantics and Davidsonian semantics addressing such logical/philosophical issues as well, but most linguistically oriented research is kept separate from it.) This means that if you take up the project of learning more about Situation Semantics, you can look forward to some serious interdisciplinarity.

12.2 Relationships with Other Varieties of Semantics

As I mentioned in earlier chapters, not all semanticists are formal semanticists. There are perspectives on semantics within linguistics which don't accept the formal semantic commitment to truth-conditional meaning. Overall, the relationships between formal semantics as a scholarly endeavor and the other linguistic theories (especially the idea theories, as well as social-practice theories) is a cold one. The fields mostly ignore one another's existence, and when they mention the others' perspectives, it's usually to make a dismissive comment or argue how wrong those perspectives are. I'm really not certain whether this is as it should be. Perhaps the job of each approach is to argue as strongly as it can that the others are wrong, so that whichever theory is actually right (and I say it's formal semantics!) will eventually be proven so. But on the other hand, it could be that no approach yet invented is right, and so at some point we should be ready to synthesize apparently incompatible ideas. One can't say at this point. However, I can say that there should be more sharing of ideas at the level of individual linguistic topics. Often, advocates of one approach simply ignore the results of research in others, and this leads to the duplication of effort and to avoidable mistakes. For example, to suggest a case which highlights some of the most fruitful work in formal semantics, it would be wise for any semanticist, of whatever persuasion, to keep track of the rich literature on tense, aspect, and modality which has been developed within the formal semantics perspective. In contrast, to suggest a case which highlights an area of relative weakness in formal semantics, it is wise for formal semanticists to remain attuned to the mass of work on lexical meaning developed within other perspectives.

12.3   Relationships with Other Fields

In this book we've time and again discussed three scholarly fields: syntax, pragmatics, and the philosophy of language. These are the intellectual areas with which formal semantics makes the closest contact. New ideas in any of them can have a direct impact on how semanticists think about language, both in a general way and in studying particular features of language (relative clauses, modals, pronouns, whatever). Semanticists tend to know a fair amount about all three, though a particular semanticist will likely not know all three equally well. Rather, there are syntactically oriented semanticists, who may be less interested in pragmatics and philosophy; philosophically oriented semanticists, who may know less about syntax; and so forth. But overall, formal semantics is actively engaged with all three, and much of the most creative work gets done where they interact closely.

Formal semantics also has connections to other areas of intellectual inquiry. Three of the most important here are logic, computer science, and cognitive science. The links to logic have been downplayed in this book, because they relate to the formalism which I have aimed to avoid. However, it should be worthwhile to discuss them briefly. When formal semantics is practiced with its formalism intact, it draws these tools largely from the tradition of logic. The fundamental goal of logic is to characterize valid patterns of reasoning, steps of inference which will lead from true premises (you have to find some true premises on your own; logic won't help you with that) to true conclusions. Since human language is ambiguous and vague, it's hard to explain precisely which kinds of inference are valid by looking solely at English sentences – something may be valid if an ambiguous sentence is understood one way but not another. Therefore, logicians have developed artificial, "logical" languages which can represent in standard, unambiguous ways the premises, inferences, and conclusions which their theories of logic are all about. These artificial languages are not much like any human language, as any linguist will tell you, but with a little practice one can learn to take a variety of sentences of a human language, like English, and translate them into a convenient logical language. (The most popular logical languages are known as *propositional calculus* and *predicate calculus*, by the way; many logical languages more sophisticated than these are on the market, not all of them relevant to linguists.) Since sentences of these logical languages are supposed to have meaning, logicians have developed an understanding of the semantics of logical languages. And since the whole point of logic is to be precise, not ambiguous and vague like human languages, this semantic understanding is itself very precise.

One of the discoveries which gave rise to formal semantics was the fact that the very precise understanding of semantics which works for logical languages can be applied to human languages as well. Richard Montague's early work in semantics was instrumental in establishing this point.[8] In fact, sometimes formal semantics is practiced by translating sentences of a human language (like English) into a logical language through a detailed translation procedure, reversing what students of logic are taught to do. In other cases, the ideas which logicians have for how to understand the semantics of their logical languages are applied directly to human languages, treating them, in effect, as logical languages which are just much richer than anything logicians have invented.

Formal semantics is linked to computer science for both intellectual and practical reasons. On the intellectual side, computer languages are formal languages very much like the languages of logic. Because computer programs have to be made to do predictable things inside an engineered pile of electronic components, computer languages have to be understood just as precisely as logical languages are. For these reasons, the motivations for using logic to help with the job of doing semantics within linguistics are also relevant for using computer science. We can treat human languages like English as computer languages, or at least draw on insights which have been gained from thinking about computer languages as we think about human languages. On the practical side, we have the need to make computers deal with humans and the products of human civilization in a reasonable way; since humans communicate using (human) language, it seems useful to try to get computers to understand human language, at least to some extent. To take a concrete example, it would be great if we could perfect automatic machine translation, getting computers to translate from one human language to another for us. Or: it would be very helpful if computers could understand language well enough to make short summaries for us of texts which we don't have time to read. As long as computer scientists are interested in this kind of project, there will be a need to work with linguists, including semanticists.

It is worth mentioning a kind of affinity that formal semanticists of a certain sort have with logicians and computer scientists. There are semanticists who just love logic, computer programming, and thinking in a formal, mathematical way. So these people tend to get along with logicians and computer scientists, and they enjoy learning about these other fields for their own sake. It even happens that formal semanticists end up working in computer science programs, philosophy programs where the study of logic is valued, and information technology companies.

Cognitive science is an interdisciplinary field with the focus on understanding the human mind. The most important component disciplines are linguistics, psychology, neuroscience, philosophy, and computer science. We are a long way from really understanding the mind, and cognitive scientists – really anyone who studies any aspect of the mind from a scientific perspective – have a variety of approaches to learning more about it. Three such approaches are: (i) study the human brain; (ii) study human behavior; and (iii) create models of things humans can do. As an example of (i), one might study what goes on in the brain as people understand language; as for (ii), one could study what aspects of language people find it easy or difficult to understand; and as for (iii), one can create a model of language, either "on paper" or by programming a computer to display some human-like understanding of language. The traditional job of linguists, including semanticists, is to create the models of language "on paper." This by itself is an important contribution to cognitive science because the ability of people to understand and produce language is one of humans' most impressive mental abilities. Moreover, one can only examine what goes on in the brain or in behavior as people understand or produce language if one knows what language is really like. For example, suppose we want to understand what goes on when people talk about possible, but not actual, situations. We would need to have them do something with modal language, listening to, reading, or producing some sentences with modal words like *must, could, possibly,* and so forth. In this context, it's going to be useful to know about such important modal concepts as "epistemic," "deontic," "necessity," and "possibility." In these ways, linguists of all kinds, and this includes formal semanticists, are essential contributors to cognitive science.

Now it's time to bring this book to a close. I hope to have shown you that when linguists study meaning, they find many unexpected facts and fascinating puzzles. Formal semantics has been my medium because I believe that, despite its reputation as being quite technical and difficult, its fundamental ideas concerning meaning are extremely insightful and understandable even without the benefit of formal tools. By explaining its ideas (at least as I see them) in this non-formal way, I hope to have made them more accessible to all with an interest in how language works.

NOTES

1 I should mention that I'm focusing here on how the concept of model plays a role in linguistic semantics. Logicians and mathematicians are very interested in model theory as well, but from a quite different perspective.
2 I thank Steve Kuhn for suggesting this example. A good linguistics reference on some of these concerns is Bach (1986).
3 This kind of direct statement of truth-conditions traces back to Tarski (1944). For more detail on the Davidsonian approach to semantics, see Davidson (1967a). For a discussion and critiques, see Evans and McDowell (1976); Soames (1992).
4 Some basic works in this area include: Barwise (1981); Barwise and Perry (1983); Perry (1993). An important critique is Soames (1990).
5 An important alternative tradition of using situations, discussed in the sentences just below, was initiated by Kratzer (1989).
6 Situation Semanticists don't write states of affairs with pluses. They put the parts into angled brackets in a particular order: <<barking, t, Shelby, True>>. But the main idea is that these four individual things are just clustered into a conglomeration which is used to classify situations. I think the "+" suggests the right idea in this less formal context.
7 See Cooper, Mukai, and Perry (1990), as well as their later volumes 2 and 3.
8 See Montague (1970a; 1970b; 1973), all reprinted in Montague (1974).

Appendix: Answers to Selected Exercises

1 A sentence of the form *p or q* denotes the set of worlds formed by adding the set denoted by *p* to the set denoted by *q*. This is the union of those two sets. A sentence of the form *It is not the case that p* denotes the set of worlds not in the set denoted by *p*. This is the complement of the original set.

2 (a) *Contradiction*: The sentence denotes the empty set:

Tautology: The sentence denotes the set of all worlds:

Compatible: The sets denoted by the sentences overlap:

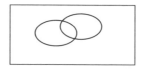

(b) • *p* entails *p or q*: Since *p or q* denotes the union of the *p*-set and the *q*-set, everything in the *p*-set must be in the *p-or-q*-set. That is, the *p*-set is a subset of the *p-or-q*-set. Entailment specifies the subset relation.

- *p* and *It is not the case that p* are contradictory: *It is not the case that p* denotes the set of worlds not in the *p*-set. Therefore, there is no world in both the *p*-set and the *not-p*-set, i.e., there is no overlap between the sets. Contradictoriness specifies the no-overlap relation.
- *p and q* entails *p*: Since *p and q* denotes the intersection of the sets denoted by *p* and *q*, everything in the *p-and-q*-set must be in the *p*-set. That is, the *p-and-q*-set is a subset of the *p*-set. Entailment specifies the subset relation.
- If *p* entails *q*, and *q* and *r* are contradictory, then *p* and *r* are contradictory: If *p* entails *q*, then everything in the *p*-set is in the *q*-set. If *q* and *r* are contradictory, then nothing in the *q*-set is in the *r*-set. This implies that nothing in the *p*-set is in the *r*-set either. That is, the *p*-set and *r*-set don't overlap. Contradictoriness specifies the no-overlap relation.

3

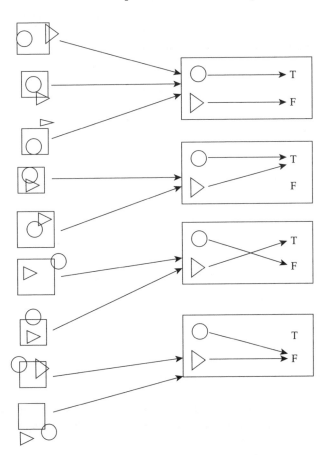

4   The function above could be written in λ calculus as:

[λ*w* . [λ*x* . *x* is inside the square in *w*]]

5   w1 → {A+B}
w2 → {B+C}
w3 → {A+B, B+C, A+C, A+B+C}
w4 → ∅

6   E ⊆ T:

This afternoon the baby woke up early.

Something occurred to me today.

I ate my dinner while riding on the train.

T ⊆ E:

This afternoon, the baby seemed sick.

Something has been bothering me today.

Once upon a time, there was a sleepy rabbit.

7   States:

Mary is tall.

Shelby smells funny.

Achievements:

Allen realized something.

The cat died.

Accomplishments:

Greg painted a tree.

The bird built a nest.

Activities:

Veronica ran and ran.

The ant moved food from one chamber to the other.

8   Consequence 2: If X *believes* S is true, than X's belief worlds are a
subset of the worlds in which S is true. If S contradicts T, then no

world is both an S-world and a T-world. But since every one of X's belief worlds is an S-world, none of X's belief worlds is a T-world. Therefore X doesn't believe T. (The same goes for *want*.)

Consequence 3: If X *believes* S is true, than X's belief worlds are a subset of the worlds in which S is true. If S entails T, then every S-world is also a T-world. And since every one of X's belief worlds is an S-world, every one of X's belief worlds is also a T-world. Therefore X believes T. (The same goes for *want*.)

9   Two PLUS two is four:

<2 _ 2 = 4, +>

Better with λ calculus: <[λR.2 R 2 = 4], +>

TWO plus TWO is four:

<_+_= 4, 2>

With λ calculus: <λx.x + x = 4, 2>

Two plus two IS four:

<2 + 2_4, =>

With λ calculus: <λR.2 + 2 R 4, =>

10   We put *John left work early again* into these constructions:

negation: *John didn't leave work early again.*

if clause: *If John left work early again, he'll be fired.*

modal sentence: *John probably left work early again.*

All of these imply that John left work early before, so the proposition that John left work early before is probably a presupposition.

11   It is raining, and Hannibal ate a bone too.

First we calculate C + *It is raining*: the proposition that it is raining is added to the Common Ground, removing worlds in which it isn't raining from the Context Set. Let's call this new Context Set C'. Then we calculate C' + *Hannibal ate a bone too*. Because of *too*, this is only felicitous if the C' entails that some other individual besides Hannibal ate a bone. The contribution of *It is raining* is irrelevant to whether or not some other individual ate a bone, so adding *Hannibal ate a bone too* will only be felicitous if the original Context Set C already entailed that some other individual ate a bone. If it did, we add the proposition that Hannibal ate a bone to the Common Ground, removing worlds in which he didn't from C', giving us an even newer Context Set C".

Hannibal ate a bone too, and Shelby also ate a bone.

First we calculate C + *Hannibal ate a bone too*: because of *too*, this is only felicitous if C entails that some individual other than Hannibal ate a bone. If C does entail this, then the proposition that Hannibal ate a bone is added to the Common Ground, removing worlds in which he didn't eat a bone from the Context Set. Let's call this new Context Set C'. Then we calculate C' + *Shelby also ate a bone*. Because of *also*, this is only felicitous if C' entails that some other individual besides Shelby ate a bone. We know that C' entails this, for two reasons: C had to entail that some other individual ate a bone, in order for the presupposition of *too* to be satisfied. And C' has to entail this because it was created by adding the proposition that Hannibal ate a bone to the Common Ground. Therefore, it's felicitous to add *Shelby ate a bone* to the Common Ground, and we do so, removing worlds in which he didn't eat a bone from C'. This gives us an even newer Context Set C".

References

Abusch, D. (1994). The scope of indefinites. *Natural Language Semantics* 2, 83–136.

Austin, J. (1962). *How to do Things with Words*. Cambridge, MA: Harvard University Press.

Bach, E. (1986). Natural language metaphysics. In R. Barcan Marcus, G. J. W. Dorn, and P. Weingartner, eds., *Logic, Methodology, and Philosophy of Science VII*. Amsterdam: North Holland, 573–95.

Bach, E. (1989). *Informal Lectures on Formal Semantics*. Albany, NY: SUNY Press.

Barwise, J. (1981). Scenes and other situations. *Journal of Philosophy* 77, 369–97.

Barwise, J. and J. Perry (1983). *Situations and Attitudes*. Cambridge, MA: MIT Press.

Block, N. (1986). Advertisement for a semantics for psychology. In P. French, T. Uehling, and H. Wettsetin, eds., *Midwest Studies in Philosophy. Vol. 10: Studies in the Philosophy of Mind*. Minneapolis: University of Minnesota Press, 615–78.

Block, N. (forthcoming). Holism, mental and semantic. In E. Craig, ed., *The Routledge Encyclopedia of Philosophy*. London and New York: Routledge.

Brandom, R. (1983). Asserting. *Noûs* 17, 637–50.

Brandom, R. (1994). *Making It Explicit*. Cambridge, MA: Harvard University Press.

Brandom, R. (2000). *Articulating Reasons: An Introduction to Inferentialism*. Cambridge, MA: Harvard University Press.

Burge, T. (1979). Individualism and the mental. In P. French and H. Wettstein, eds., *Midwest Studies in Philosophy: Studies in Metaphysics*. Minneapolis: University of Minnesota Press, 73–122.

Burge, T. (1982). Other bodies. In A. Woodfield, ed., *Thought and Object*. New York: Oxford University Press, 97–120.

Carlson, G. (1977). Reference to kinds in English. University of Massachusetts at Amherst Ph.D. dissertation. Can be downloaded from semanticsarchive.net

Chierchia, G. and S. McConnell-Ginet (2000). *Meaning and Grammar: An Introduction to Semantics*, 2nd edn. Cambridge, MA: MIT Press.

Chomsky, N. (1970). Deep structure, surface structure, and semantic interpretation. In R. Jakobson and S. Kawamoto, eds., *Studies in General and Oriental Linguistics*. Tokyo: TEC Corporation, 183–216.

Cooper, R., K. Mukai, and J. Perry, eds. (1990). *Situation Theory and Its Applications.* *Vol. 1.* Chicago: University of Chicago Press, and Stanford, CA: CSLI.

Cresswell, M. and A. von Stechow (1982). De re belief generalized. *Linguistics and Philosophy* 5, 503–35.

Davidson, D. (1967a). Truth and meaning. *Synthese* 17, 304–23.

Davidson, D. (1967b). The logical form of action sentences. In N. Rescher, ed., *The Logic of Decision and Action.* Pittsburgh: University of Pittsburgh Press, 81–120.

Davis, S. ed. (1991). *Pragmatics.* Oxford: Oxford University Press.

Dietrich, W. (1955). *Erweiterte Form, Präteritum und Perfektum im Englischen: Eine Aspet- und Tempusstudie.* Munich: Max Hueber.

Donnellan, K. (1966). Reference and definite descriptions. *Philosophical Review* 75, 281–304.

Dowty, D. (1977). Towards a semantic analysis of verb aspect and the English "imperfective progressive." *Linguistics and Philosophy* 1, 45–78.

Dowty, D. (1979). *Word Meaning and Montague Grammar.* Dordrecht: Reidel.

Dowty, D. (1990). Thematic proto-roles, argument selection, and lexical semantic defaults. *Language* 67(3), 547–619.

Dresner, E. (2002). Holism, language acquisition, and algebraic logic. *Linguistics and Philosophy* 25, 419–52.

Enç, M. (1991). The semantics of specificity. *Linguistic Inquiry* 22, 1–25.

Evans, G. (1973). The causal theory of names. *Aristotelian Society: Supplementary Volume* 47, 187–208.

Evans, G. (1980). Pronouns. *Linguistic Inquiry* 11, 337–62.

Evans, G. (1982). *The Varieties of Reference.* Oxford and New York: Clarendon Press.

Evans, G. and J. McDowell, eds. (1976). *Truth and Meaning: Essays in Semantics.* Oxford: Oxford University Press.

Fauconnier, G. (1975). Implication reversal in a natural language. In F. Guenthner and S. Schmidt, eds., *Formal Semantics and Pragmatics for Natural Language.* Dordrecht: Reidel, 289–300.

Fauconnier, G. (1985). *Mental Spaces: Aspects of Meaning Construction in Natural Language.* Cambridge, MA: MIT Press.

Field, H. (1977). Logic, meaning, and conceptual role. *Journal of Philosophy* 69, 379–408.

Fodor, J. (1975). *The Language of Thought.* New York: Crowell.

Fodor, J. and E. Lepore (1992). *Holism: A Shoppers' Guide.* Oxford: Blackwell.

Fodor, J. D. and I. Sag (1982). Referential and quantificational indefinites. *Linguistics and Philosophy* 5, 355–98.

Gazdar, G. (1979). *Pragmatics: Implicature, Presupposition, and Logical Form.* New York: Academic Press.

Gazdar, G. (1981). Speech act assignment. In A. K. Joshi, I. A. Sag, and B. L. Webber, eds., *Elements of Discourse Understanding.* New York: Cambridge University Press, 64–83.

Ginzburg, J. (1995a). Resolving questions, part I. *Linguistics and Philosophy* 18(5), 459–527.

Ginzburg, J. (1995b). Resolving questions, part II. *Linguistics and Philosophy* 18(6), 567–609.

Green, G. (1996). *Pragmatics and Natural Language Understanding*, 2nd edn. Hillsdale, NJ: Lawrence Erlbaum.

Grice, H. P. (1957). Meaning. *Philosophical Review* 66, 377–88.

Grice, H. P. (1975). Logic and conversation. In P. Cole and J. L. Morgan, eds., *Syntax and Semantics. Vol. 3: Speech Acts*. New York: Academic Press, 41–58. Repr. in H. P. Grice (1989). *Studies in the Ways of Words*. Cambridge, MA: Harvard University Press, 22–40.

Groenendijk, J. and M. Stokhof (1982). Semantic analysis of wh-complements. *Linguistics and Philosophy* 5, 175–233.

Groenendijk, J. and M. Stokhof (1984). Studies in the semantics of questions and the pragmatics of answers. Ph.D. dissertation, University of Amsterdam.

Hamblin, C. L. (1973). Questions in Montague English. *Foundations of Language* 10, 41–53.

Hamblin, C. L. (1971). Mathematical models of dialogue. *Theoria* 37, 130–55.

Han, C. H. (1998). The structure and interpretation of imperatives: mood and force in Universal Grammar. Ph.D. dissertation, University of Pennsylvania.

Harman, G. (1987). (Non-solipsistic) conceptual role semantics. In E. Lepore, ed., *New Directions in Semantics*. London: Academic Press, 55–81.

Hausser, R. (1980). Surface compositionality and the semantics of mood. In F. Kiefer and J. Searle, eds., *Speech Act Theory and Pragmatics*. Dordrecht: Reidel, 71–95.

Heim, I. (1982). The semantics of definite and indefinite noun phrases. Ph.D. dissertation, University of Massachusetts.

Heim, I. (1985). E-type pronouns and donkey anaphora. *Linguistics and Philosophy* 13, 137–78.

Heim, I. (1990). On the projection problem for presuppositions. In S. Davis, ed., *Pragmatics*. Oxford: Oxford University Press, 397–405.

Heim, I. (1992). Presupposition projection and the semantics of attitude verbs. *Journal of Semantics* 9, 183–221.

Heim, I. and A. Kratzer (1997). *Semantics in Generative Grammar*. Oxford and New York: Blackwell.

Inoue, K. (1979). An analysis of the English present perfect. *Linguistics* 17, 561–89.

Jackendoff, R. (1990). *Semantic Structures*. Cambridge, MA: MIT Press.

Jackendoff, R. (1992). *Languages of the Mind*. Cambridge, MA: MIT Press.

Jacobs, J. (1983). *Fokus und Skalen: Zur Syntax und Semantik der Gradpartikel im Deutschen*. Tübingen: Niemeyer.

Kadmon, N. (2001). *Formal Pragmatics: Semantics, Pragmatics, Presupposition and Focus*. Malden, MA, and Oxford: Blackwell.

Kadmon, N. and F. Ladman (1993). Any. *Linguistics and Philosophy* 16, 353–422.

Kamp, H. (1981). A theory of truth and semantic representation. In J. Groenendijk, T. Janssen, and M. Stokhof, eds., *Formal Methods in the Study of Language*. Amsterdam: Mathematisch Centrum, 277–322.

Karttunen, L. (1969). Pronouns and variables. In *Papers from the Fifth Regional Meeting of the Chicago Linguistics Society*. Chicago: CLS, 108–15.

Karttunen, L. (1977). Syntax and semantics of questions. *Linguistics and Philosophy* 1, 3–44.

Karttunen, L. (2003). Discourse referents. In J. Gutiérrez-Rexach, ed., *Semantics: Critical Concepts in Linguistics. Vol. III*. New York and London: Routledge, 20–39. Also in J. D. McCawley, ed. (1976). *Syntax and Semantics 7: Notes from the Linguistic Underground*. New York: Academic Press, 363–85.

Karttunen, L. and S. Peters (1979). Conventional implicature. In C.-Y. Oh and D. Dinneen, eds., *Syntax and Semantics. Vol. 11: Presupposition*. New York: Academic Press, 1–56.

Kennedy, C. (1999). *Projecting the Adjective: The Syntax and Semantics of Gradability and Comparison*. New York: Garland Press. (1997 University of California at Santa Cruz Ph.D. dissertation.)

Klein, E. and I. Sag (1985). Type-driven translation. *Linguistics and Philosophy* 8, 63–201.

Klein, W. (1994). *Time in Language*. London: Routledge.

Kratzer, A. (1977). What "must" and "can" must and can mean. *Linguistics and Philosophy* 1, 337–55.

Kratzer, A. (1981). The notional category of modality. In H. J. Eikmeyer and H. Reiser, eds., *Worlds, Words, and Contexts: New Approaches in Word Semantics*. Berlin: Walter de Gruyter, 38–74.

Kratzer, A. (1989). An investigation of the lumps of thought. *Linguistics and Philosophy* 12, 607–53.

Kratzer, A. (1991). Modality. In A. von Stechow and D. Wunderlich, eds., *Semantics: An International Handbook of Contemporary Research*. Berlin and New York: Walter de Gruyter, 639–50.

Kripke, S. (1972). Naming and necessity. In D. Davidson and G. Harman, eds., *Semantics for Natural Language*. Dordrecht: Reidel, 253–355. Also pub. 1982 as *Naming and Necessity*, Oxford: Blackwell.

Kripke, S. (1977). Speaker's reference and semantic reference. In P. A. French, T. E. Uehling, Jr, and H. K. Wettstein, eds., *Contemporary Perspectives in the Philosophy of Language*. Minneapolis: University of Minnesota Press, 6–27.

Ladusaw, W. (2002). On the notion affective in the analysis of negative-polarity items. In P. Portner and B. Partee, eds., *Formal Semantics: The Essential Readings*. Oxford: Blackwell, 457–70.

Lakoff, G. (1987). *Women, Fire, and Dangerous Things*. Chicago: University of Chicago Press.

Lakoff, G. and M. Johnson (1980). *Metaphors We Live By*. Chicago: University of Chicago Press.

Landman, F. (1992). The progressive. *Natural Language Semantics* 1, 1–32.

Larson, R. K. and G. Segal (1995). *Knowledge of Meaning: An Introduction to Semantic Theory*. Cambridge, MA: MIT Press.

Larson, R. K. and P. Ludlow (1993). Interpreted logical forms. *Synthese* 95, 305–55.

Levin, B. and M. Rappaport Hovav (1995). *Unaccusativity: At the Syntax-Lexical Semantics Interface.* Linguistic Inquiry Monograph 26. Cambridge, MA: MIT Press.

Levinson, S. (1983). *Pragmatics.* Cambridge and New York: Cambridge University Press.

Lewis, D. (1970). General semantics. *Synthese* 22, 18–67. Repr. in D. Davidson and G. Harman, eds. (1972). *Semantics of Natural Language.* Dordrecht: Reidel, 169–218.

Lewis, D. (1979). Scorekeeping in a language game. *Journal of Philosophical Logic* 8, 339–59.

Lewis, D. (1986). *On the Plurality of Worlds.* Oxford and New York: Blackwell.

Linebarger, M. (1987). Negative polarity and grammatical representation. *Linguistics and Philosophy* 10, 325–87.

Link, G. (1983). The logical analysis of plural and mass terms: a lattice-theoretic approach. In R. Bäuerle, C. Schwarze, and A. von Stechow, eds., *Meaning, Use, and Interpretation of Language.* Berlin: Walter de Gruyter, 302–32.

Ludlow, P. (2000). Interpreted logical forms, belief attribution, and the dynamic lexicon. In K. M. Jaszczolt, ed., *Pragmatics of Propositional Attitude Reports.* Oxford: Elsevier, 31–42.

Lycan, W. G. (1984). *Logical Form in Natural Language.* Cambridge, MA: Bradford Books/MIT Press.

Martin, R. (1987). *The Meaning of Language.* Cambridge, MA: MIT Press.

McCoard, R. (1978). *The English Perfect: Tense-Choice and Pragmatic Inferences.* Amsterdam: North Holland.

Montague, R. (1970a). English as a formal language. In B. Visentini et al., eds., *Linguaggi nella Società e nella Tecnica: Edizioni di Comunità.* Milan: Edizioni di Comunità, 189–224. Repr. in R. Montague (1974). *Formal Philosophy: Selected Papers of Richard Montague,* ed. and intro. R. H. Thomason. New Haven, CT: Yale University Press, 188–221.

Montague, R. (1970b). Universal Grammar. *Theoria* 36, 373–98. Repr. in R. Montague (1974). *Formal Philosophy: Selected Papers of Richard Montague,* ed. and intro. R. H. Thomason. New Haven, CT: Yale University Press, 222–46.

Montague, R. (1973). The proper treatment of quantification in ordinary English. In K. J. J. Hintikka, J. M. E. Moravcsik, and P. Suppes, eds., *Approaches to Natural Language.* Dordrecht: Reidel, 221–42. Repr. in R. Montague (1974). *Formal Philosophy: Selected Papers of Richard Montague,* ed. and intro. R. H. Thomason. New Haven, CT: Yale University Press, 247–70.

Montague, R. (1974). *Formal Philosophy: Selected Papers of Richard Montague,* ed. and intro. R. H. Thomason. New Haven, CT: Yale University Press.

Parsons, T. (1990). *Events in the Semantics of English.* Cambridge, MA: MIT Press.

Partee, B. (1973). Some structural analogies between tenses and pronouns in English. *Journal of Philosophy* 70(18), 601–9.

Partee, B. (1986). Noun phrase interpretation and type-shifting principles. In J. Groenendijk, D. de Jongh, and M. Stokhof, eds., *Studies in Discourse Representation Theory and the Theory of Generalized Quantifiers.* Dordrecht: Foris, 115–43.

Perry, J. (1993). *The Problem of the Essential Indexical and Other Essays*. New York: Oxford University Press.

Pinker, S. (1994). *The Language Instinct: How the Mind Creates Language*. New York: William Morrow.

Portner, P. (1998). The progressive in modal semantics. *Language* 74(4), 760–87.

Portner, P. (2003). The (temporal) semantics and (modal) pragmatics of the perfect. *Linguistics and Philosophy* 26, 459–510.

Portner, P. (forthcoming). The semantics of imperatives within a theory of clause types. In *Proceedings of the 14th Conference on Semantics and Linguistic Theory*. Ithaca, NY: Cornell Linguistics Department.

Portner, P. and K. Yabushita. (1998). The semantics and pragmatics of topic phrases. *Linguistics and Philosophy* 21, 117–57.

Putnam, H. (1975). The meaning of "meaning." In K. Gunderson, ed., *Language, Mind, and Knowledge*. Minneapolis: University of Minnesota Press, 131–93. Repr. in H. Putnam (1979), *Mind, Language, and Reality*. Cambridge: Cambridge University Press, 215–71.

Quine, W. V. O. (1953). Two dogmas of empiricism. In W. V. O. Quine, *From a Logical Point of View*. Cambridge, MA: Harvard University Press, 20–46.

Quine, W. V. O. (1960). *Word and Object*. Cambridge, MA: MIT Press.

Reichenbach, H. (1947). *Elements of Symbolic Logic*. New York: Macmillan.

Reinhart, T. (1982). Pragmatics and linguistics: an analysis of sentence topics. *Philosophica* 278, 53–94.

Reinhart, T. (1997). Quantifier scope: how labor is divided between QR and choice functions. *Linguistics and Philosophy* 20, 335–97.

Reis, M. (1999). On sentence types in German: an enquiry into the relationship between grammar and pragmatics. *IJGLSA* 4(2), 195–236.

Richard, M. (1990). *Propositional Attitudes*. Cambridge: Cambridge University Press.

Rooth, M. (1985). Association with focus. Ph.D. dissertation, University of Massachusetts at Amherst.

Rooth, M. (1992). A theory of focus interpretation. *Natural Language Semantics* 1, 75–116.

Russell, B. (1919). *Introduction to Mathematical Philosophy*. London: George Allen and Unwin. Relevant section repr. in A. P. Martinich, ed. (1985). *The Philosophy of Language*. New York and Oxford: Oxford University Press, 213–19.

Sadock, J. (1978). On testing for conversational implicature. In P. Cole, ed., *Syntax and Semantics. Vol. 9: Pragmatics*. New York: Academic Press, 281–98.

Saeed, J. (2003). *Semantics*, 2nd edn. Malden, MA: Blackwell.

Salmon, N. (1986). *Frege's Puzzle*. Cambridge, MA: MIT Press.

Searle, J. R. (1965). What is a speech act? In M. Black, ed., *Philosophy in America*. New York: Allen and Unwin, 221–39.

Searle, J. R. (1969). *Speech Acts*. Cambridge: Cambridge University Press.

Searle, J. R. (1975a). A taxonomy of illocutionary acts. In K. Gunderson, ed., *Language, Mind, and Knowledge: Minnesota Studies in the Philosophy of Science. Vol. 3*. Minneapolis: University of Minnesota Press, 1–29.

Searle, J. R. (1975b). Indirect speech acts. In P. Cole and J. L. Morgan, eds., *Syntax and Semantics. Vol. 3: Speech Acts.* New York: Academic Press, 59–82.

Smith, C. (1999). Activities: states or events? *Linguistics and Philosophy* 22, 479–508.

Soames, S. (1989). Presupposition. In D. Gabbay and F. Guenthner, eds., *Handbook of Philosophical Logic. Vol. 4: Topics in the Philosophy of Language.* Dordrecht: Reidel, 553–616.

Soames, S. (1990). Lost innocence. *Linguistics and Philosophy* 8, 59–71.

Soames, S. (1992). Truth, meaning, and understanding. *Philosophical Studies* 65, 17–35.

Soames, S. (2002). *Beyond Rigidity: The Unfinished Semantic Agenda of Naming and Necessity.* Oxford: Oxford University Press.

Stalnaker, R. (1974). Pragmatic presupposition. In M. Munitz and P. Unger, eds., *Semantics and Philosophy.* New York: New York University Press, 197–213.

Stalnaker, R. (1978). Assertion. *Syntax and Semantics* 9, 315–32.

Stalnaker, R. (1984). *Inquiry.* Cambridge, MA: MIT Press.

Stanley, J. (1997). Names and rigid designation. In B. Hale and C. Wright, eds., *A Companion to the Philosophy of Language.* Oxford and Malden, MA: Blackwell, 555–85.

Tarski, A. (1944). The semantic conception of truth. *Philosophy and Phenomenological Research* 4, 341–75.

van der Sandt, R. A. (1992). Presupposition projection as anaphora resolution. *Journal of Semantics* 9, 333–77.

von Stechow, A. (1991). Current issues in the theory of focus. In A. von Stechow and D. Wunderlich, eds., *Semantics: An International Handbook of Contemporary Research.* Berlin: Walter de Gruyter, 804–35.

Wittgenstein, L. (1953). *Philosophical Investigations,* trans. G. E. M. Anscombe. New York: Macmillan.

Zwarts, F. (1998). Three types of polarity. In F. Hamm and E. Hinrichs, eds., *Plurality and Quantification.* Dordrecht and Boston: Kluwer, 177–238.

Index